Instructor's Resources

Residential Housing & Interiors

Clois E. Kicklighter, Ed.D.

Dean Emeritus, School of Technology and
Professor Emeritus of Construction Technology
Indiana State University
Terre Haute, Indiana

Joan C. Kicklighter, CFCS

Author of Instructional Materials in
Family and Consumer Sciences
Naples, Florida

D1519115

Publisher
The Goodheart-Willcox Company, Inc.
Tinley Park, Illinois

Contents

Introduction

This *Instructor's Resource Portfolio* is part of the *Residential Housing & Interiors* learning package. It provides a variety of materials to help you make learning about *Residential Housing & Interiors* interesting and exciting for students. This learning package is also designed to assist you in achieving the following selected learning objectives:

To teach concepts. A variety of strategies are provided to help you teach the concepts in each chapter. You can select the strategies that are best suited for your specific class as well as individual students. Also, a number of suggestions are provided to let you present the text material using different methods to meet a variety of learning objectives.

To strengthen learning. The various activities provided in this learning package are designed to strengthen student learning by presenting concepts in several different ways, such as through teacher-lead class discussion, visual aids, field trips, guest speakers, examples of housing materials, and chapter review questions.

To expand learning. A wide range of activities is provided to meet the needs of students with varying levels of ability. The more challenging activities may be used to stimulate exceptional students and give them a chance to apply knowledge from the text to experiences beyond the classroom.

To use technology. A number of activities give students an opportunity to use the latest technology in solving problems, producing drawings, and preparing presentation plans. While some activities lend themselves to traditional drafting methods, others may be completed on a computer-aided design system. Students who have access to such systems will have the opportunity to gain additional knowledge and experience.

To demonstrate understanding. Activities are provided to give students the opportunity to demonstrate their understanding through design, analysis, and description. Various activities in the *Student Activity Guide* give students a chance to show their mastery of concepts presented in the text and in class by creating designs, analyzing housing related problems, and describing various features associated with housing systems, styles, and furnishings.

To use problem-solving techniques. Realistic activities designed to help students move from abstract to actual problem-solving situations are provided. These activities help students develop problem-solving techniques—such as performing calculations, doing research, creating projects, or writing reports—that will enable them to practice the art of reasoning and provide them with the practical knowledge and skills necessary for living.

Using the Text

Residential Housing & Interiors introduces students to the exciting world of planning, building, decorating, and landscaping a home. The text presents the many housing options available and explains how the living, sleeping, and service areas of a home can work together to satisfy individual and family needs. Information is provided to help students make wise decisions about planning a home and selecting materials, furniture, and treatments for it. Adaptations for people with special needs have been integrated throughout the text. A chapter on computer applications acquaints students with the many important roles computers play in housing today beyond information searches, including designing, testing, and managing projects. Students will learn about the systems and elements of residential structures, climate control, exteriors, remodeling, landscaping, professional methods for presenting housing ideas, and job opportunities in the broad field of housing.

This new edition of *Residential Housing & Interiors* represents a comprehensive revision of the existing text. The 2005 edition includes three new chapters.

- Chapter 21, "Communication, Security, and Home Automation," covers information and communication systems, signal and communication systems, structured wiring, security systems, home automation, and low-voltage switching.

- Chapter 23, "Designing for Health and Safety," covers smoke and fire detection, carbon monoxide detection, radon issues, moisture and mold problems, weather- and nature-related safety, and general home safety.

- Chapter 30, "Keeping a Job and Advancing a Career," deals with topics such as job performance, safety on the job, continuing education, good communication techniques, ethics, teamwork, leadership, entrepreneurship, self-employment, conflict resolution, the importance of meeting clients' needs, and managing home and work responsibilities.

In addition to the new chapters, content has been added in other areas, most notably on the following topics: Art Deco and Twenty-First Century furniture styles (Chapter 11), green building (Chapter 22), remodeling (Chapter 26), and career paths and a career in interior design (Chapter 29).

Other changes in the 2005 text include the addition of key terms, chapter summaries, Internet resources, and suggested activities for each chapter. More than 200 new, full-color photos and illustrations and 10 new section headings were also added to this edition.

Residential Housing & Interiors is designed to be used with several different housing courses, not just one specific course outline. It may also be used as a reference or resource for housing and architectural drawing classes or for outside the classroom. It is organized, concise, and easy to read, which makes it simple to use. Each chapter is fully illustrated with drawings and many color photographs.

Students should be encouraged at the beginning of the course to thoroughly study the text and become familiar with its contents. They should review the topics to be covered as well as relevant terms in the Glossary and Index to assure understanding of concepts. This will help them find information quickly and easily and save valuable class time needed for instruction and other learning activities. Students may also need to perform a number of activities outside the classroom due to the limited amount of instruction time and the vast quantity of subject matter provided in the text. Each chapter in the text includes the following features:

- **Objectives.** A list of learning objectives begins each chapter so students know what will be expected of them after studying the chapter and how they will benefit from mastering the material.

- **Key Terms.** Key terms are listed after the objectives. They appear in bold type in the text when initially discussed. The student is immediately made aware that the term is important and that he or she should become familiar with the definition. An explanation of each term is provided when it is first referenced. Each key term is also defined in the Glossary.

- **Text Body.** The body of the text is divided into main heads and subheads. The main heads identify the major concepts in the chapter. These concepts are discussed in detail in the subheads. Each chapter is arranged in a logical sequence to aid in mastering the material and establishing a foundation for continued learning.

- **Chapter Summary.** A summary is provided at the end of each chapter to review the major concepts covered.

- **Review Questions.** The review questions at the end of each chapter cover the basic information presented. These short-answer questions are designed to help students review, organize, and apply key information discussed in the text. You may wish to assign these questions as a homework assignment or quiz. You may also wish to supplement these questions with other study and evaluation strategies.

Answers to the review questions appear in this *Instructor's Resource Portfolio.* You may have students search out answers to questions they do not know, or you may wish to go over answers with students. Give students an opportunity to raise questions of their own so you can clarify information and explain the answers to any questions students may have missed.

- **Suggested Activities.** The activities proposed at the end of each chapter enable students to learn more about different aspects of housing and interiors. They are designed to provide hands-on experiences or allow students to research further designs, materials, elements, and methods.

- **Internet Resources.** Several Web sites are listed at the end of each chapter for additional sources of information related to the chapter content. They include sites for information on manufacturers, trade and professional associations, government agencies, and trade publications.

Using the *Student Activity Guide*

The *Student Activity Guide* is divided into chapters that correspond to those in the text. Each chapter consists of activities designed to help students master the subject matter presented in the text, expand their knowledge beyond the text, and strengthen their learning. The activities will also help you determine how students are progressing.

After students have read the chapter in the text, discuss the concepts presented in the chapter and supplement the text material with additional information. When you are satisfied that students have a basic understanding of the text material, have them complete the various types of activities in the *Student Activity Guide*. These activities encourage students to review the chapter's main concepts, explore community resources, and become exposed to the many mechanical and electrical systems and building practices currently used in residential housing.

Each chapter begins with "Check Your Understanding" to provide an opportunity for students to demonstrate their mastery of the chapter content. The review includes questions, multiple-choice answers, sentence completion, and matching exercises. Students should work through this review without looking in the text. When they have completed the activity, they can use the text to check their answers and strengthen areas where they lack understanding.

The remaining exercises are designed to create student interest and reinforce chapter content through application. Some activities give students a chance to perform many of the same problem-solving tasks as professionals. Other activities enable students to further refine the techniques presented in the text. A wide variety of activities are included to meet the needs of students with varying levels of ability. In addition, the activities require students to develop design ideas.

Answers to the activities provided in the *Student Activity Guide* are listed in this *Instructor's Resource Portfolio*. You may wish to review the answers with the students. This will enable you to answer student questions and further clarify the more challenging material.

The pages in the *Student Activity Guide* are perforated for easy removal and are drilled to allow students to place them in their notebooks for future use.

Using the *Instructor's Resource Portfolio*

This *Instructor's Resource Portfolio* for *Residential Housing & Interiors* suggests various ways to present the text material to students. Additional resources, evaluation techniques, effective communication skills, and sources for supplementary teaching materials are also included.

The *Instructor's Resource Portfolio* is divided into chapters that correspond to the chapters in the text. Each chapter contains a number of specific suggestions for teaching the concepts covered in the text chapter. The suggested activities enable students to relate these concepts to practical situations. Each chapter in this *Instructor's Resource Portfolio* contains the following components:

- **Objectives.** Students will be able to accomplish these objectives after completing the chapter activities.

- **Teaching Materials.** A list of all text, *Student Activity Guide*, and *Instructor Resources* materials available to supplement each chapter is provided. The list includes the names of all activities in the *Student Activity Guide* that relate to the chapter. The list also includes reproducible masters, transparency masters, and chapter test masters.

- **Instructional Concepts and Student Activities.** A variety of teaching strategies and student learning experiences are presented according to the major chapter headings. Discussion topics are recommended as well as supplementary exercises, such as inviting guest speakers, conducting field trips, and showing videos. Suggested student activities require application of the facts, principles, and concepts presented in each content area.

Several of the teaching strategies recommended are discussed further in "Using Other Resources" on page 8. Outside sources to contact for additional teaching materials are listed under "Sources for Supplementary Teaching Materials" on pages 9-14.

- **Answer Keys.** Answers are provided for the Review Questions in the text, the "Check Your Understanding" review in the *Student Activity Guide*, and the Chapter Mastery Tests that conclude each chapter of this manual. In addition, full-page reproductions of some *Student Activity Guide* exercises are included in the Answer Key showing "Solutions" and, for activities with more than one possible approach/answer, "Typical Solutions." The "Typical Solutions" can also be used as handouts to generate discussion among students regarding the different ways they addressed the issue.

- **Reproducible Masters.** Reproducible masters are included in each chapter to enhance the presentation of concepts. Some masters are designated as transparency masters for use with an overhead projector. The masters can also be used as student handouts. Often these summaries, illustrations, and graphs can encourage creative and critical thinking and serve as a basis for class discussion of important concepts.

- **Chapter Mastery Tests.** The major concepts presented in each chapter of the text are covered in the Chapter Mastery Tests. Review techniques include questions, multiple-choice answers, and sentence completion.

All materials are in a convenient three-ring binder so reproducible materials can be removed easily. Handy dividers included with the binder help you organize materials so you can quickly find the items you need.

Using the Correlation of *National Standards for Housing, Interiors, and Furnishings* with *Residential Housing & Interiors*

The National Standards for Family and Consumer Sciences Education is a comprehensive guide that provides family and consumer sciences educators with a structure for identifying what learners should be able to do. This structure is based on knowledge and skills needed for work life and family life, as well as family and consumer sciences careers.

The National Standards Components include 16 areas of study, each with a comprehensive standard that describes the overall content of the area. Each comprehensive standard is subdivided into several content standards that describe what is expected of the learner. Competencies further define the knowledge, skills, and practices of the content standards and provide the basis for measurement criteria.

By studying the *Residential Housing & Interiors* text, students will be prepared to master most of the competencies listed for the area of study called "Housing, Interiors, and Furnishings." To identify how this can be accomplished, a correlation chart is included here on pages 21-30. If you want to prepare students to meet the National Standards for Family and Consumer Sciences Education, this chart will interest you.

Using the *Instructor's Resource CD* with **Exam**View Test Generator

The *Instructor's Resource CD* includes all the contents of the *Instructor's Resource Portfolio* plus the **Exam**View Test Generator. The CD format allows you to view and print resource pages exactly as they appear in the *Instructor's Resource Portfolio* from your computer. Links in the table of contents take you directly to specific pages. To produce overhead transparencies, simply print transparency master pages onto acetate film designed for your printer.

The **Exam**View Test Generator database includes all test master questions from the *Instructor's Resource Portfolio* plus an additional 25 percent new questions prepared just for this new product. Program features guide you step-by-step through the creation of a formatted test. You can generate a test with randomly selected questions, choose specific questions from the database, or add your own questions to create customized tests for your classroom needs. You can also make different versions of the same test to use during different class periods. Answer keys are generated automatically to simplify grading.

Using the *Instructor's PowerPoint Presentations CD*

The new *Instructor's PowerPoint® Presentations CD* provides slide presentations designed for display in the classroom. The presentations are tied to material in the text and highlight key concepts and visual materials. They can be used with the PowerPoint Viewer utility, which is included with the CD. Presentations are provided for each chapter in the text. They are intended as special lecture supplements to generate student interest and classroom discussion.

Using Other Resources

Students can understand better when they see, feel, analyze, and use examples. Providing articles, illustrations, samples of materials, guest speakers, and field trips related to housing and interiors can reinforce student learning, add a dimension of realism, and contribute to students' personal experiences.

Publications are a good source of information and visual aids to reinforce student learning. Magazines are good sources of pictures depicting interior treatments, types and styles of housing, and landscape designs. Floor plans for students to evaluate and articles about housing can often be found in magazines and newspapers. Current issues of magazines and journals are good sources for student research and design. Suggested publications include:

Better Homes and Gardens
Computers for Design and Construction
Consumer Reports
Custom Builder
Exteriors
Historic Preservation
Home
House and Garden
Housing and Society (Journal of American Association of Housing Educators)
Journal of the American Planning Association
Journal of Family and Consumer Sciences
Money
New Shelter
Progressive Architecture
Sunset
What's New in Family and Consumer Sciences?

Samples of building materials and decorative treatments for students to examine in class make the learning experience more realistic. Paint stores, home improvement centers, carpeting stores, and upholstery and drapery shops are good sources of samples, such as paint chips, wallpaper books, flooring samples, and carpet and fabric remnants. These may be free, purchased for a nominal fee, or available for short-term loan.

Professionals in your community can be used to enhance classroom instruction and students' personal experiences. These talented individuals often are willing to share their housing expertise with the class through discussions or demonstrations. Suggested professionals include interior designers, architects, landscape designers, residential building contractors, lighting specialists, and kitchen planning designers. Your local community college or university may also be a good source for career information in housing and interior design fields.

Field trips give students a first-hand look at the housing industry. Students can also gain a close-up view of the important functions performed by professionals in the housing field. Visits to home improvement shows, historical or art museums, building planning centers, furniture stores, building sites, or ornamental nurseries can expand student knowledge.

Sources for Supplementary Teaching Materials

These are companies, associations, and government groups whose main purpose is to enlighten the public, provide information, and generally publicize the field, products, or purpose of their association, group, or company. The following list is not meant to be comprehensive but includes a number of housing resources that should help the teacher in gathering ideas and materials to enhance the teaching/learning process.

Companies, Associations, and Government Groups

A.O. Smith Water Products Company
hotwater.com

About, Inc.'s Color, Design, and Style Index
interiordec.about.com/cs/designcolorstyle

Acorn Stairlifts
acornstairlifts.com

Air Conditioning and Refrigeration Institute
ari.org

Alside, Inc.
alside.com

Aluminum Company of America (ALCOA) Building Products, Inc.
alcoahomes.com

American Association of Textile Chemists and Colorists
aatcc.org

American ConForm Industries
smartblock.com

American Fiber Manufacturers Association/Fiber Economics Bureau, Inc.
fibersource.org

American Institute of Architects
aia.org

American Institute of Building Design
aibd.org

American Institute of Constructors
aicnet.org

American Iron and Steel Institute
steel.org

American Lighting Association
americanlightingassoc.com

American Society for Testing and Materials
astm.org

American Society of Interior Designers
asid.org

American Society of Landscape Architects
asla.org

American Solar Energy Society
ases.org

Anchor Retaining Wall Systems
anchorwall.com

Antique Furniture Dealers
rubylane.com

Architectural Ornament, Inc.
architectural-ornamentation.com

Archtek Telecom Corp.
archtek.com

Arcways, Inc.
arcways.com

Armstrong World Industries, Inc.
armstrong.com

ART Inc., publisher of Chief Architect® software
chiefarch.com

Asphalt Institute
asphaltinstitute.org

ASTM International, formerly the American Society for Testing Materials
astm.org

ATAS International, Inc., a manufacturer of metal roofing
atas.com

Autodesk, Inc., publisher of AutoCAD®
autodesk.com

Avis America
avisamerica.com

B.F. Goodrich's FlowGuard Gold
flowguardgold.com

Baker Furniture
kohlerinteriors.com

Ball and Ball
ballandball-us.com

Bartley Collection Ltd.
bartleycollection.com

Bently Systems Inc.
bentley.com/products

Boise Cascade Engineered Wood Products
bcewp.com

Boral Bricks Inc.
boralbricks.com

Brass Light Gallery
brasslight.com

Broyhill Furniture Industries, Inc.
broyhillfurn.com

Building Systems Councils of National Association
of Home Builders
buildingsystems.org

California Closets
calclosets.com

California Redwood Association
calredwood.org

Caradco
caradco.com

Carpet and Rug Institute
carpet-rug.com

Carrier Corporation
carrier.com

Cast Stone Institute
caststone.org

Cemplank
cemplank.com

Center for Furniture Craftsmanship
woodschool.org

Centers for Disease Control and Prevention
cdc.gov

Ceramic Tile Institute of America
ctioa.org

Compaq Computers, a Hewlett-Packard Company
compaq.com

Congoleum Corporation
congoleum.com

Connecticut Valley School of Woodworking
schoolofwoodworking.com

Consumer Electronics Association TechHome
Division
techhome.org

Cooper Wiring Devices
eagle-electric.com

Cor-A-Vent, Inc.
cor-a-vent.com

Cultured Stone
culturedstone.com

Dell Inc.
dell.com

Design Basics, Inc.
designbasics.com

Design-Build Institute of America
dbia.org

Earthship Biotecture
earthship.org

Echelon Corporation
echelon.com

ELAN Home Systems.
elanhomesystems.com

Eldorado Stone
eldoradostone.com

Elk Corporation of America
elkcorp.com

ELK Products, Inc.
elkproducts.com

Energy Star Program,
energystar.gov

EnergyGuide Program
ftc.gov/bcp/conline/edcams/appliances/eg.htm

Eric Crown Design Group
designgroupstudio.com

Federal Emergency Management Agency
fema.gov

Forest Products Laboratory
fpl.fs.fed.us

Geist Manufacturing, Inc.
flexiduct.com

General Electric
ge.com/product/home/lighting.htm

National Hardwood Lumber Association
natlhardwood.org

National Institute of Building Sciences
nibs.org

National Oceanic and Atmospheric Administration
(National Weather Service)
noaa.gov

National Paint and Coatings Assn.
paint.org

National Precast Concrete Association
precast.org

National Radon Safety Board
nrsb.org

National Safety Council
nsc.org

Natuzzi
natuzzi.com

North American Insulation Manufacturers Association
naima.org

Owens Corning
owenscorning.com

Painting and Decorating Contractors of America
pdca.org

Pease Entry Systems
peasedoors.com

Pella Corporation
pella.com

Portland Cement Association
concretehomes.com and portcement.org

Pozzi Wood Windows
pozzi.com

Price Pfister
pricepfister.com

Professor J.L. Morton, Color Matters®—Design-Art
colormatters.com/colortheory.html

Progress Lighting
progresslighting.com

Raynor Garage Doors
raynor.com

Reemay, Inc.
reemay.com

Renewable Energy Policy Project
crest.org

Reynolds Building Products
reynoldsbp.com

Sauder Woodworking Company
sauder.com

Schulte Corporation
schultestorage.com

Sea Gull Lighting Products, Inc.
seagulllighting.com

Smarthome™, Inc.
smarthome.com

Society for Protective Coatings
sspc.org

SoftPlan Systems, Inc.
softplan.com

Southern Pine Council
southrnpine.com

Sterling Plumbing, a Kohler Company
sterlingplumbing.com

Studer Residential Designs
studerdesigns.com

The Engineered Wood Association
apawood.org

The Hoover Company
hoovercompany.com

The McGraw-Hill Companies, Inc. construction
products marketplace
sweets.com

The Reinforced Earth Company
recousa.com

The Sater Design Collection, Inc.
saterdesign.com

The Siemon Company
homecabling.com

The Trane Company
trane.com

The Weather Channel
weather.com

Thomasville Furniture Industries, Inc.
thomasville.com

Trex Company
trex.com

U.S. Department of Energy
energy.gov

U.S. Department of Energy, National Renewable
Energy Laboratory
nrel.gov

U.S. Department of Energy, Office of Energy
Efficiency and Renewable Energy
eren.doe.gov

U.S. Department of Housing and Urban Development
hud.gov

U.S. Department of Labor's Occupational
Information Network (O*NET)
onetcenter.org

U.S. Department of Labor's *Occupational Outlook Handbook*
bls.gov/oco/

U.S. Department of Veterans Affairs
va.gov

U.S. Environmental Protection Agency
epa.gov

U.S. Forest Products Laboratory
fpl.fs.fed.us

U.S. Green Building Council
usgbc.org

U.S. Occupational Safety and Health Administration (OSHA)
osha.gov

Vanguard Piping Systems, Inc.
vanguardpipe.com

Velux
velux.com

Ventamatic, Ltd.
bvc.com

Wausau Homes
wausauhomes.com

Western Wood Products Association
wwpa.org

Whirlpool Corporation
whirlpool.com

Windsor Windows and Doors
windsorwindows.com

X10 Home Solutions
x10.com

Trade and Technical Publications

Architectural Digest
architecturaldigest.com

Architectural Record
architecturalrecord.com

Architecture
architecturemag.com

Builder
hanleywood.com

Building Design & Construction
bdcmag.com

Building Products
hanleywood.com

Cadalyst
cadalyst.com

Computer Graphics World
cgw.pennnet.com

Concrete Construction
hanleywood.com

Construction Digest
acppubs.com

Design News
designnews.com

Environmental Building News
buildinggreen.com

Fine Homebuilding
taunton.com/finehomebuilding

Fine Woodworking
taunton.com/finewoodworking

Heating/Piping/Air Conditioning Engineering
hpac.com

Interior Design
interiordesign.net

Journal of Light Construction
hanleywood.com

Landscape Architecture
asla.org/nonmembers/lam.cfm

Masonry Construction
hanleywood.com

Modern Plastics
modplas.com

Multi-Housing News
multi-housingnews.com

Old House Journal
oldhousejournal.com

Preservation
nationaltrust.org/magazine

Professional Builder
housingzone.com/pb

Qualified Remodeler
qrmagazine.com

Remodeling
hanleywood.com

Woodshop News
woodshopnews.com

Woodsmith
woodsmith.com

In addition to these sources, students should have access to other reference materials including the following: the American National Standards Institute (ANSI) manuals, Architectural Graphic Standards, Timesaver Standards for architectural design data, the Sweets architectural files, and texts on architecture, design, drafting, construction, manufacturing, materials, and processes. These references should be available to students in the classroom or the school library. *Note: Phone numbers and Web addresses may have changed since publication.*

Strategies for Successful Teaching

By using a variety of teaching strategies, you can make *Residential Housing & Interiors* exciting and relevant for your students. As you plan your lessons and classroom activities, you may also want to keep the following points in mind.

Using Effective Communication Skills

Select a variety of instructional strategies that stimulate interest in learning. Move around the classroom and communicate with students at their desks. Offer advice and support, inform them of their progress, and use praise and encouragement freely.

A variety of techniques can be used to improve teaching and create and maintain student interest. One is motivating your students. Motivation is any factor that starts an individual toward a goal and sustains him or her until the goal is reached. Motivated students are seldom bored and are more eager to learn.

Another technique is creating enthusiasm and excitement in the classroom. Enthusiasm sets the stage for learning and helps students maintain interest in the subject. It keeps their morale high and results in better recall of the material studied. For example, you can create interesting bulletin board displays or demonstrate drawing techniques. When students view the activities as meaningful and not just busy work, the learning experience becomes more exciting.

It is important to encourage students to succeed. Students who are actively involved in class activities generally learn better and are more successful. Plan activities that let students achieve as much as possible. This will give them a positive attitude about learning. Try to predict where failure might occur in the learning process and put forth an extra effort to help students succeed. Let students know that you have confidence in them and are there to help. This extra attention will inspire them to work harder.

Stay alert to new developments in the field of housing and interiors, particularly in your own community, and share this knowledge with your class. Read the latest journals and housing-related publications to learn about new designs and innovations. Visit building materials centers to see the latest materials on the market and gather brochures. Be aware of the latest computer-aided software and drawing equipment as well as Internet sites worth exploring.

Helping Your Students Develop Critical Thinking Skills

Today's students are likely to work in several career areas and hold many different jobs. They must be prepared to solve complex problems, make difficult decisions, and assess ethical implications. In other words, students must be able to use critical thinking skills, the higher-order thinking skills that Benjamin Bloom listed as follows:

- analysis—breaking down material into its component parts so that its organizational structure may be understood

- synthesis—putting parts together to form a new whole

- evaluation—judging the value of material for a given purpose

In a broader perspective, students must be able to use reflective thinking to decide what to believe and do. According to Robert Ennis, students should be able to do the following:

- Define and clarify problems, issues, conclusions, reasons, and assumptions.

- Judge the credibility, relevance, and consistency of information.

- Infer or solve problems and draw reasonable conclusions.

To think critically, students must possess knowledge that goes beyond simply memorizing or recalling information. Critical thinking requires individuals to use common sense and experience, apply their knowledge, and recognize the controversies surrounding an issue. Critical thinking also requires creative thinking to construct all the reasonable alternatives, possible consequences, influencing factors, and supporting arguments. Unusual ideas are valued and perspectives outside the obvious are sought.

The teaching of critical thinking does not require exotic and highly unusual classroom approaches. Complex thought processes can be incorporated in the most ordinary and basic activities, even reading, writing, and listening, if these activities are carefully planned and well executed.

You can help your students develop their analytical and judgmental skills by going beyond what they see on the surface. Rather than allowing students to blindly accept what they read or hear, encourage them to examine ideas in ways that show respect for others' opinions and different perspectives. Encourage students to think about points raised by others. Ask them to evaluate how new ideas relate to their attitudes about various subjects.

Debate is an excellent way to thoroughly explore an issue. You may want to divide the class into two groups, each examining an opposing side. You can also have students explore an issue from all sides in small groups. With both methods, representatives can be chosen to summarize the key thoughts expressed within each group.

Helping Students Develop Decision-Making Skills

An important aspect in the development of critical thinking skills is learning how to solve problems and make decisions. Important decisions lie ahead for your students, particularly related to their future education and career choices. Chapters 29 and 30 of *Residential Housing & Interiors* will help students prepare for career success.

Using Cooperative Learning

The use of cooperative learning groups in your classroom gives students an opportunity to practice teamwork skills, which are highly valued in the community and the workplace. During cooperative learning activities, students learn interpersonal and small-group skills that will help them function as part of a team. These skills include leadership, decision-making, trust building, communication, and conflict management.

When planning for cooperative learning, you will have a particular goal or task in mind. First, specify the objectives for the lesson. Then, match small groups of learners based on the task and assign each person a role. Group members should be selected to include a mix of abilities and talents so opportunities for students to learn from one another exist. As groups work together over time, individuals' roles should rotate so everyone has an opportunity to practice and develop different skills.

The success of the group is measured not only in terms of group outcome, but also in terms of the successful performance of each member in his or her role. Interdependence is a basic component of any cooperative learning group. Students understand that one person cannot succeed unless everyone does. The value of each group member is affirmed as learners work toward the group's goal.

You will also need to monitor the effectiveness of the groups, intervening as necessary to provide task assistance or help with interpersonal or group skills. Finally, evaluate the group's achievement and help members discuss how well they collaborated.

Helping Students Recognize and Value Diversity

Your students will be entering a rapidly changing workplace—not only in matters pertaining to technology, but also in the diverse nature of its workforce. The majority of the new entrants to the workforce are women, minorities, and immigrants, all representing many different views and experiences. The workforce is aging, too, as most people in the workforce have decades of experience. Because of these trends, young workers must learn how to interact effectively with a variety of people who are unlike them in many ways.

The appreciation and understanding of diversity is an ongoing process. The earlier and more frequently young people are exposed to diversity, the more quickly they can develop skills to bridge cultural differences. If your students are exposed to various cultures within your classroom, the process of understanding cultural differences can begin. This is the best preparation for success in a diverse society. In addition, teachers find the following strategies for teaching diversity helpful:

- Actively promote a spirit of openness, consideration, respect, and tolerance in the classroom.

- Use a variety of teaching styles and assessment strategies.

- Use cooperative learning activities whenever possible, making sure group roles are rotated so everyone has leadership opportunities.

- When grouping students, have each group's composition as diverse as possible with regard to gender, race, age, and nationality. If groups present information to the class, make sure all members have a speaking part.

- Make sure one group's opinions are not over-represented during class discussions. Seek opinions of under-represented groups or individuals if necessary.

- If a student makes a sexist, racist, or other comment that is likely to be offensive, ask the student to rephrase the comment in a manner that it will not offend other members of the class. Remind students that offensive statements and behavior are inappropriate in the classroom.

- If a difficult classroom situation arises involving a diversity issue, ask for a time-out and have everyone write down his or her thoughts and opinions about the incident. This helps to calm the class down and allows you time to plan a response.

- Arrange for guest speakers who represent diversity in gender, race, and ethnicity, even though the topic does not relate to diversity.

- Have students change seats occasionally throughout the course and introduce themselves to their new "neighbors" so they become acquainted with all their classmates.

- Several times during the course, ask students to make anonymous, written evaluations of the class. Have them report any problems that may not be obvious.

Effective Evaluation

Evaluation is an important step in the teaching/learning process. Evaluation includes determining how students are performing as well as assessing their feelings about the class. As a conscientious teacher, you will want to be aware of students' thoughts and how they are growing intellectually.

The overall goal of effective teaching is to assist students in meeting the required objectives. A combination of your efforts and student learning can accomplish this goal. The students' ability to learn, plus the effectiveness of the teaching, is evident by an evaluation of the technical skills obtained, the concepts learned, and the mental processes of identifying and solving problems that students have developed.

The evaluation process begins with a clear statement of the overall objectives for the course. Students need to know exactly what they will be expected to know and do. You should clearly state what class behavior is acceptable and explain various class procedures. In addition, students should have a clear understanding of how they will be evaluated.

Evaluation is an ongoing process that continues throughout the class term. A variety of evaluation tools and methods are used, including reviews, tests, progress charts, and individual- as well as group-project evaluations.

A vital part of the evaluation process is immediate feedback. The best way to achieve this is by carefully observing student performance and commenting quickly on student work, providing both positive remarks and suggestions for improvement. This helps students know if they are correctly applying the knowledge learned.

Using a variety of evaluation methods permits students to express their understanding in different ways. Students with good eye-hand coordination frequently can perform successfully using drawing equipment. Those who can visualize a completed project before even starting the drawing process may be successful using the computer. Other students can perform better on written work. Provide opportunities for each student to indicate what he or she has learned.

The evaluation should always be based on guidelines and models. For example, guidelines are presented in the text for good traffic circulation. When evaluating designs for floor plans, base the evaluation on how closely the design follows these guidelines. Also, the examples in the text should be used as models for students to pattern their work after. When evaluating students' work, use the models for comparison while encouraging creativity.

The weight, or emphasis, given to various scores from evaluation devices should vary among the different projects based on their relative importance. Values should be given to projects when they are assigned so students know the worth of each. For example, a set of plans for a structure might have greater value than a chapter test.

Evaluate student performance with a degree of flexibility. Extra attention and time may be required for some students to complete their projects. Have the laboratory classroom available for student use after class hours to give students extra time to complete projects when necessary and to provide time for advanced students to work on special projects.

Assessment Techniques

Various forms of assessment are used with students to fully evaluate their achievements. Written tests have traditionally been used to evaluate performance. This method of evaluation is good to use when assessing knowledge and comprehension. Other methods of assessment are preferable for measuring the achievement of the higher-level skills of application, analysis, synthesis, and evaluation.

The text includes the following opportunities for assessing student achievements:

- A *Chapter Review* section follows each chapter summary to evaluate students' recall of key concepts.

- Activities concluding each chapter provide opportunities to assess students' abilities to use critical thinking, problem solving, and application.

In the *Student Activity Guide*, each chapter begins with "Check Your Understanding" to provide an opportunity for students to demonstrate their mastery of the chapter content. The remaining exercises are designed to reinforce chapter content through application. Some activities give students a chance to perform many of the same problem-solving tasks as professionals.

In the instructor's resources, the following means of assessing learning are found:

- In each chapter's list of student activities, Item #2 directs students to assemble a housing notebook, sometimes called portfolios, by collecting samples and creating materials relevant to the chapter's content.

Contents

- An objective Chapter Mastery Test for each chapter appears in the *Instructor's Resource Portfolio/CD*.

- A tool to create customized tests is available in the *Instructor's Resource CD* with **Exam***View* Test Generator.

Portfolios

Another type of performance assessment frequently used by teachers is the student portfolio. A portfolio consists of a selection of materials that students assemble to document their performance over a period of time. The purpose of the portfolio determines the type of items it should contain. Portfolios basically serve two purposes—to gauge progress or demonstrate employability.

For portfolios developed to gauge student progress in a course, items should demonstrate problem-solving and critical-thinking skills. A self-assessment summary report should be included that explains what has been accomplished, what has been learned, what strengths the student has gained, and which areas need improvement.

Items chosen for the portfolio are discussed with the teacher in light of educational goals and outcomes. When portfolios are evaluated for a grade, students should be given a portfolio rubric to follow and guidance on how creativity will affect their grade. Portfolios should remain the property of students when they leave the course.

For a job portfolio, items should provide evidence of employability and academic skills. These portfolios are appropriate for displaying at job interviews. Students select their best work samples to showcase their achievements. Some items appropriate for job portfolios are as follows:

- work samples (including sketches, diagrams, photographs, assessments, and so forth) that show mastery of specific skills

- writing samples that show communication skills

- a resume

- letters of recommendation that document specific career-related skills

- certificates of completion

- awards and recognition

Portfolio assessment is only one of several evaluation methods teachers can use, but it is a powerful tool for both students and teachers. It encourages students to make a thorough self-reflection and self-assessment. Traditional evaluation methods of tests, quizzes, and reports have their place in measuring the achievement of some course objectives, but portfolios and other assessment tools should also be used to fairly gauge the realization of other desired outcomes.

Performance Assessment

When you assign students some of the projects appearing at the end of each chapter, a different form of assessing mastery or achievement is required. One method that teachers successfully use is a rubric. A rubric consists of a set of criteria that includes specific descriptors or standards used for determining performance scores for students. A point value is given for each set of descriptors, leading to a range of possible points to be assigned, usually from 1 to 5. The criteria can also be weighted. This method of assessment reduces the guesswork involved in grading, leading to fair and consistent scoring. The standards clearly indicate to students the various levels of mastery of a task. Students are even able to assess their own achievement based on the criteria.

When using rubrics, students should see the criteria at the beginning of the assignment. Then they can focus their effort on what needs to be done to reach a certain performance or quality level. They have a clear understanding of your expectations of achievement.

Though you will want to design many of your own rubrics, several generic versions are included here on pages 18-20. The rubrics are designed to assess the following:

- individual participation

- individual reports

- group participation

These rubrics allow you to assess a student's performance and arrive at a performance score. Students can see what levels they have surpassed and what levels they can still strive to reach.

Goodheart-Willcox Welcomes Your Comments

We welcome your comments or suggestions regarding *Residential Housing and Interiors* and its ancillaries as we are continually striving to publish better educational materials. Please send any comments you may have by visiting our Website at *g-w.com* or writing to the following address:

FCS Editorial Department
Goodheart-Willcox Publisher
18604 West Creek Drive
Tinley Park, IL 60477-6243

Evaluation of Individual Participation

Name _____

Date _____

The rating scale below shows an evaluation of your class participation. It indicates what levels you have passed and what levels you can continue to try to reach.

Criteria:

1. Attentiveness

1	2	3	4	5
Completely inattentive.	Seldom attentive.	Somewhat attentive.	Usually attentive.	Extremely attentive.

2. Contribution to Discussion

1	2	3	4	5
Never contributes to class discussion.	Rarely contributes to class discussion.	Occasionally contributes to class discussion.	Regularly contributes to class discussion.	Frequently contributes to class discussion.

3. Interaction with Peers

1	2	3	4	5
Often distracts others.	Shows little interaction with others.	Follows leadership of other students.	Sometimes assumes leadership role.	Respected by peers for ability.

4. Response to Teacher

1	2	3	4	5
Unable to respond when called on.	Often unable to support or justify answers when called on.	Supports answers based on class information, but seldom offers new ideas.	Able to offer new ideas with prompting.	Often offers new ideas without prompting.

Total Points: _____ out of 20

Comments:

_____

_____

Evaluation of Individual Reports

Name _____

Date _____

The rating scale below shows an evaluation of your oral or written report. It indicates what levels you have passed and what levels you can try to reach on future reports.

Report title _____ Oral _____ Written _____

Criteria:

1. Choice of Topic

1	2	3	4	5
Slow to choose topic.	Chooses topic with indifference.	Chooses topic as assigned, seeks suggestions.	Chooses relevant topic without assistance.	Chooses creative topic.

2. Use of Resources

1	2	3	4	5
Unable to find resources.	Needs direction to find resources.	Uses fewer than assigned number of resources.	Uses assigned number of resources from typical sources.	Uses additional resources from a variety of sources.

3. Oral Presentation

1	2	3	4	5
Uses no notes or reads completely. Poor subject coverage.	Has few good notes. Limited subject coverage.	Uses notes somewhat effectively. Adequate subject coverage.	Uses notes effectively. Good subject coverage.	Uses notes very effectively. Complete coverage.

4. Written Presentation

1	2	3	4	5
Many grammar and spelling mistakes. No organization.	Several grammar and spelling mistakes. Poor organization.	Some grammar and spelling mistakes. Fair organization.	A few grammar and spelling mistakes. Good organization.	No grammar or spelling mistakes. Excellent organization.

Total Points: _____ **out of** _____

Evaluation of Group Participation

Name _____

Date _____

Group Members: _____

The rating scale below shows an evaluation of the efforts of your group. It indicates what levels you have passed and what levels you can try to reach on future group projects.

Criteria:

1. Teamwork

1	2	3	4	5
Passive membership. Failed to identify what tasks needed to be completed.	Argumentative membership. Unable to designate who should complete each task.	Independent membership. All tasks completed individually.	Helpful membership. Completed individual tasks and then assisted others.	Cooperative membership. Worked together to complete all tasks.

2. Leadership

1	2	3	4	5
No attempt at leadership.	No effective leadership.	Sought leadership from outside group.	One member assumed primary leadership role for the group.	Leadership responsibilities shared by several group members.

3. Goal Achievement

1	2	3	4	5
Did not attempt to achieve goal.	Were unable to achieve goal.	Achieved goal with outside assistance.	Achieved assigned goal.	Achieved goal using added materials to enhance total effort.

Total Points: _____ **out of 15**

Members cited for excellent contributions to group's effort are:

_____

_____

Members cited for failing to contribute to group's effort are:

_____

_____

Correlation of National Standards for *Housing, Interiors, and Furnishings* with *Residential Housing and Interiors*

In planning your program, you may want to use the chart shown here. It correlates the Family and Consumer Sciences Education National Standards with the content of *Residential Housing and Interiors*. The chart lists the competencies for each content standard within the "Housing, Interiors, and Furnishings" area. Also listed are the text topics that relate to each competency and the chapters in which they are found (with numbers shown in bold).

After studying the content of this text, students will be able to achieve the following comprehensive standard:

11.0 Integrate knowledge, skills, and practices required for careers in housing, interiors, and furnishings.

Competencies	Text Concepts
11.1.1 Determine the roles and functions of individuals engaged in housing, interiors, and furnishings careers.	**26:** Preparing remodeling, renovation, and preservation plans; the interior designer; the architect; the contractor **29:** Planners and designers; architect; architectural drafter; architectural illustrator; interior designer; model maker; landscape designer; building tradespeople; building contractor; construction technologist; skilled tradesperson; construction machinery operator; land surveyor; allied careers; government positions; real estate positions
11.1.2 Explore opportunities for employment and entrepreneurial endeavors.	**29:** Planners and designers; architect; architectural drafter; architectural illustrator; interior designer; model maker; landscape designer; building tradespeople; building contractor; construction technologist; skilled tradesperson; construction machinery operator; land surveyor; allied careers; government positions; real estate positions **30:** Entrepreneurship; characteristics of entrepreneurs; self-employment
11.1.3 Examine education and training requirements and opportunities for career paths in housing, interiors, and furnishings.	**29:** Planners and designers; architect; architectural drafter; architectural illustrator; interior designer; model maker; landscape designer; building tradespeople; building contractor; construction technologist; skilled tradesperson; construction machinery operator; land surveyor; allied careers; government positions; real estate positions preparing for a career path in housing; what is a career path? for what jobs are you suited? how do you get the job you want? **30:** Job performance; continuing your education
11.1.4 Examine the impact of housing, interiors, and furnishings occupations on local, state, national, and global economies.	**29:** Planners and designers; building tradespeople; allied careers; preparing for a career path in housing; what is a career path?

Competencies	Text Concepts
11.2.1 Determine the principles and elements of design.	**6:** Elements of design; space; line; shape and form; texture; color; principles of design; proportion and scale; balance; emphasis; rhythm
11.2.2 Determine the psychological impact the principles and elements of design have on the individual.	**6:** Goals of design; appropriateness; harmony, variety, and unity; function **7:** The psychology of color; the color spectrum; the color wheel; color characteristics; warm and cool colors; neutral colors; color harmonies
11.2.3 Determine the effects the principles and elements of design have on aesthetics and function.	**6:** Goals of design; appropriateness; harmony, variety, and unity; function, accessories in design **7:** Color characteristics; warm and cool colors; neutral colors; color systems; color harmonies; effect of light on color; effect of adjacent colors; effect of texture on color; effect of color on space; color decisions **23:** Planning the landscape, landscape design

Competencies	Text Concepts
11.3.1 Research product information including but not limited to floor coverings, wall coverings, textiles, window treatments, furniture, lighting fixtures, kitchen and bath fixtures and equipment, accessories, and building materials.	**8:** Wood; wood classification; wood materials; wood finishes; masonry; structural clay products; concrete masonry units; glass block; stone; concrete; colored concrete; exposed aggregate concrete; textured finishes; geometric patterns **9:** Metals; iron and steel; aluminum; copper; brass; bronze; lead; glass; flat glass; decorative glass; tinted glass; reflective glass; insulating glass; handblown glass; molded glass; leaded glass; ceramics; ceramic tile; roofing tile; pottery; plastics **10:** Fibers; natural fibers; manufactured fibers; yarns; fabric construction; weaving; knitting; tufting; other construction methods; dyeing fabrics; printing fabrics; fabric finishes **11:** Twenty-first century furniture styles; contemporary; traditional; casual; country; eclectic **12:** Wood furniture; wood types; wood finishes; wood furniture construction; upholstered furniture; fabrics; upholstered furniture construction; bedding; metal furniture; plastic furniture; upholstery fabric; ergonomics in furniture design **13:** Wall types; frame walls; masonry walls; wall treatments; wood siding; manufactured siding; mineral fiber shingles; wood shingles; decorative masonry; stucco or plaster; paint; wallpaper; fabric; paneling and boards; ceramic tile; mirrors

Contents

Competencies	Text Concepts
	14: Floor systems; floor treatments; flooring materials; floor coverings **15:** Ceilings and roofs; ceiling-surface materials; ceiling treatments; roofing materials **16:** Window types; window construction; window treatments; interior window treatments; exterior window treatments; door types; door construction; door treatments **18:** Artificial light; incandescent sources; halogen sources; fluorescent sources; applications of lighting; selection and placement; lighting fixtures; lighting controls **19:** Electrical-system components; signal and communication systems; the plumbing system; water supply; wastewater removal; fixtures **20:** Climate control; conventional heating systems; solar heating systems; cooling systems; insulation; fireplaces and stoves **21:** Types of system functions; monitoring functions; switching functions; programming functions; communication and recording functions; alarm functions; information and communication systems; signal and communication systems; structured wiring; security systems; systems to protect property; systems to protect occupants and property; home automation; types of home automation systems; low-voltage switching **22:** Energy-saving appliances; utility area appliances; service area appliances **23:** Smoke and fire detection; smoke detectors; fire extinguishers; carbon monoxide detectors; radon detection; radon testing; mold prevention and removal
11.3.2 Select manufacturers, products, and materials considering care, maintenance, safety, and environmental issues.	**8:** Wood; wood classification; wood materials; wood finishes; masonry; structural clay products; concrete masonry units; glass block; stone; concrete; colored concrete; exposed aggregate concrete; textured finishes; geometric patterns **9:** Metals; iron and steel; aluminum; copper; brass; bronze; lead; glass; flat glass; decorative glass; tinted glass; reflective glass; insulating glass; handblown glass; molded glass; leaded glass; ceramics; ceramic tile; roofing tile; pottery; plastics **10:** Fibers; natural fibers; manufactured fibers; yarns; fabric construction; weaving; knitting; tufting; other construction methods; dyeing fabrics; printing fabrics; fabric finishes **12:** Furniture selection; quality and cost; style; size; upholstery fabric; ergonomics in furniture design; maintenance **13:** Selection of wall treatments; function; appearance **14:** Selection of floor treatments; function; appearance **15:** Ceiling-surface materials; ceiling treatments

Competencies	Text Concepts
	16: Window selection and placement; interior window treatments; exterior window treatments; selection of window treatments; door treatments **18:** Selection and placement; lighting fixtures; lighting areas of the home **19:** Planning the electrical system; planning the plumbing system **20:** Climate control; conventional heating systems; solar heating systems; cooling systems; insulation; other factors; fireplaces and stoves **21:** Types of system functions; information and communication systems; signal and communication systems; structured wiring; security systems; systems to protect property; systems to protect occupants and property; home automation; types of home automation systems; low-voltage switching **22:** Insulation; windows and doors; roofs and walls; heating and plumbing systems; energy-saving appliances; utility area appliances; service area appliances; energy alternatives; energy management with computers; water conservation; green building **23:** Smoke and fire detection; fire prevention; smoke detectors; fire safety code requirements; fire extinguishers; carbon monoxide detection; carbon monoxide poisoning; carbon monoxide detectors; radon detection; radon in the home; radon testing; radon mitigation; moisture and mold problems; migration of water vapor; sources of water vapor; preventive measures; ventilation; health hazards associated with mold; mold prevention and removal; weather- and nature-related safety; general home safety
11.3.3 Review measuring, estimating, ordering, purchasing, and pricing skills.	(The competencies for this content standard are applicable to more advanced texts.)
11.3.4 Appraise various interior furnishings, appliances, and equipment which provide cost and quality choices for clients.	**6:** Accessories in design **12:** Furniture selection; quality and cost; style; size; upholstery fabric; ergonomics in furniture design **13:** Selection of wall treatments **14:** Selection of floor treatments **15:** Ceiling treatments **16:** Selection of window treatments; door treatments **18:** Selection and placement; lighting areas of the home **20:** Fireplaces and stoves **22:** Energy-saving appliances; utility area appliances; service area appliances

Competencies	Text Concepts
11.4.1 Read information provided on blueprints.	**2:** Circulation; types of circulation; circulation frequency; room relationships; reading house plans; description of drawings; other drawings **17:** Stair designs **25:** Planning the landscape; landscape design **27:** Presentation floor plans; presentation elevations; presentation plot plans; presentation landscape plans; presentation sections
11.4.2 Examine floor plans for efficiency and safety in areas including but not limited to zones, traffic patterns, storage, electrical, and mechanical systems.	**2:** Circulation; types of circulation; circulation frequency; room relationships **3:** Living rooms; location; size and arrangement; dining rooms; location; size and arrangement; family rooms; location; size and arrangement; entryways; patios, porches, and courts; adaptations for special needs **4:** Bedrooms; location; size and arrangement; master bedrooms; children's rooms; bathrooms; location; size and arrangement; heat and moisture considerations; adaptations for special needs **5:** Kitchens; location; size and arrangement; work centers; appliances, cabinets, and counters; kitchen designs; laundry facilities; location; size and arrangement; basements; garages and carports; location; size and design; service entries; special-purpose rooms; home offices; storage; adaptations for special needs
11.4.3 Draw an interior space to scale using correct architecture symbols and drafting skills.	**2:** Reading house plans; description of drawings; other drawings **27:** Presentation floor plans; presentation elevations; presentation plot plans; presentation landscape plans; presentation sections **28:** Computer-assisted drafting and design; plot, site, and landscape planning; kitchen and bath design **Appendix:** A-2 Topographical Symbols; A-3 Plumbing Symbols; A-4 Electrical Symbols; A-5 Climate Control Symbols; A-7 Common Sizes of Living Room Furniture; A-8 Common Sizes of Bedroom Furniture; A-9 Minimum Clearance Requirements; A-10 Common sizes of Bathroom Fixtures; A-11 Common Sizes of Kitchen Base Cabinets; A-12 Common Sizes of Kitchen Wall Cabinets; A-13 Common Sizes of Kitchen Appliances; A-15 Building Material Symbols; A-18 Common Furniture Sizes; A-19 Common Sizes of Double-Hung Windows; A-20 Common Sizes of Horizontal Sliding Windows; A-21 Common Sizes of Casement Windows; A-22 Common Sizes of Awning and Hopper Windows; A-23 Common Sizes of Picture Windows; A-24 Common Sizes of Glass Sliding Doors

Competencies	Text Concepts
11.4.4 Arrange furniture placement with reference to principles of design, traffic flow, activity, and existing architectural features.	**3:** Living rooms; location; size and arrangement; dining rooms; location; size and arrangement; family rooms; location; size and arrangement; entryways; patios, porches, and courts; patios; porches; courts; adaptations for special needs **4:** Bedrooms; location; size and arrangement; master bedrooms; children's rooms; bathrooms; location; size and arrangement; heat and moisture considerations; adaptations for special needs **5:** Kitchens; location; size and arrangement; work centers; appliances, cabinets, and counters; kitchen designs; laundry facilities; location; size and arrangement; basements; garages and carports; location; size and design; service entries; special-purpose rooms
11.4.5 Utilize applicable building codes, universal guidelines, and regulations in space planning.	**3:** Adaptations for special needs; living and family rooms; dining rooms; entryways and foyers; patios, porches, and courts **4:** Adaptations for special needs; bedrooms; bathrooms **5:** Adaptations for special needs; kitchens; clothes care centers; garages **19:** Planning the electrical system; planning the plumbing system **23:** Fire safety code requirements **26:** Preparing remodeling, renovation, and preservation plans; the interior designer; the architect; the contractor
11.4.6 Create floor plans using computer design software.	**28:** Design and analysis; computer-assisted drafting and design; kitchen and bath design; service to clients and customers; home planning aids; interior design programs

Competencies	Text Concepts
11.5.1 Explore features of furnishings that are characteristic of various historical periods.	**11:** Traditional furniture from France; Late Renaissance; Baroque; Regence; Rococo; Neoclassic; Directoire; Empire; traditional furniture from England: Early Renaissance period; Tudor; Elizabethan; Jacobean; Cromwellian; traditional furniture from England: Middle Renaissance period; Restoration; William and Mary; Queen Anne; Early Georgian; traditional furniture from England: Late Renaissance period; Late Georgian; Regency; Victorian; traditional American styles; Early American; American Georgian; Federal; Post Federal; twentieth-century furniture styles; Art Nouveau; Frank Lloyd Wright; Bauhaus; Scandinavian; Art Deco; twenty-first century furniture styles; contemporary; traditional; casual; country; eclectic

Competencies	Text Concepts
11.5.2 Consider how prosperity, mass production, and technology are related to the various periods.	**11:** Traditional furniture from France; Late Renaissance; Baroque; Regence; Rococo; Neoclassic; Directoire; Empire; traditional furniture from England: Early Renaissance period; Tudor; Elizabethan; Jacobean; Cromwellian; traditional furniture from England: Middle Renaissance period; Restoration; William and Mary; Queen Anne; Early Georgian; traditional furniture from England: Late Renaissance period; Late Georgian; Regency; Victorian; traditional American styles; Early American; American Georgian; Federal; Post Federal; twentieth-century furniture styles; Art Nouveau; Frank Lloyd Wright; Bauhaus; Scandinavian; Art Deco; twenty-first century furniture styles; contemporary; traditional; casual; country; eclectic
11.5.3 Examine the development of architectural styles throughout history.	**24:** Traditional styles; Native American; Spanish; Swedish; Dutch; German; French; English; the salt-box; the garrison; the Cape Cod; Georgian; Federal; Greek Revival; Southern Colonial; Italianate; Victorian; modern designs; the ranch house; the split-level house; contemporary designs; geodesic domes; foam domes; solar homes; earth-sheltered homes
11.5.4 Compare historical architectural details to current housing and interior design trends.	**11:** Twentieth-century furniture styles; Art Nouveau; Frank Lloyd Wright; Bauhaus; Scandinavian; Art Deco; twenty-first century furniture styles; contemporary; traditional; casual; country; eclectic **13:** Wallpaper; selection of wall treatments **24:** Modern designs; the ranch house; the split-level house; contemporary designs; geodesic domes; foam domes; solar homes; earth-sheltered homes
11.5.5 Consider future trends in architectural and furniture design and development.	**12:** Wood furniture; wood types; wood finishes; wood furniture construction; upholstered furniture; fabrics; upholstered furniture construction; bedding; metal furniture; plastic furniture; furniture selection; quality and cost; style; size; upholstery fabric; ergonomics in furniture design **24:** Contemporary designs; geodesic domes; foam domes; solar homes; earth-sheltered homes

Competencies	Text Concepts
11.6.1 Assess human needs, safety, space, and technology as they relate to housing and interior design goals.	**1:** Factors affecting housing choices; location; climate; availability; cost; taste; lifestyle; types of housing available; tract houses; custom houses; manufactured houses; mobile homes; cooperatives; condominiums **2:** Circulation; types of circulation; circulation frequency; room relationships **3:** Living rooms; location; size and arrangement; dining rooms; location; size and arrangement; family rooms; location; size and arrangement; entryways; patios, porches, and courts; patios; porches; courts; adaptations for special needs **4:** Bedrooms; location; size and arrangement; master bedrooms; children's rooms; bathrooms; location; size and arrangement; heat and moisture considerations; adaptations for special needs **5:** Kitchens; location; size and arrangement; work centers; appliances, cabinets, and counters; kitchen designs; laundry facilities; location; size and arrangement; basements; garages and carports; location; size and design; service entries; special-purpose rooms; home offices; storage; adaptations for special needs **21:** Types of system functions; monitoring functions; switching functions; programming functions; communication and recording functions; alarm functions; information and communication systems; signal and communication systems; structured wiring; security systems; home automation; low-voltage switching **22:** Energy-saving appliances; energy alternatives; energy management with computers; water conservation; green building **23:** Smoke and fire detection; fire prevention; smoke detectors; fire safety code requirements; fire extinguishers; carbon monoxide detection; carbon monoxide poisoning; carbon monoxide detectors; radon detection; radon in the home; radon testing; radon mitigation; moisture and mold problems; migration of water vapor; sources of water vapor; preventive measures; ventilation; health hazards associated with mold; mold prevention and removal; weather- and nature-related safety; earthquakes; floods; tornadoes; hurricanes; general home safety

Competencies	Text Concepts
11.6.2 Assess community, family, and financial resources needed to achieve clients' housing and interior goals.	**1:** Factors affecting housing choices; location; climate; availability; cost; taste; lifestyle; types of housing available; tract houses; custom houses; manufactured houses; mobile homes; cooperatives; condominiums; rentals **26:** Choosing to remodel; types of remodeling; changing lived-in areas; making unused space livable; adding on; buying to remodel **28:** PERT and Gantt charts for scheduling; cost estimates and financial models
11.6.3 Assess a variety of available resources for housing and interior design.	**26:** The interior designer; the architect; the contractor **28:** Service to clients and customers; home planning aids; interior design programs; CD-ROM marketing tools; Internet sources; virtual reality models
11.6.4 Critique design plans that address clients' needs, goals, and resources.	**2:** Circulation; types of circulation; circulation frequency; room relationships **3:** Living rooms; location; size and arrangement; dining rooms; location; size and arrangement; family rooms; location; size and arrangement; entryways; patios, porches, and courts; patios; porches; courts; adaptations for special needs **4:** Bedrooms; location; size and arrangement; master bedrooms; children's rooms; bathrooms; location; size and arrangement; heat and moisture considerations; adaptations for special needs **5:** Kitchens; location; size and arrangement; work centers; appliances, cabinets, and counters; kitchen designs; laundry facilities; location; size and arrangement; basements; garages and carports; location; size and design; service entries; special-purpose rooms; home offices; storage; adaptations for special needs **6:** Goals of design; appropriateness; harmony, variety, and unity; function **25:** Planning the landscape **28:** Design and analysis; computer-assisted drafting and design; plot, site, and landscape planning; kitchen and bath design; energy analysis **30:** Meeting client needs

Competencies	Text Concepts
11.7.1 Select appropriate studio tools.	**27:** Pencil rendering; ink rendering; watercolor rendering; colored pencil rendering; felt-tip marker rendering; appliqué rendering; airbrush rendering

Competencies	Text Concepts
11.7.2 Prepare renderings, elevations, and sketches using appropriate media.	**27:** Presentation drawings; exterior perspectives; interior perspectives; presentation floor plans; presentation elevations; presentation plot plans; presentation landscape plans; presentation sections **28:** Design and analysis; computer-assisted drafting and design; plot, site, and landscape planning; kitchen and bath design
11.7.3 Prepare visual presentations including legends, keys, and schedules	**27:** Other presentation methods; presentation boards; models; slide presentations; PowerPoint presentations **28:** Design and analysis; computer-assisted drafting and design; plot, site, and landscape planning; kitchen and bath design; energy analysis; selection of construction elements and processes; structural analysis; preferred construction and installation techniques; service to clients and customers; virtual reality models; project management; PERT and Gantt charts for scheduling; cost estimates and financial models; project data management; computer usage by housing professionals
11.7.4 Utilize a variety of presentation media such as photography, video, computer, and software for client presentations.	**27:** Presentation drawings; other presentation methods; presentation boards; models; slide presentations; PowerPoint presentations **28:** Service to clients and customers; home planning aids; interior design programs; CD-ROM marketing tools; Internet sources; virtual reality models **30:** Using good communication techniques; meeting client needs

(The competencies for this content standard are applicable to more advanced texts.)

Chapter 1
Fundamentals of Housing

Objectives

After studying this chapter, students will be able to

- list physical factors outside the house that affect housing choices.
- explain the relationship between lifestyle and housing choices.
- describe the seven main types of housing.
- determine the strengths and weaknesses of the different types of housing.

Teaching Materials

Text, pages 14–26

Student Activity Guide

Check Your Understanding
1-1, *Housing Choices*
1-2, *Personal Needs*
1-3, *Dwelling Features*
1-4, *Housing Types*

Instructor's Resources

Factors Affecting Housing Choices, transparency master 1-A

Costs of Home Ownership, transparency master 1-B

Housing Priorities, reproducible master 1-C

Rental Lease Agreement, transparency master 1-D

Renting an Apartment, transparency/reproducible master 1-E

Chapter 1 Mastery Test

Instructional Concepts and Student Activities

1. Have students read Chapter 1 of the text and complete the review questions.
2. Have students start a housing notebook of residential housing ideas. Ask them to collect pictures from magazines, newspapers, advertising pamphlets, or from home to illustrate the various types of housing available. Then have them label the style and type of each dwelling illustrated. Suggest they section their notebooks with a labeled divider for each chapter in the text that you plan to cover in the course.

Factors Affecting Housing Choices

3. *Factors Affecting Housing Choices*, transparency master 1-A, IR. Introduce students to the six basic factors that affect housing choices. Ask them to provide everyday examples of each factor.
4. Involve students in a discussion on the effect of factors such as location, climate, availability, cost, taste, and lifestyle on housing choices. Ask which are more important to the students.
5. *Costs of Home Ownership*, transparency master 1-B, IR. Have students review the many costs involved in home ownership. If possible, provide a realistic example of common costs in your area.
6. *Housing Choices*, Activity 1-1, SAG. Students are to explain how various factors affect housing choices.
7. *Personal Needs*, Activity 1-2, SAG. Students are to list personal needs that can be satisfied by individual, group, and support space in their housing.
8. *Housing Priorities*, reproducible master 1-C, IR. Students are to independently select the top three factors likely to affect the housing choices of each of the given households. Have students report and explain their answers.

Types of Housing Available

9. Lead a class discussion on the types of housing available: tract houses, custom houses, manufactured houses, mobile homes, cooperatives, condominiums, and rentals.
10. Ask students to describe the pros and cons of living in each type of dwelling discussed in Item 6.
11. *Dwelling Features*, Activity 1-3, SAG. Each student is to clip an advertisement for a tract or custom home and summarize the features of the home.

12. *Housing Types*, Activity 1-4, SAG. Students are to study the housing qualities listed and indicate which type of housing each describes.

13. Invite a real estate broker to speak to the class about the types of housing available in your area. After the presentation, involve the students in a discussion about the advantages and disadvantages of various types of housing.

14. *Rental Lease Agreement*, transparency master 1-D, IR. Review the key components of most housing rental agreements. Ask students if they are aware of other rental conditions or restrictions encountered by some renters.

15. *Renting an Apartment*, transparency/reproducible master 1-E, IR. Have students total the costs involved in renting an apartment for the first time. (Some students may be able to provide firsthand information.) Ask students to check the cost of the security deposit, monthly rent, and other required fees of a dwelling they would like to rent. Caution them to check the presence of all basic appliances in the dwelling (and furniture, if the dwelling is furnished). If one or more items must be purchased, ask students to include an estimate of the total cost of furniture and appliance they must buy to move into the rental space.

16. Assign one or more tasks listed in the text's *Suggested Activities* section at the end of the chapter.

Suggested Evaluation Techniques

16. *Check Your Understanding*, SAG. Have students complete as many questions as possible without referring to the text. Then have them find answers to questions they do not know.

17. Administer the *Chapter 1 Mastery Test*.

Answer Key

Text

Review Questions, page 25

1. location, climate, availability, cost, personal taste, and lifestyle

2. unstable or uncontrolled growth of a community; lower price range of surrounding homes; turnover rate on resale of homes; undesirable level of upkeep on neighboring homes; lack of facilities, such as schools, places of worship, shopping areas, and public services; or location too far from place of work

3. North Dakota house: more insulation, more steeply sloped roof to prevent snow buildup, fewer windows, and cozy interior
Arizona house: walls of thick masonry or another material that releases heat from the house at night and wide roof overhangs to shade the house

4. individual space: sleeping, dressing, studying, and relaxing in privacy; group space: family recreation, conversation, dining, and entertaining; support space: preparing food and doing laundry

5. tract house: designed before it is sold, may exist first as a model, less expensive than a custom house, and may have little individuality
custom house: designed and built to meet the needs and desires of a specific household, different from all other houses, and more expensive than tract houses

6. size and activities of household members, site on which the house will be built, ability of the designer, cost, and the materials to be used

7. advantages: lower costs, reduced building time, high quality construction, and optional features available
disadvantages: limited selection, special installation equipment needed, and expensive shipping costs

8. high moving expense, need for professional movers, and highway restrictions

9. cooperative: owners of each apartment run the complex as a corporation, owners decide on maintenance and other issues that affect the entire complex, and owners may vote on whether a person is allowed to move into an apartment
condominium: each owner is in control of only his or her apartment, some community property is shared, an outside firm manages maintenance of group property, and owners do not vote on new residents

10. ready availability, convenient location, very affordable, no long-term commitment required, and little or no upkeep and maintenance responsibilities

Student Activity Guide

Check Your Understanding, pages 7–9

1. Maine house: ample insulation, tight shell to keep cold air out, steep roof to prevent snow buildup, and fewer windows to reduce heat loss
Arkansas house: masonry construction to aid in cooling, gently sloping roof since snow is not a problem, more or larger windows to aid in ventilation, and wider overhangs to shade the sides of the house

2. thick masonry wall that moderates the inside temperature by absorbing heat during the day and releasing it at night
3. maturity, different life experiences, friends and associates, and housing trends
4. (Student response. See pages 17-19 in the text.)
5. (List five:) schools, health care facilities, transportation, shopping areas, places of worship, recreation facilities, fire and police protection, adequate garbage collection and utilities, work opportunities
6. repairs or upkeep, insurance, and taxes
7. individual, group, and support
8. cooperatives: buyers purchase stock in a corporation and receive a lease to an apartment, corporation manages and runs the apartment building, value of the apartment determines the amount of stock purchased, owners pay a monthly fee for property taxes and maintenance costs, corporation takes care of maintenance and repairs, owners generally vote on whether a prospective buyer may purchase an apartment, and owners must abide by the decisions of the group
condominiums: owners buy an apartment and a share of the common ground, owners receive a deed to and pay taxes on the property, owners pay a monthly fee to cover maintenance costs, owners can sell apartments without approval of the other owners, and owners cast votes on matters affecting common areas in proportion to the values of their respective properties
9. tract
10. custom
11. manufactured
12. mobile
13. condominiums
14. rentals (*or* apartments)
15. location
16. urban (*or* city)
17. support
18. design
19. precuts
20. code

Dwelling Features, Activity 1-3
Typical solution on page 34

Housing Types, Activity 1-4
1. rentals
2. tract houses
3. manufactured houses
4. cooperatives
5. custom houses
6. mobile homes
7. tract houses
8. rentals
9. manufactured houses
10. custom homes
11. condominiums
12. mobile homes
13. custom houses

Instructor's Resources

Chapter 1 Mastery Test
1. D
2. A
3. C
4. B
5. C
6. D
7. D
8. D
9. lifespace
10. taste
11. lifestyle
12. individual
13. tract
14. custom
15. stock
16. condominium
17. (Student response. See page 16 in the text.)
18. Heat loss is greater through glass than through walls.
19. Wide overhangs shade the walls and thus reduce heat buildup.
20. Trailers, mobile homes, motor homes, and houseboats are considerations because they offer personalized comfort for their occupants while providing the ultimate in mobility.
21. individual space: sleeping, dressing, studying, and relaxing in privacy; group space: family recreation, conversation, dining, and entertaining; support space: preparing food and doing laundry
22. tract houses, custom houses, manufactured houses, mobile homes, and multifamily dwellings (cooperatives, condominiums, and rentals)
23. (List four:) Buyers can see exactly what they are buying. A firm price can generally be negotiated before construction begins. The subdivision is generally planned as a whole. Tract houses usually cost less. The home's value often increases as the development grows.
24. They usually require less expense and effort in upkeep than other types of housing, offer a variety of lifestyles, and are readily available.

Dwelling Features
Activity 1-3

Typical Solution

At home on a hillside, you'll just love the excitement of living in this 4-bedroom, 3½-bath beauty. Every room has an interesting shape. From the foyer, view the recessed ceilings of the dining room, the bump-out windows of living room, and the family room with patio and fireplace. Beyond the central stairwell lies the angular kitchen with skylit breakfast nook. The master bedroom suite is down a short hall. Each bedroom upstairs has direct access to a full bath. And, don't worry about carrying a heavy laundry basket down the stairs. A centrally located chute delivers dirty clothes to the laundry room. First floor has 1,593 sq. ft.; second floor, 818 sq. ft.; basement, 863 sq. ft.; and garage, 720 sq. ft.

Factors Affecting Housing Choices

- ## Location

- ## Climate

- ## Availability

- ## Cost

- ## Taste

- ## Lifestyle

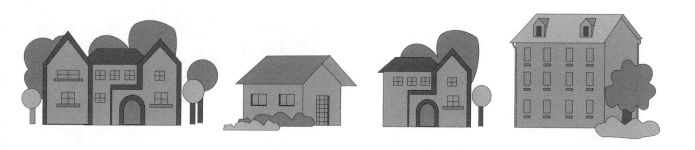

Costs of Home Ownership

Monthly mortgage payment—usually for 25-30 years

Mortgage insurance—a highly variable monthly fee assessed by the lender

Property tax—depends on state and county decisions

Utility costs—includes electric, gas, and water use and waste disposal

Maintenance costs—the upkeep of the structure and its systems

Property insurance such as flood insurance

Other possible costs:

- Homeowner association fees
- Condominium assessment fees

Source: Government National Mortgage Association (Ginnie Mae)

Housing Priorities

Name _____

Date _____

Complete the chart by selecting the top three factors that you believe are likely to affect the housing choices of the individuals or groups listed below. Compare your answers to those of your classmates.

Housing Factors

A. Location   D. Cost

B. Climate   E. Taste

C. Availability   F. Lifestyle

Households	Top Three Priorities
Example: Newlyweds	D, A, F
1. Boating enthusiasts	
2. Active, retired couple	
3. Young couple planning to have children	
4. Large family with an ailing grandparent	
5. Aspiring artist and painter	
6. Single parent with two school-age children	
7. Single professional having a job transfer	
8. Young family wanting to live near relatives	

Rental Lease Agreement

General information—dwelling address, list of contents (appliances and furnishings), and names of landlord and tenant

Key dates—occupancy date, length of lease, monthly rent due-date, and date of signed agreement

Financial figures—required security deposit, monthly rent, additional fees, and penalty for late payment

Important directions
- When and how to pay rent
- Conditions of the security-deposit refund
- Lease-renewal provisions
- Clause on assigning or subletting the dwelling
- Tenant/landlord rights in terminating the lease
- Prohibited possessions (pets?) and restricted behavior (noise?)
- Responsibilities for repairs, maintenance, and utility payments
- Final inspection procedures

Renting an Apartment

Security deposit: _____

Monthly rent: _____

Additional monthly fees for
- utilities: _____
- waste disposal: _____
- access to recreational
  facilities: _____
- grounds maintenance:
- other: _____ _____

Cost of needed furniture
and/or appliances: _____

Total "move-in" costs: _____

Fundamentals of Housing

Chapter 1 Mastery Test

Name _____

Date _____

Score _____

Multiple Choice: Select the best response and write the letter in the preceding blank.

_____ 1. Housing refers to _____.
  A. a dwelling
  B. everything within a dwelling
  C. everything surrounding a dwelling
  D. All of the above.

_____ 2. Housing choices are affected by factors such as _____.
  A. location, climate, availability, and cost
  B. lifestyle, personal taste, cost, and social history
  C. climate, availability, personal taste, and social level
  D. personal taste, lifestyle, ethnic background, and family history

_____ 3. Most city homes are designed as compact, multilevel structures because _____.
  A. added height provides more comfort in the city
  B. taller homes are more attractive
  C. most city lots are small
  D. city ordinances require it

_____ 4. Examples of group-space activities include _____.
  A. family recreation, conversation, studying, and entertaining
  B. dining, conversation, family recreation, and entertaining
  C. relaxing, conversation, preparing food, and doing laundry
  D. family recreation, sleeping, dressing, and doing laundry

_____ 5. Manufactured houses are available in several forms and degrees of completion. They include _____.
  A. modular components, prefabs, and stick-built
  B. precuts, kit houses, and prototypes
  C. modular components, prefabs, kit houses, and precuts
  D. roof panels, floor panels, wall sections, kitchens, and baths

_____ 6. One of the factors *not* associated with manufactured housing is _____.
  A. limited selection
  B. the need for special equipment to install large modules
  C. the expense of shipping large modules
  D. poor construction and design

_____ 7. The main advantage of a mobile home is _____.
  A. property taxes are not charged for mobile homes
  B. anyone can move a mobile home
  C. a wide variety of floor plans is available
  D. the purchase price is comparatively low and very little upkeep is required

_____ 8. Condominium ownership includes _____.
  A. the purchase of a share of common ground along with the living unit
  B. property taxes that must be paid by the respective owner(s)
  C. a joint interest in all the shared property and facilities
  D. All of the above.

(continued)

Name _____

Completion: Complete the following sentences by writing the missing words in the preceding blanks.

_____ 9. People and housing are inseparable, and for that reason, the term _____ is sometimes used to describe housing.

_____ 10. A sense of what is fitting, harmonious, or beautiful describes good _____.

_____ 11. Truly functional dwelling space is a logical extension of the _____ of the household's occupants.

_____ 12. Sleeping, dressing, studying, and relaxing in privacy are examples of _____ space.

_____ 13. A house built by a developer who subdivides a large piece of land into lots and builds several houses using just a few basic plans is an example of _____ houses.

_____ 14. A _____ house is different from all other houses and is built to meet the needs of a specific household.

_____ 15. For those who cannot afford to hire an architect to design their homes, _____ plans from magazines or other sources may be modified to meet their needs.

_____ 16. A unit owned within a multifamily dwelling is a _____.

Short Answer: Provide brief answers to the following questions or statements.

17. What questions might a person ask when evaluating features that add or detract from the quality of life in a neighborhood? _____

_____

_____

_____

_____

_____

_____

_____

_____

_____

_____

_____

_____

18. Why is the amount of a dwelling's exterior glass a consideration in a cold climate? _____

_____

(continued)

Name _____

19. Why do homes in warm climates generally have wide overhangs? _____

_____

20. What types of housing might a highly mobile family seek in an area where apartments, single-family dwellings, and condominiums are unavailable? Explain. _____

_____

_____

_____

21. Identify the three types of space inside a home and the primary purpose of each. _____

_____

_____

_____

_____

_____

22. Identify the basic types of housing that are generally available in most areas. _____

_____

_____

_____

23. List four advantages of tract houses. _____

_____

_____

_____

_____

24. Why are apartments generally popular with young singles, newly married couples, and highly mobile people? _____

_____

_____

_____

_____

Chapter 2
Evaluating Floor Plans

Objectives

After studying this chapter, students will be able to
- map a circulation pattern and evaluate its quality.
- identify the specific activities and areas involved in family, work, service, and guest circulation patterns.
- determine the utility of a floor plan in relationship to a family's needs.
- identify the seven types of drawings included in a set of house plans and explain their purposes.
- interpret the symbols on a plot plan, foundation/basement plan, floor plan, exterior elevation, electrical plan, and construction detail drawing.

Teaching Materials

Text, pages 27–41

Student Activity Guide

Check Your Understanding
2-1, *Basic Areas*
2-2, *Types of Circulation*
2-3, *Circulation Evaluation Chart*
2-4, *Room Relationships*
2-5, *Reading House Plans*

Instructor's Resources

Examining Room Relationships, transparency/reproducible master 2-A
Drawings Included in a Set of Plans, reproducible master 2-B
Climate-Control Plan, transparency master 2-C
Plumbing Plan, transparency master 2-D
Chapter 2 Mastery Test

Instructional Concepts and Student Activities

1. Have students read Chapter 2 of the text and complete the review questions.

2. Ask students to collect floor plans showing good circulation patterns from magazines, newspapers, or builder literature. Have them identify the strengths of each plan and file them in their housing notebooks for future reference.
3. Discuss the three main areas of the home: living, sleeping, and service.
4. *Basic Areas*, Activity 2-1, SAG. Students are to identify and shade each of the three basic areas of a dwelling using different colors.

Circulation

5. Lead a class discussion on circulation, which is the route that people follow as they move from one place to another in the home.
6. Ask students to identify and describe the four basic types of circulation patterns: family, work, service, and guest.
7. *Types of Circulation*, Activity 2-2, SAG. Students are to map the four basic types of circulation patterns in the floor plan.
8. *Circulation Evaluation Chart*, Activity 2-3, SAG. Students are to evaluate the quality of each type of circulation in the floor plan used in Item 7.
9. Discuss the importance of circulation frequency in the evaluation of a floor plan.
10. Explain the functional relationships between various rooms or areas of the home. Involve the class in listing the natural relationships between certain rooms.
11. *Room Relationships*, Activity 2-4, SAG. Students are to study the relationship of the living room to other rooms in the floor plan and list positive and negative points about the relationship.
12. *Examining Room Relationships*, transparency/reproducible master 2-A, IR. Have students use the handouts to carefully evaluate the floor plan's room relationships. Review their evaluations in class. Ask students to identify the household composition and type of lifestyle that seems most suited to this house plan.

Reading House Plans

13. *Drawings Included in a Set of Plans*, reproducible master 2-B. Use as a handout to give students a concise overview of the individual drawings covered in greater depth in the text.

14. Lead a class discussion on the various plans generally found in a set of construction drawings. Identify the standard features included in each drawing. Provide copies of a typical set of house plans for each student or group of students to examine as you discuss the drawings. (You may also make transparencies of Figures 2-7 through 2-12 in the text to use for this discussion.)

15. *Reading House Plans,* Activity 2-5, SAG. Students are to analyze the floor plan to determine whether it includes all the basic features that should appear on this type of drawing.

16. Summarize the importance of examining circulation and room relationships in house plans to make a useful evaluation of a particular house design.

17. *Climate-Control Plan,* transparency master 2-C, IR. Acquaint students with the features of a climate-control plan's drawing, which is an optional part of a set of construction plans.

18. *Plumbing Plan,* transparency master 2-D, IR. Acquaint students with the features of a plumbing plan's drawing, which is an optional part of a set of construction plans.

19. Assign one or more tasks listed in the text's *Suggested Activities* section at the end of the chapter.

Suggested Evaluation Techniques

20. *Check Your Understanding,* SAG. Have students complete as many questions as possible without referring to the text. Then have them find answers to questions they do not know.

21. Administer the *Chapter 2 Mastery Test.*

Answer Key

Text

Review Questions, page 40

1. Routes with high circulation frequency should be as short and direct as possible, while routes with low circulation frequency may be longer and less direct.

2. family, work, service, and guest

3. bath located close to the bedrooms, indoor living area readily accessible to outdoor living area, related rooms close together, short and simple routes for high frequency circulation, excessive hall space avoided, and rooms not cut in half by circulation routes

4. to save steps, do tasks quickly and easily, and prevent interference and accidents resulting from cross-traffic

5. near kitchen, basement stairs, and garage

6. entry, coat closet, living room, bathroom

7. irregular architectural features and poorly located doors, windows, and closets

8. adjacent: dining area, outdoor eating area, and garage; far: bedrooms

9. plot plan, foundation/basement plan, floor plan, exterior elevations, electrical plan, construction details, and pictorial presentations

10. specifications

Student Activity Guide

Check Your Understanding, pages 15–17

1. D	20. E
2. H	21. C
3. B	22. H
4. H	23. C
5. I	24. F
6. B	25. C
7. D	26. E
8. E	27. D
9. F	28. B
10. A	29. G
11. B	30. J
12. F	31. E
13. E	32. C
14. I	33. B
15. H	34. A
16. D	35. D
17. C	36. C
18. A	37. C
19. H	38. B

39. to determine if the floor plan and circulation meet the lifestyle of the household

40. Dining room B allows sufficient wall space to place furniture.

41. (Student response.)

42. Locate the bathroom in the bedroom area as close as possible to the main entry and work area.

43. to communicate exactly how the finished structure will appear

44. climate-control plan

45. fresh water lines to water storage tank or house main, wastewater lines, water conditioning equipment, and plumbing fixtures

Basic Areas, Activity 2-1

Typical solution on page 46

Types of Circulation, Activity 2-2

Typical solution on page 47

Circulation Evaluation Chart, Activity 2-3

family circulation: good–1, 2, and 3;
average–4, 5, and 6

work circulation: good–7, 10, 12, 13, 14;
average–8, 9, 11

service circulation: good–16, 17, 18, 19, 20;
average–15

guest circulation: good–21, 22, 23

Room Relationships, Activity 2-4

1. located outside main traffic pattern, easy
   access to foyer and outside living area
   (covered porch), convenient to family room,
   and located on quiet end of house
2. more distant from dining room than is desired

Reading House Plans, Activity 2-5

1. exterior and interior walls, location of windows
   and doors, built-in cabinets and appliances,
   permanent fixtures, stairs and fireplace,
   porches, patios, decks, room names, and
   approximate room sizes
2. size of windows and doors, material symbols,
   location and size dimensions, and scale of
   the drawing. (This drawing is a presentation
   floor plan, not a construction drawing.)
3. plant features

Instructor's Resources

Chapter 2 Mastery Test

1. D
2. B
3. A
4. D
5. B
6. A
7. C
8. C
9. circulation
10. circulation frequency
11. kitchen
12. service
13. specifications
14. floor
15. pictorial presentations
16. plumbing
17. to help decide which type of housing is most
    desirable for a specific situation, how much
    space is needed, and how space should be
    divided for most effective use
18. living area: living room, dining room, family
    room, study, den, library, music room, hobby
    room, entryway, patio, and porch
    sleeping area: bedrooms, bathrooms, and
    dressing rooms
    service area: kitchen, clothes care center,
    utility room, basement, and garage
19. (List five:) A bath is located close to the
    bedrooms. The interior living area is readily
    accessible to the outdoor living area. Related
    rooms are close together. High-frequency
    circulation routes are short and simple.
    Excessive hall space is avoided. Rooms are
    not cut in half by circulation.
20. (List three:) irregular architectural features
    interrupting wall space and poorly placed
    doors, windows, and closets
21. plot plan, foundation/basement plan, floor
    plan, exterior elevations, electrical plan, con-
    struction details, and pictorial presentations
22. section drawing
23. meter and distribution panel, electrical outlets,
    light fixtures, switches, and telephone
24. to fully describe the construction of features
    that require more information

Basic Areas
Activity 2-1

Typical Solution

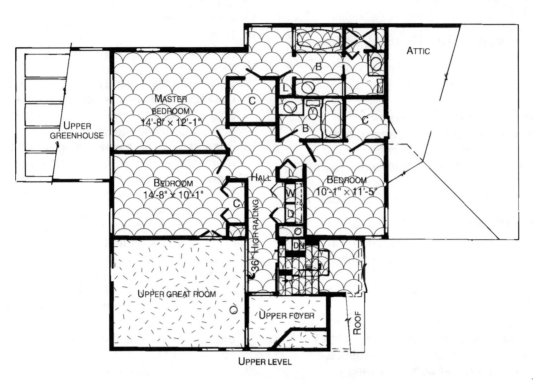

UPPER LEVEL

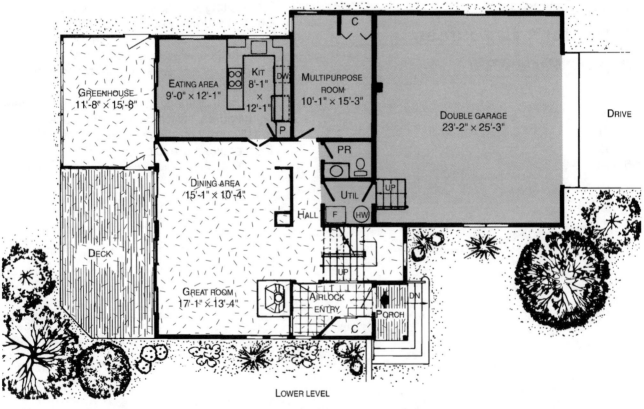

LOWER LEVEL

Living   Sleeping   Service

Types of Circulation
Activity 2-2

Typical Solution

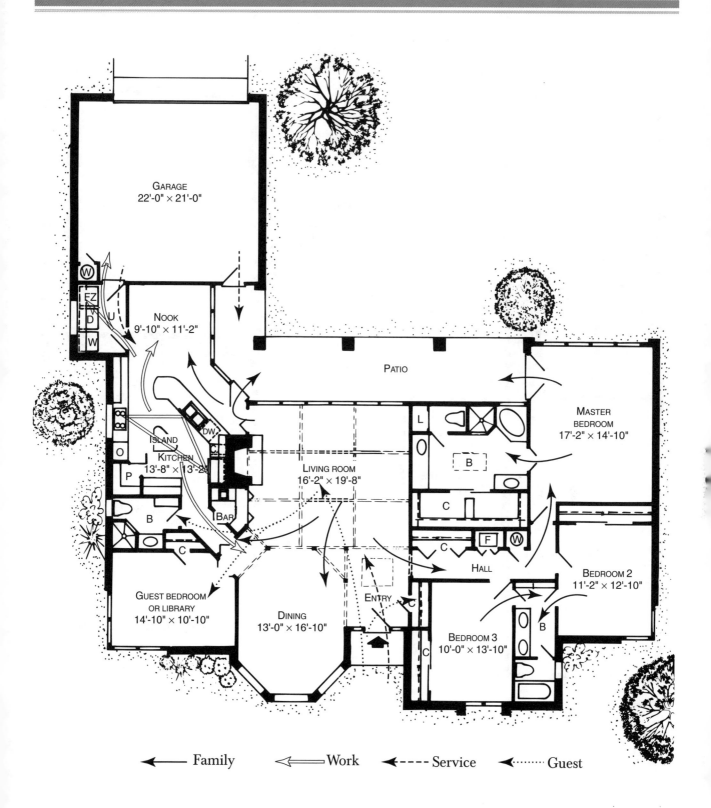

GARAGE
22'-0" × 21'-0"

NOOK
9'-10" × 11'-2"

PATIO

MASTER
BEDROOM
17'-2" × 14'-10"

ISLAND
KITCHEN
13'-8" × 13'-2"

LIVING ROOM
16'-2" × 19'-8"

BAR

HALL

BEDROOM 2
11'-2" × 12'-10"

GUEST BEDROOM
OR LIBRARY
14'-10" × 10'-10"

DINING
13'-0" × 16'-10"

ENTRY

BEDROOM 3
10'-0" × 13'-10"

← Family   ⇐ Work   ◄---- Service   ◄······· Guest

Examining Room Relationships

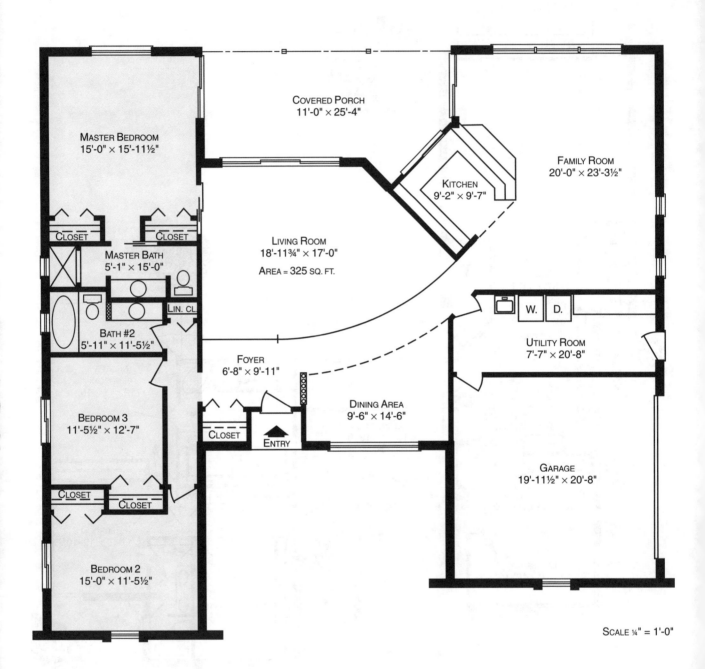

MASTER BEDROOM
15'-0" × 15'-11½"

COVERED PORCH
11'-0" × 25'-4"

FAMILY ROOM
20'-0" × 23'-3½"

CLOSET   CLOSET

MASTER BATH
5'-1" × 15'-0"

KITCHEN
9'-2" × 9'-7"

LIVING ROOM
18'-11¾" × 17'-0"

AREA = 325 SQ. FT.

LIN. CL.

BATH #2
5'-11" × 11'-5½"

W.   D.

FOYER
6'-8" × 9'-11"

UTILITY ROOM
7'-7" × 20'-8"

BEDROOM 3
11'-5½" × 12'-7"

CLOSET
ENTRY

DINING AREA
9'-6" × 14'-6"

CLOSET   CLOSET

GARAGE
19'-11½" × 20'-8"

BEDROOM 2
15'-0" × 11'-5½"

SCALE ¼" = 1'-0"

Drawings Included in a Set of Plans

Plot plan	Location of house on the site, utilities, topography, site dimensions, other buildings on the property, and a scale
Foundation plan	Foundation size and materials, excavation information, waterproofing, supporting structures, and a scale
Floor plan	Exterior and interior walls, doors and windows, patios, walks, decks, fireplaces, stairs, mechanical equipment, built-in cabinets, appliances, and a scale
Exterior elevations	View of each side of the house, exterior materials, placement of windows and doors, chimney, roofing, steps, grade line, roof pitch, and a scale
Electrical plan	Location of switches and outlets, telephone and TV jacks, service-entrance location, panel box, circuit data, electrical fixture schedule, and a scale
Construction details	Kitchen, stairs, chimneys, fireplaces, windows and doors, typical foundation walls, longitudinal section, items of special construction, and a scale
Pictorials	Presentation elevations, presentation floor plans, presentation sections, interior perspectives, exterior perspectives, and models
Optional drawings	Roof plan, roof-framing plan, floor-framing plan, heating/ventilating/cooling plan, plumbing plan, landscape plan, furniture plan, and expansion plan

Climate-Control Plan

The features of a heating, ventilating, and air-conditioning (HVAC) plan shown in a drawing include

- information on size and location of distribution pipes and ducts

- location of thermostats

- placement of registers or baseboard convectors

- type and location of climate-control equipment

- equipment schedule, if needed

- heat-loss calculations

- notes and scale of the drawing

Plumbing Plan

The features of a plumbing system shown in a drawing include

- waste line from all sinks, tubs, showers, and water closets

- vent stacks and clean-outs

- supply lines for hot and cold water

- drain and fixture locations

- size and type of pipe to be used

- water treatment devices such as a water softener

- water heater and water storage tank (if needed)

- built-in vacuum cleaning system (if appropriate)

- meter, house drain and clean-out, and house sewer

- plumbing-fixture schedule

- notes and scale of the drawing

Evaluating Floor Plans

Chapter 2 Mastery Test

Name _____

Date _____

Score _____

Multiple Choice: Select the best response and write the letter in the preceding blank.

_____ 1.   A _____ is *not* located in the living area of the home.
   A.   recreation room
   B.   study
   C.   dining room
   D.   bathroom

_____ 2.   Of the following, _____ is *not* a basic type of circulation pattern in the home.
   A.   service circulation
   B.   kitchen circulation
   C.   guest circulation
   D.   family circulation

_____ 3.   Good service circulation is provided by _____.
   A.   locating a service entrance near the kitchen and basement stairs
   B.   providing an outside access to the basement
   C.   considering the number of trips from the living room to the kitchen
   D.   placing the laundry room in a convenient location

_____ 4.   The kitchen should be close to _____.
   A.   the dining room
   B.   the garage
   C.   the basement stairs
   D.   All of the above.

_____ 5.   In a set of construction drawings, the _____ shows the location of the structure on the site.
   A.   construction details
   B.   plot plan
   C.   landscape plan
   D.   exterior elevations

_____ 6.   The _____ is generally *not* shown on a foundation/basement plan.
   A.   meridian arrow (north symbol)
   B.   direction, size, and spacing of floor joists
   C.   grade elevation
   D.   scale of the drawing

_____ 7.   Residential floor plans are generally drawn to a scale of _____.
   A.   ⅛" = 1'-0"
   B.   ¼" = 1"
   C.   ¼" = 1'-0"
   D.   1" = 20'-0"

_____ 8.   The _____ is *not* generally included on a residential exterior elevation plan.
   A.   roof feature
   B.   depth of foundation
   C.   contour of the land
   D.   chimney

(continued)

Name _____

Completion: Complete the following sentences by writing the missing words in the preceding blanks.

_____ 9. The route that people follow as they move from one place to another in the home is known as _____.

_____ 10. The number of times a route within a home is repeated in any given period of time is called _____ _____.

_____ 11. The hub of the work circulation pattern is the _____.

_____ 12. Good movement in and out of the home is a characteristic of good _____ circulation.

_____ 13. The construction drawings and a set of _____ form the basis for a legal contract between the owner and builder.

_____ 14. The _____ plan is the heart of a set of construction drawings and is used by all tradespeople.

_____ 15. The purpose of _____ _____ is to better communicate how the entire structure will appear beyond what construction drawings can show.

_____ 16. Although sometimes not included in a set of residential construction drawings, the _____ plan shows the fresh water lines, wastewater lines, and water conditioning equipment.

Short Answer: Provide brief answers to the following questions or statements.

17. Why should making a list of your housing needs and wants be the starting point in evaluating a floor plan? _____

_____

_____

18. List the three main areas of the home and the rooms included in each. _____

_____

_____

_____

19. List five principles of a good family-circulation pattern. _____

_____

_____

_____

_____

_____

20. Identify architectural considerations that reduce the usable space in a room. _____

_____

_____

_____

(continued)

Name _____

21. List the drawings that generally comprise a set of typical house plans, also called construction drawings._____

_____

_____

_____

_____

22. A floor plan is what type of drawing? _____

23. Features such as circuit data, the lighting-fixture schedule, doorbells and chime, home security systems, electrical appliances, and the scale of the drawing are generally shown on residential electrical plans. List five other features also shown on that plan. _____

_____

_____

_____

_____

_____

24. What is the purpose of construction details? _____

_____

Chapter 3
Planning Living Areas

Objectives

After studying this chapter, students will be able to

- list the rooms and activities involved in the living areas of a house.
- judge the appropriateness of a living room for a family according to its location, size, and arrangement.
- identify a dining room that meets the size and location needs of a specific family.
- determine the appropriateness of a family room's location, size, and arrangement for a family.
- recognize various types of entryways according to purpose and location.
- list possible uses and styles of patios, porches, and courts.
- identify living-area requirements for individuals with special needs.

Teaching Materials

Text, pages 42–56

Student Activity Guide

Check Your Understanding
3-1, *Room Sizes*
3-2, *Entryway and Foyer*
3-3, *Arranging Furniture*
3-4, *Designing a Patio*

Instructor's Resources

Living Areas in the Home, transparency/reproducible master 3-A

Designing Living Areas, reproducible master 3-B

Examining Living Areas, transparency/reproducible master 3-C

Universal Design for Living Areas, reproducible master 3-D

Americans with Disabilities Act, reproducible master 3-E

Chapter 3 Mastery Test

Instructional Concepts and Student Activities

1. Have students read Chapter 3 in the text and complete the review questions.
2. Ask students to collect pictures of rooms located in the living area of a home that appeal to them. Have the students add the pictures to their housing notebooks.

Living Rooms

3. *Living Areas in the Home*, transparency/reproducible master 3-A, IR. Introduce students to the areas within a home that constitute the living areas.
4. Lead a class discussion on the location, size, and arrangement of living rooms.
5. Have students, as a class or individually, create a list of considerations for good living room design in terms of location, size, and arrangement.
6. Have students identify the items they would select for a 12 by 14 ft. living room and their placement. If the living room were increased to 16 by 20 ft., what changes in furniture arrangements would they make?
7. *Room Sizes*, Activity 3-1, SAG. Students are to calculate square footages for several rooms and complete a chart seeking the smallest, average, and largest areas among the examples listed. (This will help students develop a mental relationship between length and width of various sizes of living areas.)

Dining Rooms

8. Lead a class discussion on the location, size, and arrangement of dining rooms. Have students add additional considerations to those mentioned in the text.
9. *Arranging Furniture*, Activity 3-3, SAG. Students are to plan a functional furniture arrangement for a given living room and dining room with the furniture templates provided.

Family Rooms

10. Lead a class discussion on the location, size, and arrangement of family rooms. Ask students to describe family rooms in their homes or elsewhere that exhibit good design.

11. Have students, as a class or individually, create a list of considerations for good family room design.
12. *Designing Living Areas*, reproducible master 3-B, IR. Students are to draw the two living areas of the given floor plan to scale, select appropriate furniture for a family with two teenagers, and arrange it. Choose several of the resulting designs and have the class discuss the advantages and disadvantages of each.

Entryways

13. Lead a class discussion on the function of entryways and identify the three categories: main or guest, special purpose, and service.
14. Have students, as a class or individually, list several considerations for good entryway design and placement.
15. *Entryway and Foyer*, Activity 3-2, SAG. Students are to redesign an entryway and foyer to increase efficiency.

Patios, Porches, and Courts

16. Explain the differences among patios, porches, and courts to students.
17. Use photos, pictures, or drawings to discuss the functions and features of each type of extended living area.
18. *Designing a Patio*, Activity 3-4, SAG. Students are to design a patio following several specifications.
19. *Examining Living Areas*, transparency/reproducible master 3-C, IR. Have students use the handouts to carefully evaluate the floor plan's living areas according to the principles discussed in the text. Review their evaluations in class. Ask students to identify ways to improve the plan.

Adaptations for Special Needs

20. *Universal Design for Living Areas*, reproducible master 3-D, IR. Use the handout to introduce students to the concept of universal design, with examples common to living areas. (The chart lists housing features for people with special needs beyond those covered in the text.)
21. Have each student evaluate his or her home to determine how well suited it is for people with special needs.
22. *Americans with Disabilities Act*, reproducible master 3-E, IR. Use as a handout to acquaint students with provisions of the *Americans with Disabilities Act*.
23. Assign one or more tasks listed in the text's *Suggested Activities* section at the end of the chapter.

Suggested Evaluation Techniques

24. *Check Your Understanding*, SAG. Have students complete as many questions as possible without referring to the text. Then have them find answers to questions they do not know.
25. Administer the *Chapter 3 Mastery Test*.

Answer Key

Text

Review Questions, page 55

1. conversation, recreation, dining, entertaining, enjoying hobbies, relaxing
2. living room, dining room, family room, entryway, foyer, patio, porch, and special purpose rooms (library, music room, or hobby room)
3. by having the main entryway open into a hall or foyer, by changing floor level between the living room and other areas, by locating entrances at one end of the room
4. seating for two or three people, piano, desk, or reading area for one person
5. to avoid circulation across a conversation area
6. an open plan because it makes a small home appear more spacious
7. between the living room and kitchen
8. 120 sq. ft., 180 sq. ft.
9. in basement, in attic, near living room, near kitchen, near a pool or outdoor recreation area
10. comfortable furniture that is durable, easily cleaned, and versatile
11. near the center of the house with access to an entry hall or foyer to establish better circulation inside the house
12. Texas: north side, Minnesota: south side
13. at least 4 to 5 ft.
14. hard surfaces or low-pile carpeting

Student Activity Guide

Check Your Understanding, pages 25–27

1. C	6. F	11. B
2. G	7. A	12. H
3. D	8. D	13. I
4. A	9. F	14. D
5. D	10. E	

15. (List four:) conversation, recreation, dining, entertaining, enjoying hobbies, relaxing
16. (List four:) living room, dining room, family room, entryway/foyer, patio or porch, special purpose rooms (library, music room, or hobby room)

17. have main entryway open into a hall or foyer, change floor level between the living room and other areas

18. closed plan: special area reserved just for dining, fewer distractions from other rooms, quieter, private, more formal
    open plan: usually more spacious, less confining, informal, accommodates larger groups of people, allows interaction of host and guests during food preparation

19. to facilitate the movement of food at serving time and permit guests to move easily from living room to dining room.

20. 180

21. 8

22. 8'-8"

23. (Student response. See pages 47-49 in the text.)

24. 12 by 16 ft. or larger; enough space for the number of people who will use the room and the activities planned for it; adequate storage for games, hobbies, and other recreation activities; furniture that is comfortable, durable, serviceable, and compatible with the room's activities; interior treatments that are durable, easy to clean, and suitable for activities; and carpeting when noise or warmth is a consideration

25. main

26. 8, 10

27. 10, 14

28. secondary

29. 16, 18

30. circulation

31. lever

32. ramp

Room Sizes, Activity 3-1

1. (Answers appear in the Activity.)
2. 120, 270, 195
3. 192, 400, 296
4. 35, 120, 78
5. 80, 192, 136
6. 140, 400, 270
7. 48, 240, 144

Entryway and Foyer, Activity 3-2

Typical solution on page 58

Arranging Furniture, Activity 3-3

Typical solution on page 59

Designing a Patio, Activity 3-4

Typical solution on page 60

Instructor's Resources

Chapter 3 Mastery Test

1.	B	5.	B
2.	D	6.	C
3.	A	7.	D
4.	D	8.	B

9. noise
10. primary
11. secondary
12. kitchen
13. open
14. 200
15. 2
16. quiet
17. foyer
18. (Student response.)
19. household size, special activities and hobbies, and budget
20. (List five:) number of people to use it; how it will be used; when it will be used; furniture planned; size of other rooms in the house; and the presence of an adjacent patio, porch, deck, or balcony
21. locating it within view from the conversation circle and allowing no circulation between it and the conversation circle
22. between living room and kitchen; to conveniently serve food from the kitchen and allow guests to assemble from the living room
23. table and chairs; buffet, hutch, corner cabinets and serving carts
24. 12 by 16 ft. size or larger; enough space for the number of people who will use the room and the activities planned for the room; adequate storage for games, hobbies, and other recreation activities; furniture that is comfortable, durable, serviceable, and compatible with the room's activities; interior treatments that are durable, easy to clean, and suitable for activities; and carpeting when noise or warmth is a consideration
25. Porches are raised above ground and covered by a roof, which provides shelter for guests and protection for the entryway.
26. living and family room at grade level, proper clearance around furniture, firm seat cushions on furniture, elevated chair seats, tables with pedestal legs, nonslip and hard-surface flooring, 90° opening for entry door, levers instead of knobs, and ramps for wheelchairs

Entryway and Foyer
Activity 3-2

Typical Solution

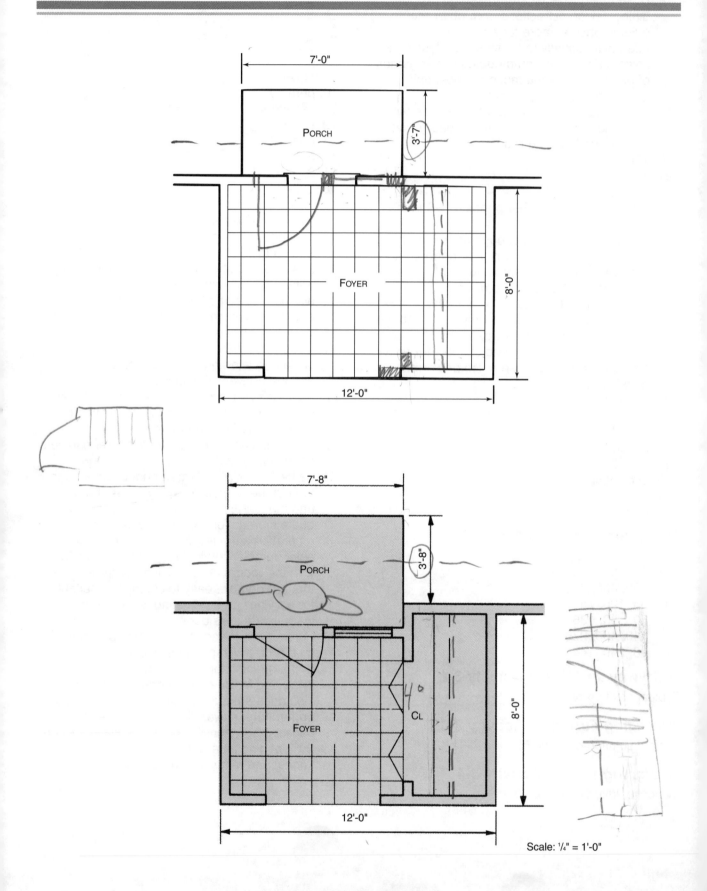

Scale: ¼" = 1'-0"

Arranging Furniture
Activity 3-3

Typical Solution

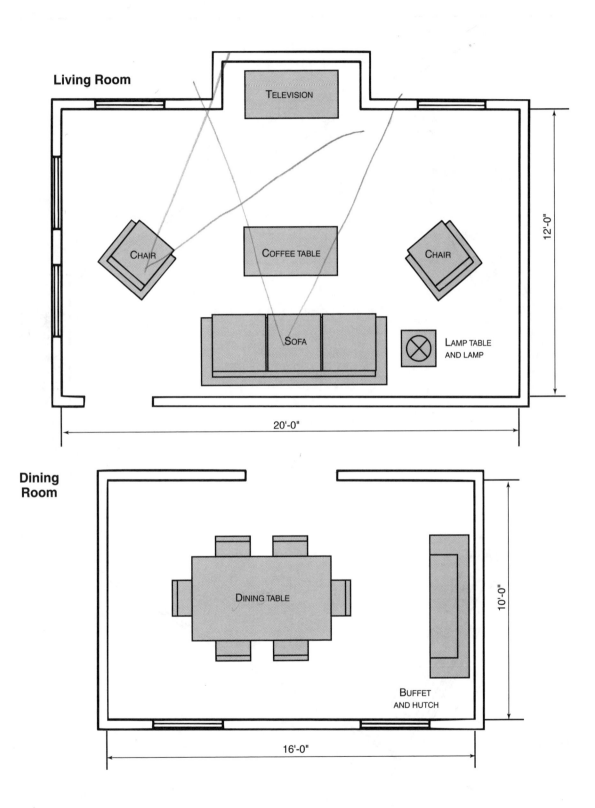

Living Room

TELEVISION

CHAIR

COFFEE TABLE

CHAIR

SOFA

LAMP TABLE
AND LAMP

12'-0"

20'-0"

**Dining
Room**

DINING TABLE

BUFFET
AND HUTCH

10'-0"

16'-0"

Designing a Patio
Activity 3-4

Typical Solution

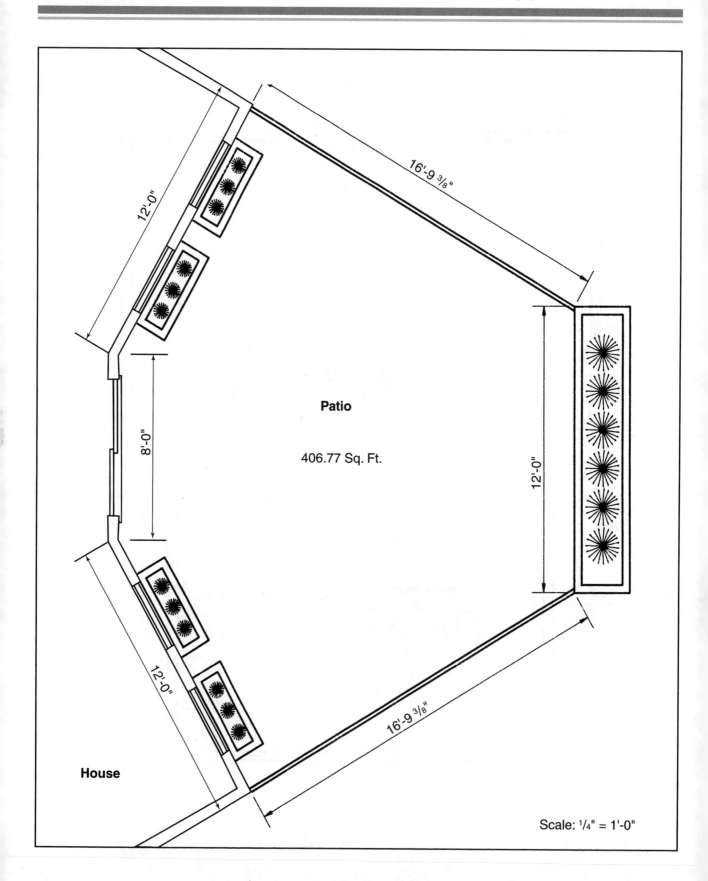

12'-0"

16'-9 3/8"

8'-0"

Patio

406.77 Sq. Ft.

12'-0"

12'-0"

16'-9 3/8"

House

Scale: 1/4" = 1'-0"

Living Areas in the Home

- Living room

- Dining room

- Family room

- Entryway or foyer

- Patio, porch, and court

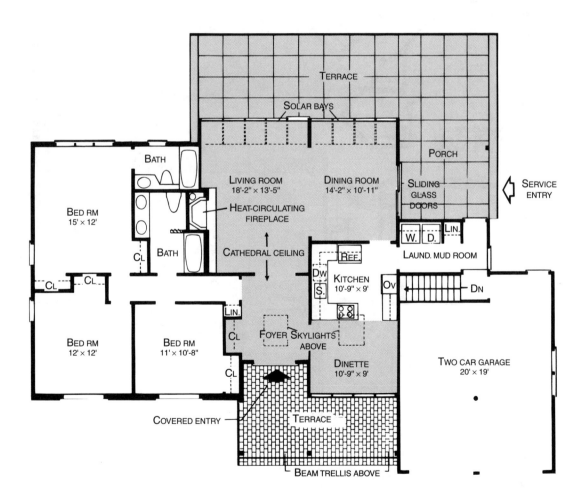

Designing Living Areas

Name _____

Date _____

Incorporate living room, dining room, and family room furniture in the two shaded areas of this floor plan. First, draw the shaded areas to a ¼ *in. = 1 ft.* scale on graph paper. On a separate piece of paper, list and number the furniture pieces you would choose and identify their approximate sizes. (Refer to "A-7, Common Sizes of Living Room Furniture" and "A-18, Common Furniture Sizes" in the text's appendix.) Finally, use correctly scaled furniture templates on your floor plan or draw the furniture to scale.

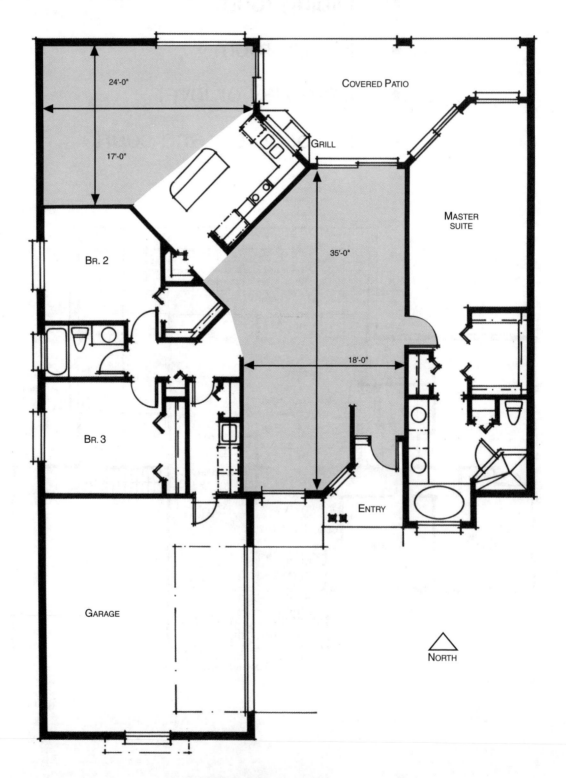

Examining Living Areas

Name _____

Date _____

Study the living areas of this house plan and evaluate them according to the principles discussed in the text. Write your comments on a separate piece of paper. Also identify ways to improve the plan.

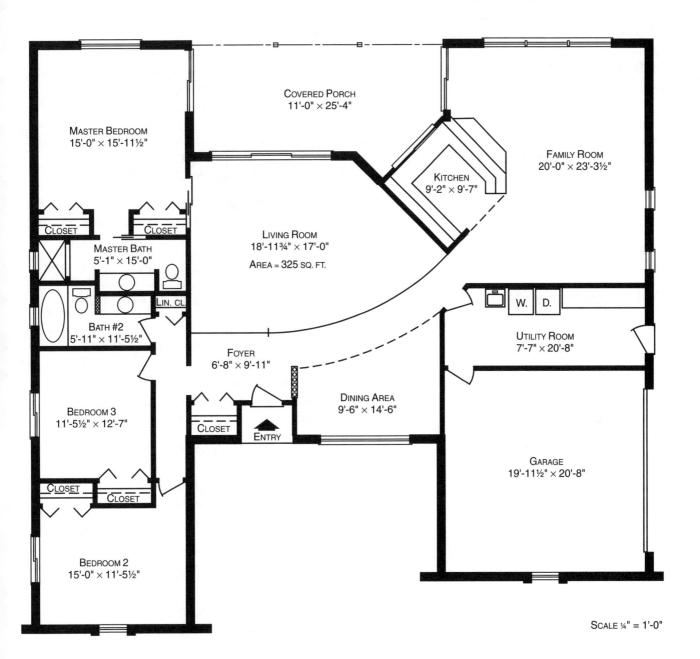

MASTER BEDROOM
15'-0" × 15'-11½"

COVERED PORCH
11'-0" × 25'-4"

FAMILY ROOM
20'-0" × 23'-3½"

CLOSET

CLOSET

KITCHEN
9'-2" × 9'-7"

MASTER BATH
5'-1" × 15'-0"

LIVING ROOM
18'-11¾" × 17'-0"

AREA = 325 SQ. FT.

LIN. CL.

BATH #2
5'-11" × 11'-5½"

W.   D.

UTILITY ROOM
7'-7" × 20'-8"

FOYER
6'-8" × 9'-11"

DINING AREA
9'-6" × 14'-6"

BEDROOM 3
11'-5½" × 12'-7"

CLOSET

ENTRY

CLOSET

CLOSET

GARAGE
19'-11½" × 20'-8"

BEDROOM 2
15'-0" × 11'-5½"

SCALE ¼" = 1'-0"

Universal Design for Living Areas

Universal design is a concept focusing on designs that make the environment more usable for everyone, hence the term *universal*. Your text discussed several such features for living areas, but additional features are described here. No single house is expected to include all the universal-design features possible, but when more are included, a house becomes more usable.

Feature	Description
Stepless entrances	Stepless entrances for preferably all, but at least most, home entrances. (If only one exists, consider passage through a garage, patio or raised deck.)
Integrated stepless entrances	Driveway and garage elevated to floor level so vehicles do the climbing. Graded site to create earth berms, bridges, and sloping walks. (If ramps are used, integrate them into the design.) Leveled bridges from entry to uphill point.
Other entrance features	Maximum rise of ½ in. at entrance thresholds. View of visitors—through sidelights, wide-angle door viewers, TV monitors, windows in doors, and/or windows nearby—for everyone, including children and seated users. A place to put packages while opening doors (such as a built-in shelf, bench, or table) with knee space located on the outside next to the door. Covered entrys such as porches, awnings, long roof overhangs, and/or carports to provide shelter while unlocking and opening doors. A way for visitors to communicate with residents, such as lighted doorbell at a reachable height, intercom with cordless telephone link, and/or hard-wired intercom. A 5 by 5 ft., level, clear space inside and outside an entry door for maneuvering while opening or closing the door. (Can be smaller if automatic power door is provided.)

Feature	Description
Other entrance features *(continued)*	Good lighting at entry doors, including focused light on the lockset, general illumination for seeing visitors at night, and/or motion-detector controls that turn on lights when someone approaches. Large, high-contrast, well-lighted address/house number located in a prominent place.
Interior circulation	Passage routes at least 42 in. wide to provide maneuvering room in hallways and archways.
Hardware	Easy-to-use varieties requiring little or no strength or flexibility such as the following: lever-type door handles, push plates, loop-handle pulls on drawers and cabinet doors, touch latches, and magnetic latches in lieu of mechanical keyless locks. (No knobs)
Sliding doors	Exterior sliding doors with the frame and threshold dropped into the subfloor, or finished flooring ramped to the top of the threshold track on both sides. Pocket doors between rooms that, when fully open, should extend at least 2 in. outside the door jamb and have open-loop handles for easy gripping. By-passing closet doors, with each panel creating an opening at least 32 in. clear.
Windows	A 36 in. maximum sill height to allow an extended view. Crank-operated types, or power operators when possible. Preferably casement, awning, hopper, and jalousie styles.
Special optional feature	Power operators on exterior doors when possible.

Source: Center for Universal Design, North Carolina State University

Americans with Disabilities Act

Background

On July 26, 1990, the *Americans with Disabilities Act (ADA)* became law. Under the ADA, it is illegal to discriminate against disabled persons in the areas of employment, public and private transportation, and access to public and commercial buildings. The physical access requirements of the ADA affect both existing places of public access and new construction.

Public Accommodations Covered Under the ADA

Title III of the ADA covers privately owned "public accommodations" such as the following: hotels and motels, restaurants and clubs, theaters, convention centers, shopping centers, banks, insurance offices, hospitals and offices of health care providers, law offices, accountant offices, day care facilities, and recreation centers.

Modifications to Affected Establishments

For establishments affected by the ADA, reasonable modifications such as the following may be required: removal of architectural and communication barriers including

- installing ramps and curb cuts
- widening doors
- eliminating turnstiles
- installing raised toilet seats and grab bars
- installing flashing alarm lights and telecommunication devices for people who are deaf
- adding raised elevator buttons for people who are blind
- providing parking that will accommodate people in wheelchairs

In addition, depending on the use of the area, the paths of travel to bathrooms, telephones, drinking fountains, and other facilities may also need to be made accessible.

Public Accommodations Not Covered Under the ADA

Public accommodations do not include the following: multifamily housing, which is covered under the *Federal Fair Housing Act of 1988*; private clubs; religious organizations; and public entities such as state or local governments or divisions thereof, which are governed by different standards under Title II of the ADA.

Planning Living Areas

Chapter 3 Mastery Test

Name _____

Date _____

Score _____

Multiple Choice: Select the best response and write the letter in the preceding blank.

_____ 1. The living area of a home does *not* include the _____.
- A. family room
- B. kitchen
- C. living room
- D. entryway

_____ 2. When choosing the location of the living room in a house, _____ should be considered.
- A. the view
- B. the location of the main entry
- C. the location of the dining room
- D. All of the above.

_____ 3. The primary purpose of a dining room is to _____.
- A. set aside a place for eating
- B. display collections
- C. provide an area for games and hobbies
- D. All of the above.

_____ 4. The ideal size for a dining room is determined by _____.
- A. the number of people to be served at one time
- B. the furniture intended
- C. the amount of space needed for circulation
- D. All of the above.

_____ 5. The minimum dining area size for four people is about _____ sq. ft.
- A. 60
- B. 80
- C. 100
- D. 120

_____ 6. From the edge of an occupied dining table to a wall, buffet, or hutch, approximately _____ in. of space are needed for serving.
- A. 24 to 32
- B. 32 to 36
- C. 36 to 44
- D. 44 to 50

_____ 7. When choosing the location of a family room, it is important to remember that _____.
- A. family rooms should be located near the living room
- B. family rooms should be located near the kitchen
- C. family rooms should be located in the basement
- D. no set rules exist for the location of a family room

_____ 8. The type of entry that provides access to a private garden or patio is a _____.
- A. side entry
- B. special-purpose entry
- C. service entry
- D. main entry

(continued)

Name _____

Completion: Complete the following sentences by writing the missing words in the preceding blanks.

_____   9. The living room should be located so _____ from the kitchen does not interfere with quiet activities in the living room.

_____   10. The dominant furniture grouping in the living room is called the _____ conversation area.

_____   11. A _____ furniture grouping allows an area for quiet reading or more intimate conversation away from the main conversation circle.

_____   12. Many homes built today provide an area for informal dining in the _____ and more formal dining in a dining room.

_____   13. In the _____ plan, the dining area is an extension of the living room or kitchen.

_____   14. A dining room that has several pieces of furniture and is considered very large will exceed _____ sq. ft.

_____   15. To seat people comfortably at a dining table, approximately _____ ft. of table length should be allowed per person.

_____   16. When categorized by function, there are three types of patios: play, living, and _____ patios.

_____   17. A main entry that opens into an entry hall or _____ is preferable to one that opens directly into a living room.

Short Answer: Provide brief answers to the following questions or statements.

18. How do the living areas of a home serve both household members and guests? Give an example.

_____

_____

_____

_____

_____

19. What factors determine the number and types of rooms included in the living area of the home?

_____

_____

_____

_____

_____

20. List the five factors that influence the ideal size of the living room. _____

_____

_____

_____

_____

_____

(continued)

Name_____

21. What should be considered when locating a fireplace in a living room? _____

_____

_____

_____

_____

_____

_____

_____

22. Where is the ideal location for the dining room? Explain. _____

_____

23. In the dining room, what are the basic pieces of furniture? other possible pieces? _____

_____

_____

_____

24. List the design features characteristic of the ideal family room. _____.

_____

_____

_____

_____

_____

25. How do porches differ from patios? _____

_____

_____

_____

_____

26. List several ways to make the living area of the home more usable for people with disabilities.

_____

_____

_____

_____

_____

_____

_____

_____

Chapter 4
Planning Sleeping Areas

Objectives

After studying this chapter, students will be able to

- describe the two main types of bedroom plans.
- recognize a well-designed bedroom.
- arrange bedroom furniture in a style that is attractive and functional.
- list the three main types of bathrooms and the fixtures they include.
- recognize the need for special features in the bathroom due to heat and moisture.
- identify sleeping-area requirements for individuals with special needs.

Teaching Materials

Text, pages 57–68

Student Activity Guide

Check Your Understanding
4-1, *Bedroom Furniture Sizes*
4-2, *Bedroom Arrangements*
4-3, *Room Clearances*
4-4, *Bathroom Layout*

Instructor's Resources

Sleeping Areas in the Home, transparency/reproducible master 4-A

Designing Sleeping Areas, reproducible master 4-B

Examining Sleeping Areas, transparency/reproducible master 4-C

Redoing Bathrooms for Wheelchair Use, reproducible master, 4-D

Universal Design for Bathrooms, reproducible master 4-E

Chapter 4 Mastery Test

Instructional Concepts and Student Activities

1. Have students read Chapter 4 in the text and complete the review questions that follow.
2. Have students collect pictures from magazines or sales literature that show good design in bedrooms and bathrooms. Students are to identify the outstanding design elements of each room and add the pictures to their housing notebooks.

Bedrooms

3. *Sleeping Areas in the Home*, transparency/reproducible master 4-A, IR. Introduce students to the areas of a house that constitute the sleeping areas.
4. Lead a class discussion on the location, size, and arrangement of bedrooms.
5. Have students, as a class or individually, make a list of considerations for good bedroom design.
6. Have students develop a checklist of guidelines for furniture arrangement and clearances for bedrooms.
7. *Bedroom Furniture Sizes*, Activity 4-1, SAG. Students are to use catalogs to identify standard sizes of bedroom furniture.
8. Lead a class discussion on the relationship of closets, doors, and windows to bedroom design.
9. Discuss with students the unique requirements of master bedrooms and children's bedrooms.
10. *Bedroom Arrangements*, Activity 4-2, SAG. Students are to prepare a functional furniture arrangement for two specific types of bedrooms using the furniture templates provided. Encourage students to refer to their housing notebooks for ideas.
11. *Designing Sleeping Areas*, reproducible master 4-B, IR. Students are to draw the sleeping areas of the given floor plan to scale, select appropriate furniture for a family with two teenagers, and arrange it. Choose several resulting designs and have the class discuss the advantages and disadvantages of each.

Bathrooms

12. Lead a class discussion on the location, size, and arrangement of bathrooms.
13. Show students pictures of various styles of bathroom fixtures, such as water closets, lavatories, tub/showers, saunas, whirlpool baths, and bidets.
14. *Room Clearances*, Activity 4-3, SAG. Students are to identify the recommended sizes, distances, or clearances for bedroom furniture and bathroom fixtures.
15. *Examining Sleeping Areas*, transparency/reproducible master 4-C, IR. Have students use the handouts to carefully evaluate the floor plan's sleeping areas according to the principles discussed in the text. Review their evaluations in class. Ask students to identify ways to improve the plan.
16. *Bathroom Layout*, Activity 4-4, SAG. Students are to prepare a well-planned layout for both a small and a large bath using standard fixtures and recommended clearances. Have students refer to the ideas in their housing notebooks for developing suitable solutions.
17. Discuss with students heat and moisture considerations in the bathroom.
18. Invite a housing designer to speak to the class about functional bathroom design. Give students an opportunity to ask questions and discuss good bathroom design.

Adaptations for Special Needs

19. Lead a class discussion on considerations in bedrooms and bathrooms for people with special physical needs.
20. *Redoing Bathrooms for Wheelchair Use*, reproducible master 4-D, IR. Students are to combine the two bathrooms shown into a redesigned space that can be used by a person in a wheelchair. Students are to use graph paper and the appropriate scale to display their ideas.
21. *Universal Design for Bathrooms*, reproducible master 4-E, IR. Use as a handout to reinforce the concept of universal design and provide examples common to bathrooms. (The chart lists housing features for people with special needs beyond those covered in the text.)
22. Assign one or more tasks listed in the text's *Suggested Activities* section at the end of the chapter.

Suggested Evaluation Techniques

23. *Check Your Understanding*, SAG. Have students complete as many questions as possible without referring to the text. Then have them find out answers to questions they do not know.
24. Administer the *Chapter 4 Mastery Test*.

Answer Key

Text

Review Questions, page 67

1. grouped plan: concentrates bedrooms into one area, is compact, creates a quiet zone, and allows all bedrooms to share a bath
split plan: separates one bedroom from the others and permits greater privacy for the master bedroom, live-in relatives, and overnight guests
2. Step 1: Draw the dimensions of the bedroom on graph paper showing windows and doors in their correct positions. Step 2: Make scaled drawings of the furniture to be placed in the room and cut them out. Step 3: Place the bed. Step 4: Place the remaining furniture, keeping circulation paths clear.
3. A. 22 in.
   B. 22 in.
   C. 40 in.
   D. 33 in.
   E. 42 in. circle
4. an entry door in a corner that preserves wall space, high windows that allow furniture placement underneath, or little wall space devoted to a closet
5. Freestanding closets are not attached to walls. Built-in closets are built into walls. Walk-in closets are built into walls and deeper than 4 ft.
6. furniture, storage, and space requirements to meet changing needs; flexibility in room arrangements; and privacy in a shared space
7. half bath: water closet and lavatory; three-quarters bath: water closet, lavatory, and shower; full bath: water closet, lavatory, and bathtub with or without a shower
8. centrally located to all areas of the house
a full bath upstairs near the sleeping areas and a half bath downstairs near the living and service areas
9. easier to clean under and around it, and more accessible to people with disabilities
10. wide ledge for sitting, grab rails, and a nonskid bottom
11. window or exhaust fan
12. a 5 by 5 ft. area, which is 25 sq. ft.
13. thermostatically controlled device

Student Activity Guide

Check Your Understanding, pages 35–38

1. B
2. A
3. D
4. C

5. A
6. A
7. B
8. C
9. D
10. sleeping, storage, dressing
11. the grouped plan, which locates all bedrooms in one area, versus the split plan, which separates the master bedroom from the others
12. near the bedroom entrance so it can easily be reached without walking around furniture
13. 4 ft.
14. provide ventilation and privacy, prevent drafts across the bed, allow placement of furniture below
15. Children's needs change as they grow. Young children need floor space to play and storage that is within reach. Older children need tables or desks for studying and may have special hobby needs.
16. saunas, whirlpool baths, laundry facilities, and exercise equipment
17. vanity base or wall-hung units
18. grab rails, nonskid bottoms
19. Showers require less space and are less costly.
20. skid-proof steps for safe access, minimum clearance space of 30-42 in. for entering and exiting
21. window, exhaust fan
22. beyond reach
23. the need for waterproof, easily cleaned surfaces
24. bed
25. 22
26. mattress
27. 40
28. 42
29. 24, 30
30. armoires
31. 100
32. full
33. 15
34. 24
35. 30, 42
36. 40

Bedroom Furniture Sizes, Activity 4-1
Typical solution on page 74

Bedroom Arrangements, Activity 4-2
Typical solution on page 75

Room Clearances, Activity 4-3
Solution on page 76

Bathroom Layout, Activity 4-4
Typical solution on page 77

Instructor's Resources

Chapter 4 Mastery Test
1. D
2. D
3. C
4. B
5. B
6. D
7. B
8. hallway
9. 6
10. 4
11. L
12. 24
13. lavatory
14. 30
15. to provide privacy for sleeping, bathing, and dressing
16. number, sex, and ages of family members
17. number and age of people using the room, activities to be performed in addition to sleeping and dressing, and furniture.
18. Step 1: draw the dimensions of the bedroom on graph paper showing windows and doors in their correct positions. Step 2: make scaled drawings of the furniture to be placed in the room and cut them out. Step 3: place the bed. Step 4: place the remaining furniture, keeping circulation paths clear.
19. to provide proper ventilation and privacy, allow placement of furniture below, and prevent drafts from blowing across the bed
20. half bath: water closet and lavatory; three-quarters bath: water closet, lavatory, and shower; full bath: water closet, lavatory, and bathtub with or without a shower
21. in a place that is easily accessible to all areas of the home (Student response.)
22. 5 ft. sq. area for wheelchair turnaround space, closet rods that are 40-42 in. high, adjustable shelves, shelves no deeper than 16 in., and clothes hooks no higher than 40 in. from the floor
23. firm mattress, bed that is adjustable or the same height as the wheelchair, 10-13 in. of clearance under the bed for wheelchair footrests, and bedside controls for lights and phone
24. 5 ft. sq. area for wheelchair turnaround space, mirrors tilted or lowered for people who are seated, medicine cabinets no higher than 50½ in. from the floor, 36 in. wide space for water closet installation, and a 20 in. high seat on the water closet

Bedroom Furniture Sizes
Activity 4-1

Typical Solution

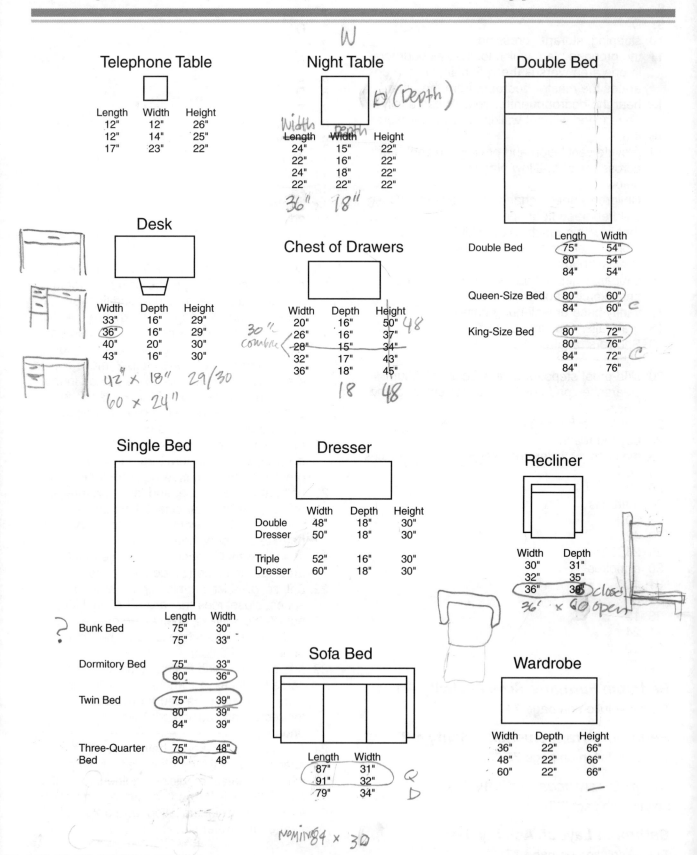

Telephone Table

Length	Width	Height
12"	12"	26"
12"	14"	25"
17"	23"	22"

Night Table

W

D (Depth)

Width   *Depth*

Length	Width	Height
24"	15"	22"
22"	16"	22"
24"	18"	22"
22"	22"	22"

36"   18"

Double Bed

	Length	Width
Double Bed	75"	54"
	80"	54"
	84"	54"
Queen-Size Bed	80"	60"
	84"	60" *C*
King-Size Bed	80"	72"
	80"	76"
	84"	72" *C*
	84"	76"

Desk

Width	Depth	Height
33"	16"	29"
36"	16"	29"
40"	20"	30"
43"	16"	30"

42" x 18"   29/30

60 x 24"

Chest of Drawers

Width	Depth	Height
20"	16"	50" *48*
26"	16"	37" *48*
28"	15"	34"
32"	17"	43"
36"	18"	45"

30" Combine

18   48

Single Bed

	Length	Width
Bunk Bed	75"	30"
	75"	33"
Dormitory Bed	75"	33"
	80"	36"
Twin Bed	75"	39"
	80"	39"
	84"	39"
Three-Quarter Bed	75"	48"
	80"	48"

?

Dresser

	Width	Depth	Height
Double Dresser	48"	18"	30"
	50"	18"	30"
Triple Dresser	52"	16"	30"
	60"	18"	30"

Recliner

Width	Depth
30"	31"
32"	35"
36"	36" *closed*

36' x 60 open

Sofa Bed

Length	Width
87"	31"
91"	32" *Q*
79"	34" *D*

NOMIN 84 x 30

Wardrobe

Width	Depth	Height
36"	22"	66"
48"	22"	66"
60"	22"	66"

Bedroom Arrangements
Activity 4-2

Typical Solution

Teen Bedroom

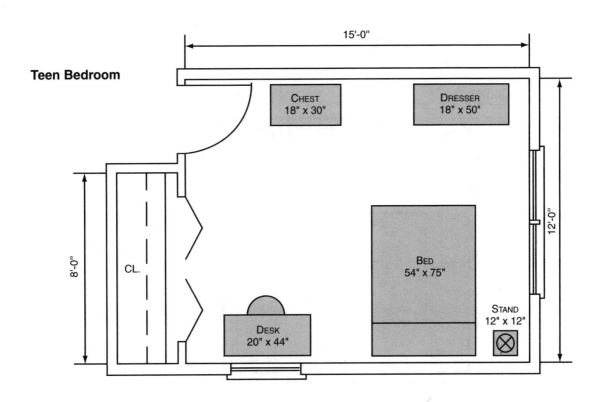

15'-0"

CHEST
18" x 30"

DRESSER
18" x 50"

12'-0"

8'-0"

CL.

BED
54" x 75"

DESK
20" x 44"

STAND
12" x 12"

Adult Bedroom

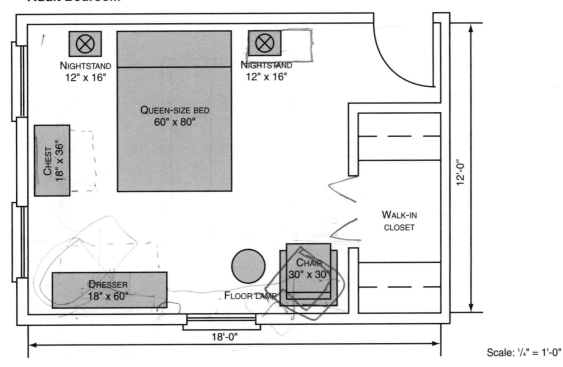

NIGHTSTAND
12" x 16"

NIGHTSTAND
12" x 16"

QUEEN-SIZE BED
60" x 80"

CHEST
18" x 36"

12'-0"

WALK-IN
CLOSET

CHAIR
30" x 30"

DRESSER
18" x 60"

FLOOR LAMP

18'-0"

Scale: ¼" = 1'-0"

Room Clearances
Activity 4-3

Solution

Bedroom

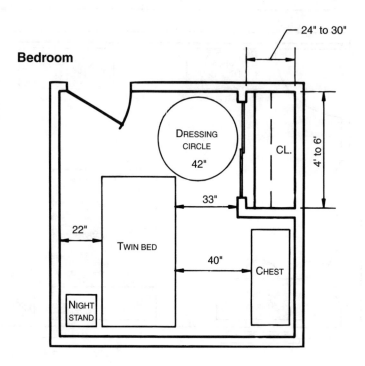

Bathroom

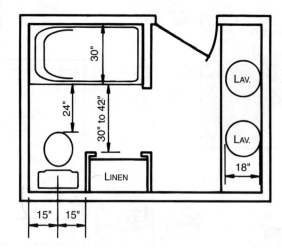

Scale: ¼" = 1'-0"

Bathroom Layout
Activity 4-4

Typical Solution

Small Bath

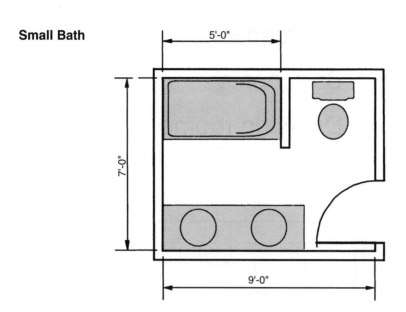

Large Bath

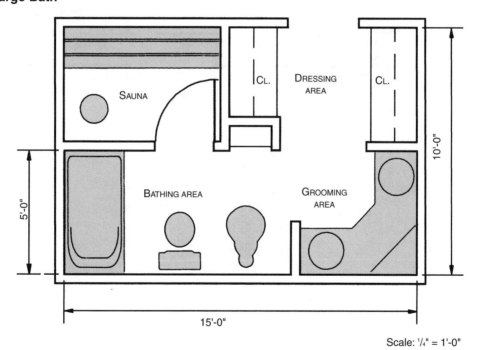

Scale: 1/4" = 1'-0"

Sleeping Areas in the Home

- Bedrooms
- Bathrooms
- Dressing rooms

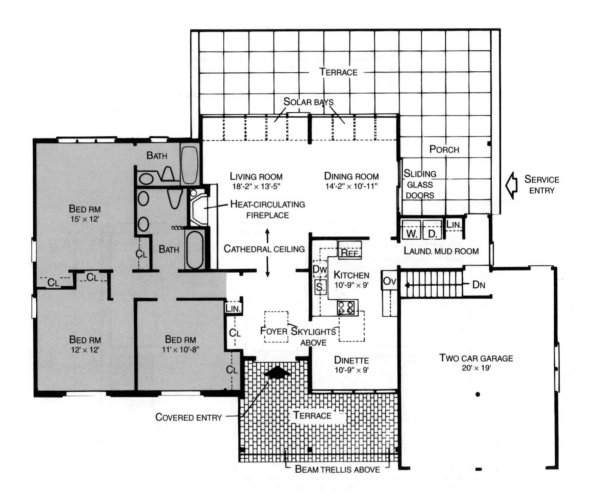

Designing Sleeping Areas

Name _____

Date _____

Incorporate bedroom furniture in the two shaded areas of this floor plan. First, draw the shaded areas to a ¼ *in. = 1 ft.* scale on graph paper. On a separate piece of paper, list and number the furniture pieces you would choose and identify their approximate sizes. (Refer to "A-8, Common Sizes of Bedroom Furniture" in the text's appendix.) Finally, use correctly scaled furniture templates on your floor plan or draw the furniture to scale.

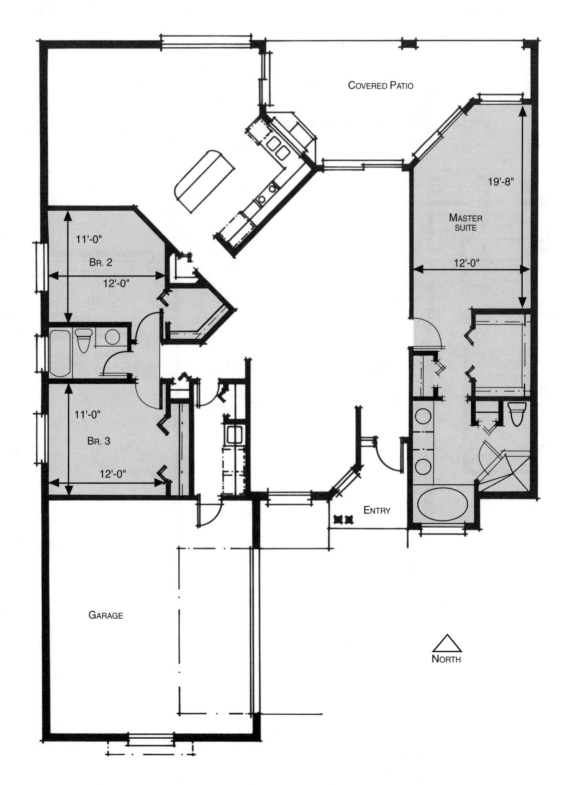

Examining Sleeping Areas

Name _____

Date _____

Study the sleeping areas of this house plan and evaluate them according to the principles discussed in the text. Write your comments on a separate piece of paper. Also identify ways to improve the plan.

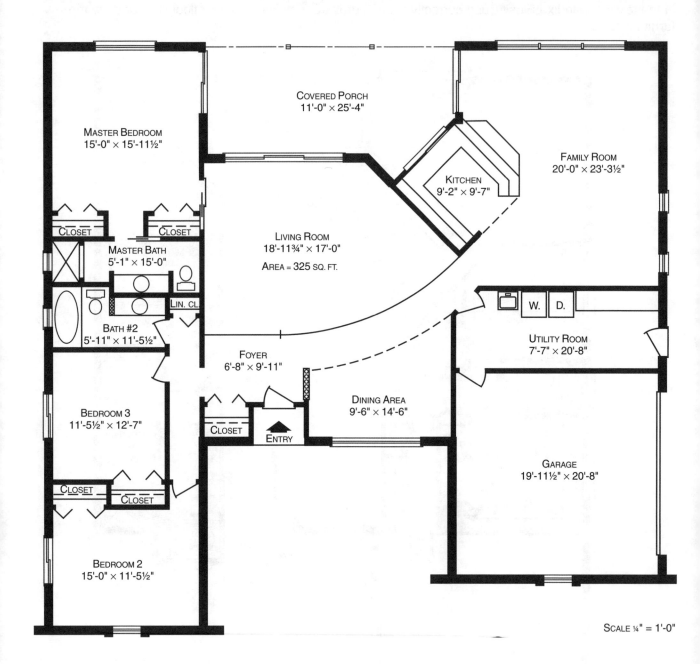

MASTER BEDROOM
15'-0" × 15'-11½"

COVERED PORCH
11'-0" × 25'-4"

FAMILY ROOM
20'-0" × 23'-3½"

CLOSET   CLOSET

KITCHEN
9'-2" × 9'-7"

MASTER BATH
5'-1" × 15'-0"

LIVING ROOM
18'-11¾" × 17'-0"

AREA = 325 SQ. FT.

LIN. CL.

BATH #2
5'-11" × 11'-5½"

W.   D.

UTILITY ROOM
7'-7" × 20'-8"

FOYER
6'-8" × 9'-11"

DINING AREA
9'-6" × 14'-6"

BEDROOM 3
11'-5½" × 12'-7"

CLOSET   ENTRY

CLOSET   CLOSET

GARAGE
19'-11½" × 20'-8"

BEDROOM 2
15'-0" × 11'-5½"

SCALE ¼" = 1'-0"

Redoing Bathrooms for Wheelchair Use

Name _____

Date _____

Study the two bathrooms of this house plan and design a single bathroom from the combined space that provides appropriate clearances for wheelchair use. On a separate sheet of paper, use a ¼ in. = 1 ft. scale to draw your redesign. (Use the appropriate clearances and principles discussed in your text.)

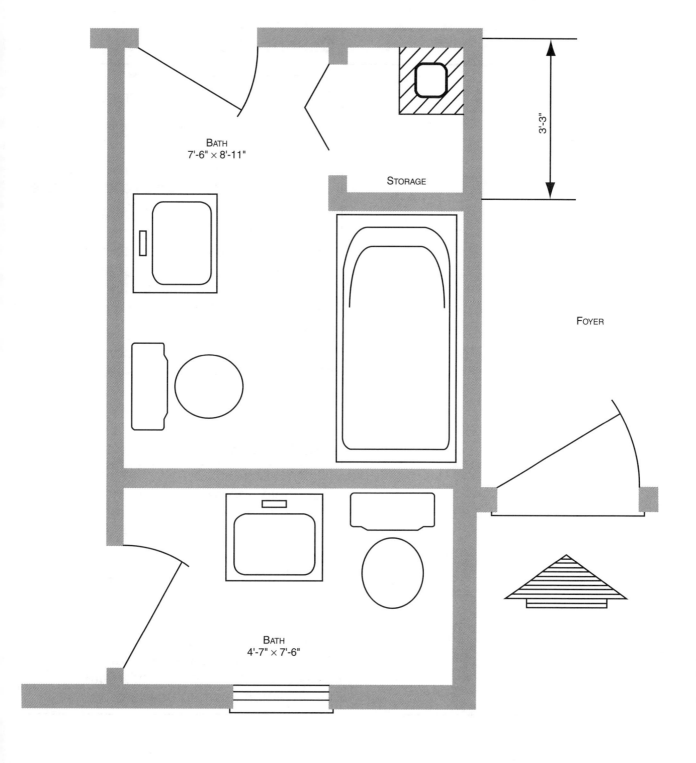

Universal Design for Bathrooms

Universal design focuses on designs that make the environment more usable for everyone. Your text discussed several such features, but additional bathroom features are described here. No single house is expected to include all the universal-design features possible, but when more are included, a house becomes more usable.

In a home with more than one bathroom, all should meet the following criteria, including bathrooms on the second floor.

Features	Description
General	At least one bathroom must have one of the following accessible bathing fixtures: • deep, curbless, shower at least 5 by 3 ft. (5 by 4 ft. preferred) • a waterproof floor, floor drain, and tub with integral seat (which allows people to sit in tub/shower without needing additional equipment) Other bathrooms in the same house may have a tub with an integral seat or a 3 by 3 ft. transfer shower with L-shaped folding seat and ½ in. maximum lip (curb) in lieu of fixtures described above. When more than one bathroom has the same type of bathing fixture (tub/shower or shower), at least one shower should be arranged for left-hand use.
Fixture controls	Single-lever water controls should be at all plumbing fixtures and faucets. Handheld showerheads are necessary in all tubs and showers. (If fixed heads are also present, a single-lever diverter valve is needed.) An adjustable-height, movable, handheld showerhead or 60 in. flexible hose allows easy use by people of all heights. Offset tub/shower controls located near adjacent, clear floor space allow easy access outside the tub, with no inconvenience when used inside.

Features	Description
Lavatory	Knee space under a lavatory may be open space or a clearing achieved by removing the vanity, or moving fold-back or self-storing doors. Pipe protection is needed to prevent contact with hot or sharp surfaces. Bowls mounted in countertop lavatories should be as close to the front edge as possible. Wall-hung lavatories should have appropriate pipe protection. Color contrast is needed between counter-tops and front edges or cabinet faces.
Walls	Broad blocking in walls around toilet, tub, and shower • allows for future placement and relocation of grab bars • assures adequate load bearing • eliminates the need to open the wall and add blocking later Grab bars, if installed, need *not* be stainless steel or chrome. Colors are available to match decor.
Floor	A 30 by 48 in. clear floor space is needed at each fixture, but spaces may overlap. Color contrast between floor surfaces and trim allows easy recognition of the floor/wall juncture, which aids in depth perception.
Mirror	Long mirrors should have their bottoms no more than 36 in. above the finished floor, with their tops, at least 72 in. high.

Source: Center for Universal Design, North Carolina State University

Planning Sleeping Areas

Chapter 4 Mastery Test

Name _____

Date _____

Score _____

Multiple Choice: Select the best response and write the letter in the preceding blank.

_____ 1. Of the following, _____ are generally *not* included in the sleeping area.
   A. bedrooms
   B. bathrooms
   C. dressing rooms
   D. exercise rooms

_____ 2. Bedrooms should be located _____.
   A. at the rear of the first floor or on the second floor
   B. at one end grouped together
   C. on the north side only
   D. anywhere there is privacy of sight and sound

_____ 3. To allow clearances for pulling open the drawers of a chest or dresser, _____ in. of space are recommended in front.
   A. 20
   B. 30
   C. 40
   D. 50

_____ 4. The minimum size recommended for a child's bedroom is _____ sq. ft.
   A. 90
   B. 100
   C. 110
   D. 120

_____ 5. When considering the number of baths required, a two-story house needs at least _____.
   A. one bath
   B. one and one-half baths
   C. two baths
   D. two and one-half baths

_____ 6. In addition to the typical needs a bathroom serves, space may be provided for _____.
   A. exercising
   B. sunbathing
   C. laundry
   D. All of the above.

_____ 7. The electrical switch for a bathroom exhaust fan should be placed _____.
   A. beside the light switch
   B. where it cannot be reached from the tub or shower
   C. on an inside wall
   D. anywhere there is room

Completion: Complete the following sentences by writing the missing words in the preceding blanks.

_____ 8. Ideally, each bedroom should open from a _____ instead of directly from another room.

_____ 9. The minimum closet space recommended per person is 4 to _____ ft. in length.

_____ 10. Built-in closets deeper than _____ ft. are usually considered walk-in closets.

_____ 11. An _____-shaped room can provide privacy for both children when a bedroom is shared.

(continued)

Name _____

_____ 12. A _____ in. clearance space is recommended in front of the water closet.

_____ 13. To provide knee space underneath, a _____ is available as a wall-hung or pedestal-type unit.

_____ 14. At least _____ to 42 in. of clearance space should be allowed for entering or leaving a sauna or whirlpool bath.

Short Answer: Provide brief answers to the following questions or statements.

15. What is the main purpose of the sleeping area? _____

_____

16. List the factors that determine the number and size of bedrooms needed in a residence.

_____

_____

17. What factors should be considered when determining the size of a bedroom? _____

_____

_____

_____

_____

_____

18. What steps should be followed when planning furniture arrangement in a bedroom?

_____

_____

_____

_____

19. Why are ribbon windows recommended for bedrooms? _____

_____

_____

20. List the three main types of bathrooms and the fixtures included in each. _____

_____

_____

_____

_____

_____

(continued)

Name _____

21. If a home has only one bath, where should it be located? Explain. _____

_____

_____

22. List several design considerations that are important for closets used by individuals with special physical needs. _____

_____

_____

_____

_____

23. Identify several considerations for beds for disabled family members. _____

_____

_____

_____

_____

_____

_____

24. List several design considerations for bathrooms used by individuals with special physical needs.

_____

_____

_____

_____

_____

_____

Chapter 5
Planning Service and Work Areas

Objectives

After studying this chapter, students will be able to

- describe the three centers of the work triangle and plan an efficiently arranged kitchen using any of the six common floor plans.
- evaluate the location, layout, and efficiency of laundry facilities in relationship to the lifestyle of various households.
- list possible uses and layouts of basements.
- determine the best location on a floor plan for the garage (or carport) and service entries.
- list the types and uses of special-purpose rooms, especially home offices, and storage units.
- identify requirements for service-areas used by individuals with special needs.

Teaching Materials

Text, pages 69–87

Student Activity Guide

Check Your Understanding
5-1, *Kitchen Evaluation*
5-2, *Kitchen Planning*
5-3, *Kitchen Elevations*
5-4, *Clothes Care Center*
5-5, *Special-Purpose Room*

Instructor's Resources

Service and Work Areas in the Home, transparency master 5-A

Six Common Kitchen Plans, transparency master 5-B

Evaluating Kitchen Design, reproducible master 5-C

Examining Service and Work Areas, transparency/reproducible master 5-D

Universal Design for Service and Work Areas, reproducible master 5-E

Chapter 5 Mastery Test

Instructional Concepts and Student Activities

1. Have students read Chapter 5 in the text and complete the review questions.
2. Ask students to collect pictures of kitchens, laundry facilities, basements, garages, service entries, special-purpose rooms, and storage areas. Have them add the pictures to their housing notebooks for future reference.

Kitchens

3. *Service and Work Areas in the Home*, transparency master 5-A, IR. Introduce students to the areas of a house that constitute the service and work areas.
4. Lead a class discussion on the location, size, and arrangement of kitchens.
5. Lead a class discussion on the three basic kitchen work centers—food preparation and storage center, cleanup center, cooking and serving center—and the work triangle.
6. Invite a professional kitchen designer to speak to the class on the process of designing a kitchen.
7. *Six Common Kitchen Plans*, transparency master 5-B, IR. Introduce students to the basic kitchen plans discussed in the text. Have each student identify which plan is closest to his or her home kitchen.
8. Provide your students with literature about appliances, cabinets, and counters. Have them examine this material while you discuss the types, sizes, shapes, and colors available.
9. *Kitchen Evaluation*, Activity 5-1, SAG. Students are to evaluate the design of a kitchen, identifying its strengths and weaknesses based on principles discussed in the text.
10. Discuss with students the six common kitchen floor plans: U-shaped, L-shaped, corridor, peninsula, island, and one-wall.
11. *Kitchen Planning*, Activity 5-2, SAG. Students are to plan a functional arrangement for appliances and features in a given kitchen.

12. *Evaluating Kitchen Design*, reproducible master 5-C, IR. Students are to evaluate the design of a kitchen, identifying its strengths and weaknesses based on principles discussed in the text.

13. *Kitchen Elevations*, Activity 5-3, SAG. Students are to draw an elevation view of a straight line kitchen using given height dimensions.

Laundry Facilities

14. Lead a class discussion on the location, size, and arrangement of laundry facilities. Have students evaluate the pros and cons of various arrangements.

15. *Clothes Care Center*, Activity 5-4, SAG. Students are to plan a functional arrangement of a typical clothes care center and draw an elevation view of the window wall.

16. Have students examine laundry equipment shown in product catalogs and sales brochures to become familiar with the types and sizes available.

Garages and Carports

17. Lead a class discussion on the location, size, and design of garages and carports.

18. Ask students with automobiles to measure the length and width of their automobiles, both with doors opened and closed, to illustrate the relationship of garage space to various types of automobiles.

Service Entries

19. Lead a class discussion on the location, size, and design of service entries.

20. *Examining Service and Work Areas*, transparency/reproducible master 5-D, IR. Have students use the handouts to carefully evaluate the floor plan's service and work areas according to the principles discussed in the text. Review their evaluations in class. Ask students to identify ways to improve the plan.

Special-Purpose Rooms

21. As a class or individually, ask students to list as many special-purpose rooms as they can. Then ask them to list the special requirements of each room.

22. *Special-Purpose Room*, Activity 5-5, SAG. Students are to clip a picture of a special-purpose room from a magazine and draw the floor plan of the room, identifying its unique features.

Storage

23. Ask students to identify the types of storage they have at home. List these on the board. Then, as a class, discuss any unique requirements associated with the listed types.

Adaptations for Special Needs

24. Lead a class discussion on ways to make service areas more usable for people with special physical needs.

25. *Universal Design for Service and Work Areas*, reproducible master 5-E, IR. Use the handout to reinforce the concept of universal design and provide examples common to service and work areas. (The chart lists housing features for people with special needs beyond those covered in the text.)

26. Assign one or more tasks listed in the text's *Suggested Activities* section at the end of the chapter.

Suggested Evaluation Techniques

27. *Check Your Understanding*, SAG. Have students complete as many questions as possible without referring to the text. Then have them find answers to questions they do not know.

28. Administer the *Chapter 5 Mastery Test*.

Answer Key

Text

Review Questions, page 86

1. food preparation and storage center: Tasks include storing, preparing, and mixing food. Common equipment includes a refrigerator, small appliances such as an electric mixer and food processor, mixing and measuring tools, and baking utensils and ingredients.
cooking and serving center: Tasks include cooking and serving food. Common equipment includes a cooking surface, range, and/or oven; cooking utensils; potholders; and small appliances such as a microwave oven, frypan, and toaster.
cleanup center: Tasks include rinsing food; and washing, drying, and storing dishes. Common equipment includes a sink; dishwasher; food waste disposer; dishcloths and dishwashing detergent; and cleaning, cutting, and draining utensils.

2. 22 ft.
3. when it includes a sink, under which food products should not be stored
4. its more efficient work triangle
5. sorting, pretreating, washing, drying, folding, ironing, and possibly mending clothes
6. in the kitchen, mudroom, utility room, sleeping area, basement, or a separate laundry room (Advantages and disadvantages are student response.)
7. an interior stairway at least 36 in. wide positioned to accommodate the greatest amount of traffic to and from first floor, an exterior entrance near wherever gardening and outdoor tools are used most
8. west or south, north
9. 7 ft.
10. near the kitchen
11. (Name eight:) home office, exercise room, darkroom, library, sewing room, arts and crafts studio, hobby room, workshop, music room, greenhouse, billiard room
12. built-in storage unit: advantages—uses less space and uses space more efficiently; disadvantages—offers few possibilities for furniture arrangements and is difficult to change
    freestanding storage unit: advantages—is moveable and comes in a wide variety of sizes and styles; disadvantages—ties up floor space and uses space less efficiently
13. direct entry from the street, an appropriate seating area such as a table with chairs, and a professional atmosphere
14. eye level
15. 5 ft.

Student Activity Guide

Check Your Understanding, pages 45–47

1. I	6. K	11. B
2. L	7. H	12. E
3. M	8. A	13. G
4. D	9. J	
5. F	10. C	

14. convenient to supervise or participate in nearby activities, makes kitchens appear larger
15. (List two:) dining, office work, homework, laundry
16. immediately adjacent to the sink
17. the pattern of taking food from the refrigerator-freezer, cleaning it at the sink, cooking it at the range, and returning leftovers to the refrigerator-freezer

18. (List three:) ceramic, metal, wood, plastic, stone
19. (List two:) prevent circulation from passing through the work triangle, provide ample cabinet and counter space, is the most efficient layout
20. (List two:) adapt to a variety of room plans, allow space for an eating area if the room is large, prevent interruption of the work triangle by circulation
21. in the mudroom or utility room near the service entrance; because it will be convenient for removing outdoor clothing soiled by gardening
22. D
23. A
24. C
25. D
26. A
27. 60
28. 18
29. 22
30. 12, 13
31. 16, 7
32. 10
33. freestanding
34. surge
35. audit
36. 8, 11
37. 48
38. 5

Kitchen Evaluation, Activity 5-1

1. Nearness to service entrance and dining area is good, but bathroom is too distant.
2. ample wall and base cabinets, but small food storage area
3. Work triangle from refrigerator to sink to range is good; 24 in. of countertop space is missing from one side of cooking surface.
4. good because it is less than 22 ft.
5. none
6. A lazy Susan would improve use of corner area.
7. not enough counter space, no range hood

Kitchen Planning, Activity 5-2

Typical solution on page 93

Kitchen Elevations, Activity 5-3

Typical solution on page 94

Clothes Care Center, Activity 5-4

Typical solution on page 95

Instructor's Resources

Chapter 5 Mastery Test

1.	B	4.	C	7.	D
2.	D	5.	D	8.	C
3.	B	6.	C	9.	B

10. service
11. 36
12. 24
13. 34½, 24
14. 12, 30
15. L-shaped
16. 240
17. basement
18. 36
19. to sustain all other areas of a home
20. kind and amount of food to be prepared and the activities that will take place in the kitchen
21. food preparation and storage center, cooking and serving center, and the cleanup center Additional work areas may include a mixing, eating, planning, or laundry center.
22. dishwasher and food waste disposer
23. to connect most directly to the water source and for easy loading and unloading of dishes
24. refrigerator in the food preparation and storage center, sink in the cleanup center, cooking surface in the cooking and serving center Food is taken from the refrigerator-freezer, cleaned at the sink, cooked on the range, and returned to the refrigerator-freezer as leftovers.
25. U-shaped, L-shaped, corridor, peninsula, island, and one-wall
26. incorporates work centers on three walls, is very efficient, prevents circulation from passing through the work triangle, and provides ample cabinet and counter space
27. Dampness can cause discomfort and damage stored items. It is reduced by using proper ventilation, running a dehumidifier, insulating walls with moisture-resistant insulation, or drying and heating the air.
28. 10

Kitchen Planning
Activity 5-2

Typical Solution

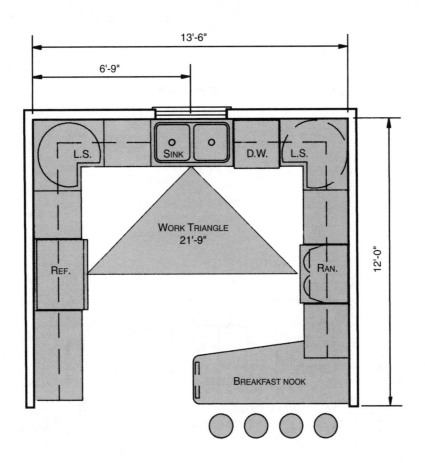

Plan View

Scale: $^1/_4$" = 1'-0"

Kitchen Elevations
Activity 5-3

Typical Solution

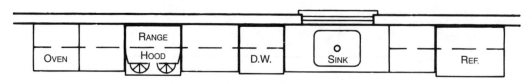

Plan View

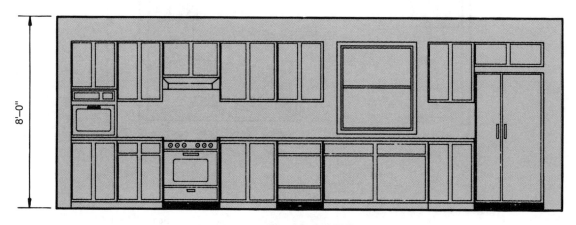

Elevation View

Scale: 1/4" = 1'-0"

Clothes Care Center
Activity 5-4

Typical Solution

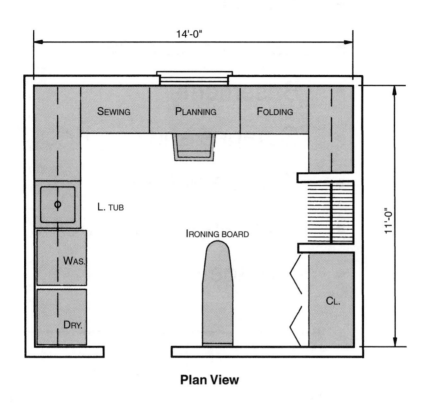

Plan View

14'-0"

11'-0"

SEWING   PLANNING   FOLDING

L. TUB

WAS.

DRY.

IRONING BOARD

CL.

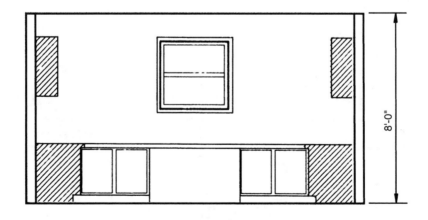

Elevation View

8'-0"

Scale: 1/4" = 1'-0"

Service and Work Areas in the Home

- Kitchens

- Laundry facilities

- Basements

- Garages and carports

- Service entries

- Special-purpose rooms

- Storage

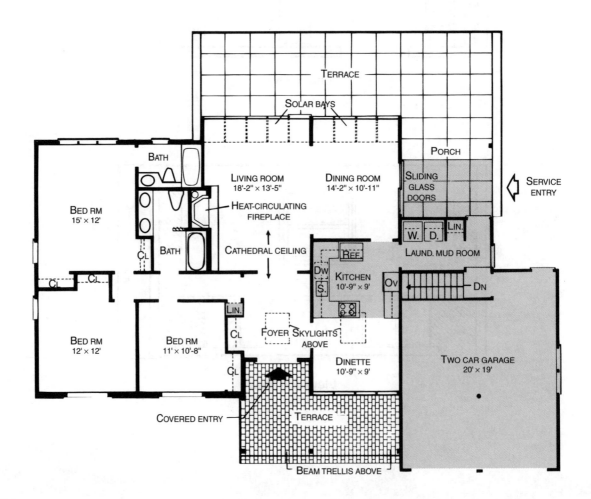

Six Common Kitchen Plans

L-Shaped Kitchen

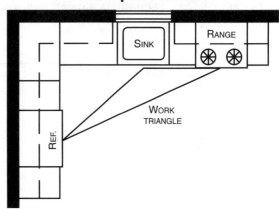

One-Wall Kitchen

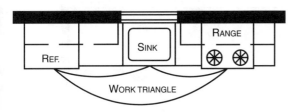

Corridor Kitchen

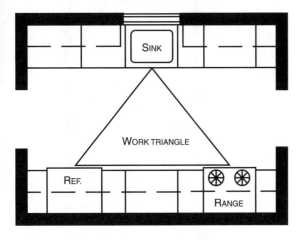

U-Shaped Kitchen

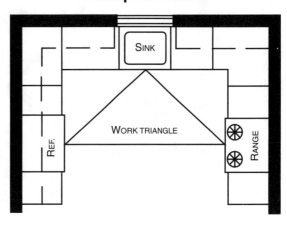

Peninsula Kitchen

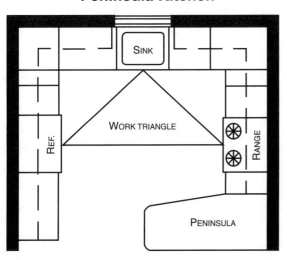

Island Kitchen

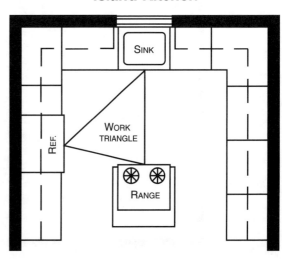

Evaluating Kitchen
Design

Name _____

Date _____

Evaluate the design of the kitchen below according to the principles discussed in the text. Identify its strength and weaknesses in terms of the following criteria: location, adequate storage, layout, and efficiency of the work triangle. On a separate piece of paper, write your evaluation as well as your recommendations for improvement.

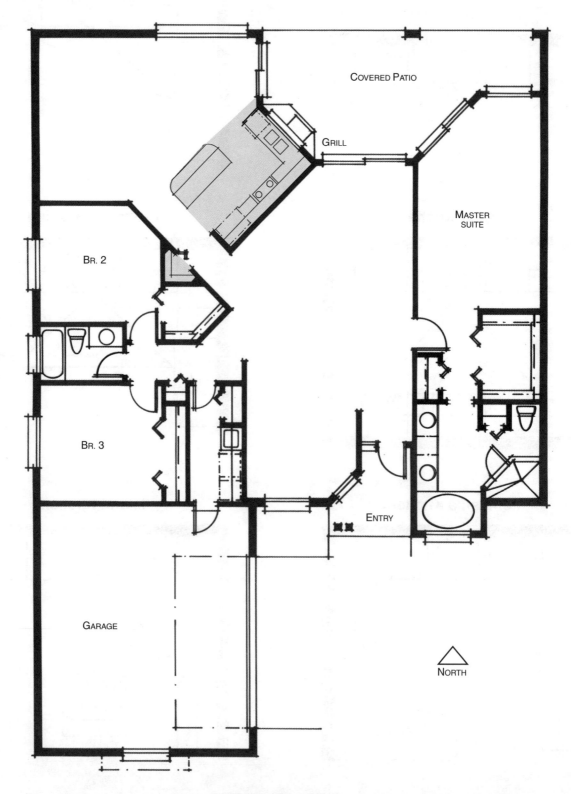

Examining Service and Work Areas

Name _____

Date _____

Study the service and work areas of this house plan and evaluate them according to the principles discussed in the text. Write your comments on a separate piece of paper. Also identify ways to improve the plan.

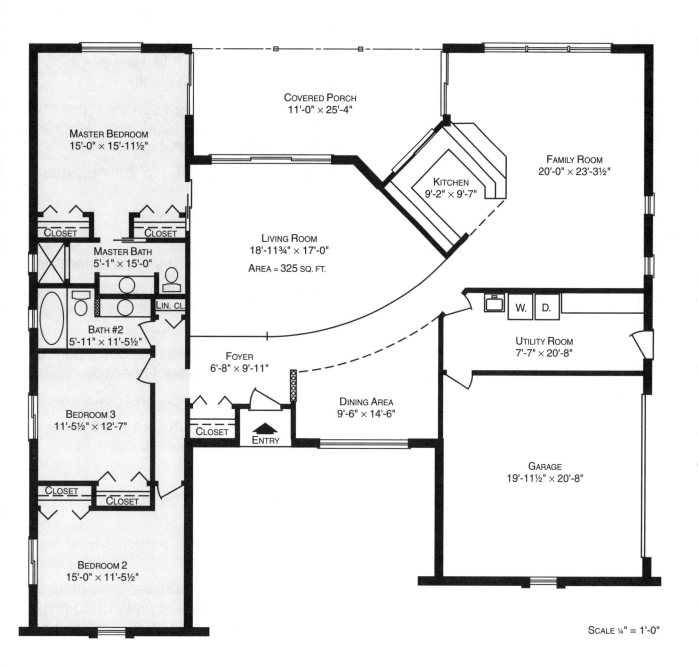

SCALE ¼" = 1'-0"

Universal Design for Service and Work Areas

Universal design focuses on designs that make the environment more usable for everyone. Your text discussed several such features, but additional features for service and work areas are described here. No single house is expected to include all the universal-design features possible, but when more are included, a house becomes more usable.

Feature	Description
Kitchens	Minimum space of 48 in. between face of cabinets and opposite wall.
	Adjustable-height work surfaces (possibly with sinks, disposals, and/or cooktops) ranging from 28-42 in. high that are
	• electrically powered to the individual user's height, or
	• mechanically adjustable in 2 in. increments
	Contrasting color edges on countertops.
	Long stretches of continuous countertop for easy sliding of heavy items between the work centers.
	Pantry storage with easy-access, pull-out and/or adjustable-height shelves.
	Front-mounted controls on appliances.
	Cooktop or range with staggered burners and front or side-mounted controls.
	Glarefree lighting.
	Refrigerators that allow easy reach of all areas such as
	• side-by-side units, particularly with pull-out shelving
	• under-counter or drawer-type units installed on a raised platform to provide storage 18-48 in. above the floor
	Dishwasher raised on a platform or drawer unit so top rack is level with adjacent countertop.
	Single-lever water controls.

Feature	Description
Laundry areas	Laundry sink and countertop no more than 34 in. above finished floor, with knee space below. Clear floor space at least 36 in. wide across front of washer and dryer, and extending at least 18 in. beyond right and left sides. (Extension can be part of under-counter knee space.)
Storage	Maximum height of 54 in. for at least half the storage space. Flexible storage options such as • adjustable-height closet rods and shelves • motorized cabinets that raise and lower • power-operated clothing carousels
Garages and carports	Power-operated overhead doors. Extra length and width inside for easy movement around parked cars (No ramp in garages). Sloping garage floor with through-the-wall/door vents at bottom of slope to release fumes (in lieu of stepped entrance with ramp from garage/patio to house interior).

Source: Center for Universal Design, North Carolina State University

Planning Service and Work Areas

Name _____

Date _____

Score _____

Chapter 5 Mastery Test

Multiple Choice: Select the best response and write the letter in the preceding blank.

_____   1.   The food preparation and storage center focuses on _____.
A. the range
B. the refrigerator-freezer
C. the sink
D. None of the above.

_____   2.   The minimum space needed next to the sink to stack soiled dishes is _____ in.
A. 12
B. 18
C. 30
D. 36

_____   3.   The minimum space needed next to the sink to drain and stack clean dishes is _____ in.
A. 12
B. 18
C. 24
D. 30

_____   4.   The recommended maximum length of the kitchen work triangle is _____ ft.
A. 18
B. 20
C. 22
D. 24

_____   5.   Suitable countertop materials include _____.
A. ceramic, laminated plastic, and stone
B. metal
C. wood, stone, and plastic
D. All of the above.

_____   6.   Base kitchen cabinets generally range from 9 to 48 in. widths in increments of _____ in.
A. 1½
B. 2
C. 3
D. 4

_____   7.   The peninsula in a peninsula kitchen can be used for _____.
A. extra storage space
B. an eating area
C. space for a built-in appliance
D. All of the above.

_____   8.   Washers and dryers range in width from 24 to _____ in.
A. 30
B. 32
C. 34
D. 36

_____   9.   To store one automobile in a garage or carport, the space needed is _____ ft.
A. 10 by 18
B. 11 by 20
C. 12 by 20
D. 12 by 21

(continued)

Name _____

Completion: Complete the following sentences by writing the missing words in the preceding blanks.

_____ 10. Ideally, the kitchen needs to be located near the _____ entrance of the home as well as the dining area.

_____ 11. A minimum length of _____ in. of counter space is needed next to the food storage area for mixing food.

_____ 12. The cooking center requires at least _____ in. of heat-resistant counter space on each side of the range to hold ingredients and utensils needed for cooking.

_____ 13. The height of a standard base kitchen cabinet is _____ in. and its depth is _____ in.

_____ 14. Generally, wall cabinets are 12 or 13 in. deep and range from _____ to _____ in. high.

_____ 15. In _____ kitchens, the work centers form a continuous line along two adjoining walls.

_____ 16. A clothes dryer will require the availability of a gas line or _____-volt electrical outlet.

_____ 17. Although a _____ can be a living or sleeping area, it is usually considered part of the service area.

_____ 18. The basement stairway should be at least _____ in. wide to accommodate large items such as water heaters, furniture, and equipment.

Short Answer: Provide brief answers to the following questions or statements.

19. Why is it necessary to make service areas as efficient as possible? _____

_____

_____

20. What factors determine the ideal size of a kitchen?_____

_____

_____

_____

21. Identify the three basic work centers in the kitchen and any additional work centers. _____

_____

_____

_____

_____

_____

_____

_____

(continued)

Name _____

22. Name the two appliances that are frequently included in the cleanup center. _____

_____

_____

23. Why should a dishwasher be located next to a sink? _____

_____

_____

24. What are the three focal points of the kitchen work triangle? How do they work together?

_____

_____

_____

_____

_____

25. List the six common kitchen plans. _____

_____

_____

_____

_____

_____

_____

26. Describe the floor plan of a U-shaped kitchen. _____

_____

_____

_____

27. Why is moisture a primary concern in basements? How can it be reduced? _____

_____

_____

_____

_____

28. Approximately what percent of the space in a house should be allocated for storage? _____

_____

Chapter 6
Design

Objectives

After studying this chapter, students will be able to

- describe the various uses and effects of space, line, shape, form, texture, and color.
- evaluate a room design according to its proportion, scale, balance, emphasis, and rhythm.
- use the elements and principles of design to create a room plan with appropriateness, harmony, variety, unity, and function.
- evaluate the selection and placement of functional and decorative accessories according to the elements, principles, and goals of design.

Teaching Materials

Text, pages 89–106

Student Activity Guide

Check Your Understanding
6-1, *Elements of Design*
6-2, *Principles of Design*
6-3, *Goals of Design*

Instructor's Resources

Design Elements, transparency master 6-A
Design Principles, transparency master 6-B
Design Goals, transparency master 6-C
Chapter 6 Mastery Test

Instructional Concepts and Student Activities

1. Have students read Chapter 6 in the text and complete the review questions.
2. Ask students to collect pictures that show good design. Have them look for examples that concentrate on the elements, principles, and goals of design. Students are to add these photos to their housing notebooks, labeling each with the design principle, element, or goal it illustrates.

Elements of Design

3. *Design Elements*, transparency master 6-A, IR. Introduce students to the factors that comprise the basic elements of design. Emphasize their relationship to the goals of design.
4. Show the *Design for Living* video from Learning Seed's catalog and have students discuss it.
5. Discuss the elements of design—space, line, shape, form, texture, and color. Ask students to show examples from their housing notebooks that illustrate the elements of design.
6. Show the *Eye for Design* video from Learning Seed's catalog and have students discuss it.
7. *Elements of Design*, Activity 6-1, SAG. Students are to illustrate each of the elements of design using a subject related to housing.

Principles of Design

8. *Design Principles*, transparency master 6-B, IR. Introduce students to the basic factors that comprise the principles of design. Emphasize their relationship to the goals of design.
9. Discuss the five main principles of design—proportion, scale, balance, emphasis, and rhythm. Ask students to show examples from their housing notebooks that illustrate the principles of design.
10. *Principles of Design*, Activity 6-2, SAG. Students are to demonstrate an understanding of proportion, scale, balance, emphasis, and rhythm by completing various exercises.

Goals of Design

11. *Design Goals*, transparency master 6-C, IR. Introduce students to the basic factors that comprise the goals of design. Emphasize their relationship to the elements and principles of design.
12. Discuss appropriateness, harmony, variety, unity, and function. Show examples and ask students to share examples from their housing notebooks.
13. *Goals of Design*, Activity 6-3, SAG. Students are to select pictures that demonstrate appropriateness and unity, and explain how those design goals are reflected in the pictures.

Accessories in Design

14. Discuss with the class the function and role of accessories in a design scheme.
15. Show the *Interiors: Rooms That Teach* video from Learning Seed's catalog and have students discuss it.
16. Assign one or more tasks listed in the text's *Suggested Activities* section at the end of the chapter.

Suggested Evaluation Techniques

17. *Check Your Understanding*, SAG. Have students complete as many questions as possible without referring to the text. Then have them find answers to questions they do not know.
18. Administer the *Chapter 6 Mastery Test*.

Answer Key

Text

Review Questions, page 105

1. One type of space, line, shape and form, texture, or color should dominate; variations should be added for interest.
2. by using full or partial walls, dividers/screens, or furniture to divide space
3. Horizontal stripes are best because they will make the room appear shorter and wider; vertical lines will make the room appear too tall and small; diagonal lines are overpowering for a small room.
4. softening, graceful effect
5. Shape is two-dimensional with length and width. Form is three-dimensional with length, width, and depth (or height).
6. Smooth surfaces reflect light, intensify colors, and make them appear lighter and brighter. Rough surfaces absorb light, subdue colors, and make them appear darker and less intense.
7. unequal amounts because that is more pleasing to the eye
8. the hutch because a tall china cabinet against a wall with a low ceiling will make the room appear crowded
9. Formal balance has identical objects placed on both sides of a central point, while informal balance has different, but equivalent, objects.
10. The focal point should dominate, but not overpower, other design aspects. No other features should compete with it.
11. repetition, gradation, transition, radiation

12. appropriateness, harmony with variety and unity, and function
13. by using a variety of lines, shapes, textures, or colors
14. The intended use or function of an object dictates a suitable form.
15. Functional accessories should be chosen and placed to meet needs and, secondarily, to serve decorative purposes.
16. Use a picture in scale with the sofa. Place it at least 6 to 8 in. above.

Student Activity Guide

Check Your Understanding, pages 55–57

1. K	10. M	19. F
2. G	11. B	20. C
3. S	12. H	21. D
4. O	13. L	22. D
5. A	14. P	23. A
6. J	15. I	24. C
7. D	16. E	25. D
8. N	17. Q	26. A
9. C	18. R	

27. space, line, shape/form, texture, color
28. Cluster furniture and accessories into primary and secondary conversation areas. Divide a room into two separate activity areas with dividers.
29. length, width, depth (or height)
30. Smooth surfaces reflect light, intensify colors, and make them appear lighter and brighter. Rough surfaces absorb light, subdue colors, and make them appear darker and less intense.
31. The focal point should dominate, but not overpower, other aspects of the room or design. No other features should compete with the focal point.
32. repetition
33. (Student response.)
34. The use of a structure, room, or object should generally determine its form.

Principles of Design, Activity 6-2

Typical solution on page 110

Instructor's Resources

Chapter 6 Mastery Test

1. B
2. C
3. B
4. D
5. B
6. space

7. horizontal
8. shape
9. texture
10. balance
11. proportion
12. harmony
13. tactile
14. (Student response. See pages 95-100 in the text.)
15. by planting shrubs or building fences to extend the living area of the house beyond its walls

16. squares, rectangles, triangles, and circles
17. (List four:) tetrahedron, cube, pyramid, cone, sphere
18. Too little variety is monotonous, while too much variety can create a disjointed, distracting appearance.
19. Choose objects that are the proper size for the space they occupy, are appropriate for human dimensions, and appear their actual size.
20. repetition, gradation, transition, and radiation

Principles of Design
Activity 6-2

Typical Solution

Proportion

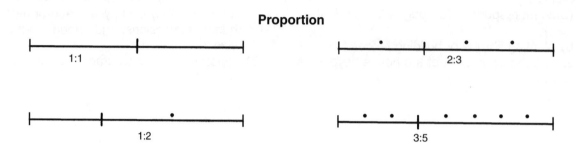

Balance

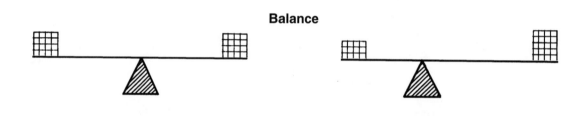

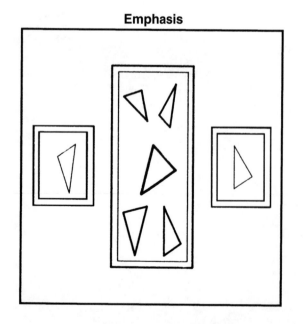

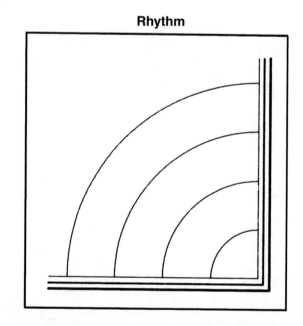

Design Elements

- **Space**
- **Line**
- **Shape**
- **Form**
- **Texture**
- **Color**

Elements of design **+** **Principles of design** **=** **Goals of design**

Design Principles

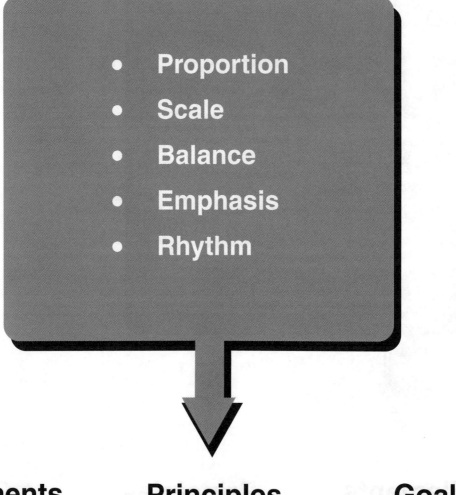

- **Proportion**
- **Scale**
- **Balance**
- **Emphasis**
- **Rhythm**

Elements of design **+** **Principles of design** **=** **Goals of design**

Design Goals

- **Appropriateness**
- **Harmony**
- **Variety**
- **Unity**
- **Function**

Elements of design **+** **Principles of design** **=** **Goals of design**

Design
Chapter 6
Mastery Test

Name _____

Date _____

Score _____

Multiple Choice: Select the best response and write the letter in the preceding blank.

_____ 1. The element of design that gives direction to a design is _____.
A. space
B. line
C. texture
D. color

_____ 2. The line that suggests action, movement, and excitement is _____.
A. vertical
B. horizontal
C. diagonal
D. curved

_____ 3. The three-dimensional element of design is _____.
A. shape
B. form
C. texture
D. color

_____ 4. The false statement about form is _____.
A. form should be considered as it relates to space
B. thinner, more delicate forms appear fragile even when built of sturdy materials
C. related forms tend to look better together than unrelated forms
D. perfect geometric forms are more pleasing than imperfect geometric forms

_____ 5. A sense of equilibrium is achieved in a design through _____.
A. form
B. balance
C. emphasis
D. rhythm

Completion: Complete the following sentences by writing the missing words in the preceding blanks.

_____ 6. _____ is affected by the number and size of forms in it.

_____ 7. _____ lines suggest informality and restfulness and make objects seem wider and lower.

_____ 8. The two-dimensional element of design is _____.

_____ 9. A surface's tactile quality is known as _____.

_____ 10. The five main principles of design include: scale, proportion, _____, emphasis, and rhythm.

_____ 11. The ratio of one part to another part or of one part to the whole is known as _____.

_____ 12. The goals of design include: appropriateness, _____, variety, unity, and function.

_____ 13. The *perception of touch* defines _____.

(continued)

Name_____

Short Answer: Provide brief answers to the following questions or statements.

14. How does each element of design play a part in the overall success of a design?_____

_____

_____

_____

_____

_____

_____

_____

15. When homes are built close together, people may feel some loss of privacy. How can this problem
    be solved? _____

_____

_____

_____

16. List the four perfect geometric shapes that are very pleasing to the eye. _____

_____

_____

_____

_____

17. Identify four common geometric forms that have application in housing. _____

_____

_____

_____

_____

18. Why does a well-designed room need a variety of textures?_____

_____

_____

_____

(continued)

Name _____

19. How should objects be chosen for housing and interiors to achieve good scale? _____

_____

_____

_____

_____

_____

20. Name the four types of rhythm in design. _____

_____

_____

_____

Chapter 7
Color

Objectives

After studying this chapter, students will be able to
* explain the perceptions linked to certain colors.
* describe the standard color wheel.
* evaluate a color according to hue, value, and intensity.
* use a color wheel to plan various color harmonies.
* describe three popular color systems.
* identify seven common color harmonies.
* explain the effect of light on color.

Teaching Materials

Text, pages 107–124

Student Activity Guide

Check Your Understanding
7-1, *Color Wheel*
7-2, *Color Characteristics*
7-3, *Neutral Colors*
7-4, *Color Harmonies*

Instructor's Resources

Color Relationships, transparency master 7-A

Monochromatic Color Harmony Using Purple, transparency master 7-B

Analogous Color Harmony Using Purple, transparency master 7-C

Complementary Color Harmony Using Purple, transparency master 7-D

Split-Complementary Color Harmony Using Purple, transparency master 7-E

Triadic Color Harmony Using Purple, transparency master 7-F

Double-Complementary Color Harmony Using Purple, transparency master 7-G

Chapter 7 Mastery Test

Instructional Concepts and Student Activities

1. Have students read Chapter 7 in the text and complete the review questions.
2. Ask students to collect examples of colors they like. Students are to add these samples to their housing notebooks, identifying the colors by name.

The Psychology of Color

3. Lead a detailed class discussion of color. Cover the impact of color on human feelings, the color wheel, color terms, and color characteristics.

The Color Spectrum

4. *Color Wheel*, Activity 7-1, SAG. Students are to develop their own color wheel using colored pencils or color samples from paint or wallpaper stores.
5. *Color Relationships*, transparency master 7-A, IR. Show students an easy way to remember the following color groups on the common color wheel:
   * An upright triangle points to the primary colors.
   * An inverted triangle points to the secondary colors.
   * A hexagon links the remaining colors, which are the intermediate colors.
6. Show *The Language of Color* video from Learning Seed's catalog and have students discuss it.

Color Characteristics

7. *Color Characteristics*, Activity 7-2, SAG. Students are to illustrate the hue, value, and intensity of each of the three primary colors using colored pencils, colored paper, or paint color samples.
8. *Neutral Colors*, Activity 7-3, SAG. Students are to illustrate the neutral and near-neutral colors using color samples or colored pencils.

Color Systems

9. Ask students to research and write an essay on one of the three color systems described in the text.

Color Harmonies

10. Discuss the basic color harmonies with the class and illustrate each with a photo, slide, or magazine picture.
11. Show the *Color Harmony for Interiors* video from Learning Seed's catalog and have students discuss it.
12. *Monochromatic Color Harmony Using Purple*, transparency master 7-B, IR. Have students discuss the color scheme that results when purple is used as a foundation color in this type of color harmony. Ask students to describe the mood created by the color harmony.
13. *Analogous Color Harmony Using Purple*, transparency master 7-C, IR. Have students discuss the color scheme that results when purple is used as a foundation color in this type of color harmony. Ask students to describe the mood created by the color harmony.
14. *Complementary Color Harmony Using Purple*, transparency master 7-D, IR. Have students discuss the color scheme that results when purple is used as a foundation color in this type of color harmony. Ask students to describe the mood created by the color harmony.
15. *Split-Complementary Color Harmony Using Purple*, transparency master 7-E, IR. Have students discuss the color scheme that results when purple is used as a foundation color in this type of color harmony. Ask students to describe the mood created by the color harmony.
16. *Triadic Color Harmony Using Purple*, transparency master 7-F, IR. Have students discuss the color scheme that results when purple is used as a foundation color in this type of color harmony. Ask students to describe the mood created by the color harmony.
17. *Double-Complementary Harmony Using Purple*, transparency master 7-G, IR. Have students discuss the color scheme that results when purple is used as a foundation color in this type of color harmony. Ask students to describe the mood created by the color harmony.
18. *Color Harmonies*, Activity 7-4, SAG. Students are to illustrate each of the standard color harmonies using their color wheel in the text as a model for colors and color locations.

19. Have each student plan a color harmony using his or her favorite color. Students are to illustrate their color harmony by using color swatches, textures, and fabrics.

Effect of Light on Color

20. Select several objects of different colors and observe their color changes under different lighting conditions. Have students record their observations.

Effect of Adjacent Colors

21. Provide an assortment of color samples and have the students place pairs of colors side-by-side to observe the effect of different pairings on the appearance of the hues. Have them record their reaction to each color pairing.

Effect of Texture on Color

22. Collect samples of a single color hue showing a variety of textures. Observe the effect of texture on the appearance of the color.

Effect of Color on Space

23. Have students make presentations to test the following principles:
    - Colors appear darker and brighter when close than when viewed at a greater distance.
    - Colors seem to gain intensity when covering large areas.
    - Some colors have a natural tendency to appear closer (*or* farther away).
    - Light and cool colors recede, while dark and warm colors advance.

Color Decisions

24. Have students bring pictures, art objects, or other source of a color harmony to class. Identify the colors and the color harmony represented.
25. Assign one or more tasks listed in the text's *Suggested Activities* section at the end of the chapter.

Suggested Evaluation Techniques

26. *Check Your Understanding*, SAG. Have students complete as many questions as possible without referring to the text. Then have them find answers to questions they do not know.
27. Administer the *Chapter 7 Mastery Test.*

Answer Key

Text

Review Questions, page 122

1. primary, secondary, and intermediate (or tertiary)
2. hue, value, and intensity
3. Warm colors make rooms seem warmer and appear smaller, while cool colors make rooms seem cooler and appear larger. warm colors: red, orange, and yellow; cool colors: green, blue, and violet
4. neutrals: white, black, and gray; near neutrals: brown, tan, and beige
5. red, yellow, and blue
6. a three-dimensional double cone
7. 100
8. monochromatic
9. complementary
10. black
11. complementary colors such as orange and blue
12. warm
13. ocher, sienna, red oxide, umber, and terre verde

Student Activity Guide

Check Your Understanding, pages 61–63

1. B	9. D	17. C
2. A	10. H	18. B
3. I	11. C	19. A
4. F	12. D	20. C
5. E	13. B	21. D
6. G	14. C	22. A
7. C	15. A	
8. J	16. D	

23. stimulates the nervous system and increases blood pressure, respiration rate, and heartbeat
    uses: as an accent color, a dominant color in a recreation or game room, or as a color to warm northern or eastern exposures
24. yellow
25. by mixing equal amounts of two primary colors

26. by adding black to a hue
27. a softening effect
28. opposite
29. advance
30. recede
31. low
32. lighter
33. warmer
34. cool

Instructor's Resources

Chapter 7 Mastery Test

1. B
2. A
3. C
4. A
5. C
6. C
7. C
8. B
9. blue
10. color wheel
11. primary
12. yellow, violet
13. neutral
14. orange
15. violet
16. Brewster
17. Ostwald
18. cooler
19. by mixing, lightening, and darkening
20. A tint is a lightened value of a hue, made by adding white to a hue. A shade is a darkened value of a hue, made by adding black to a hue.
21. by combining two colors that are directly opposite each other on the color wheel
22. Orange comes from combining yellow and red; green, from yellow and blue; and violet, from blue and red.
23. the name of the color
24. the lightness or darkness of the hue
25. the brightness or dullness of a hue
26. (Student response. See pages 120-122 in the text.)
27. The reflected rays give the object its color.
28. blue, green, violet

Color Relationships

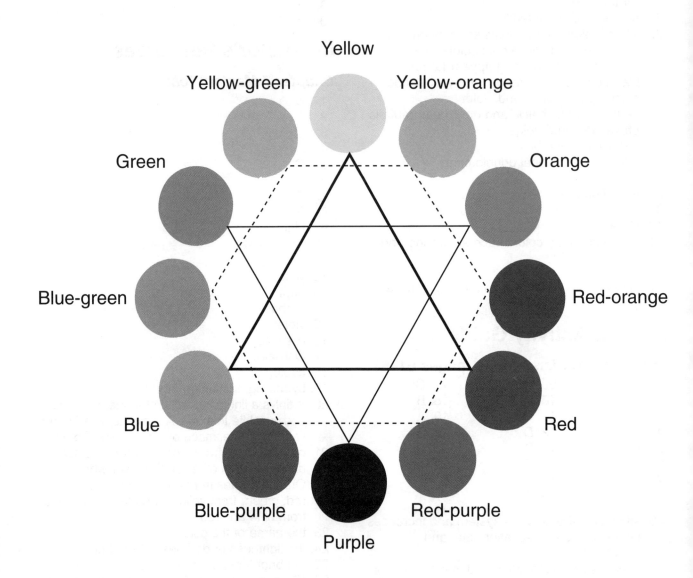

 Primary colors

 Secondary colors

 Intermediate colors

Monochromatic Color Harmony Using Purple

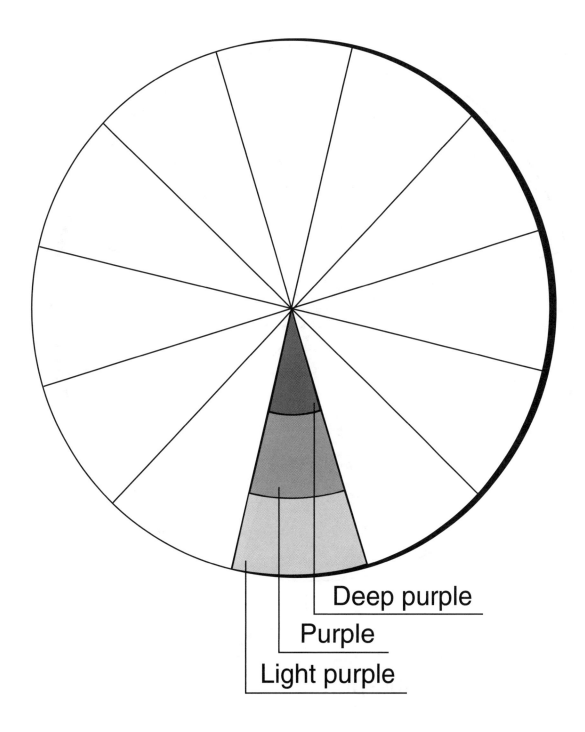

Deep purple

Purple

Light purple

Analogous Color Harmony Using Purple

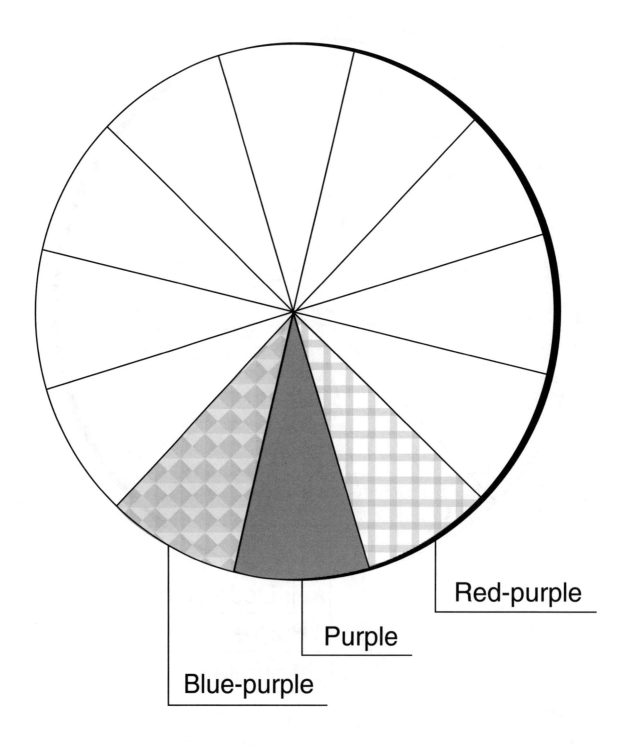

Red-purple

Purple

Blue-purple

Complementary Color Harmony Using Purple

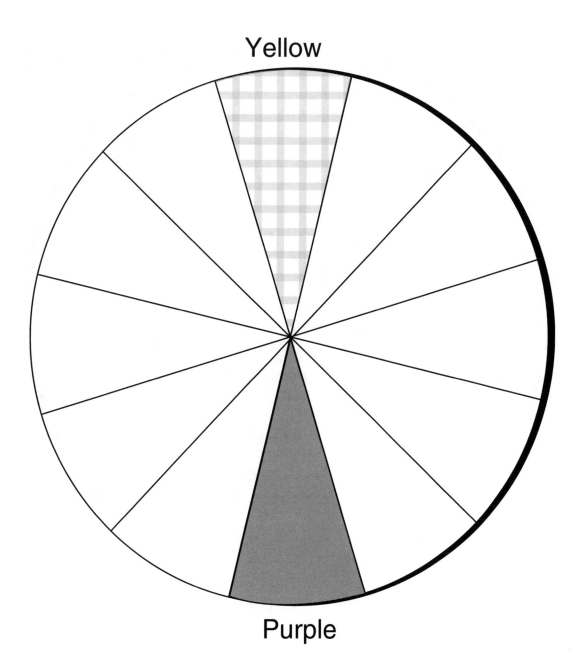

Yellow

Purple

Split-Complementary Color Harmony Using Purple

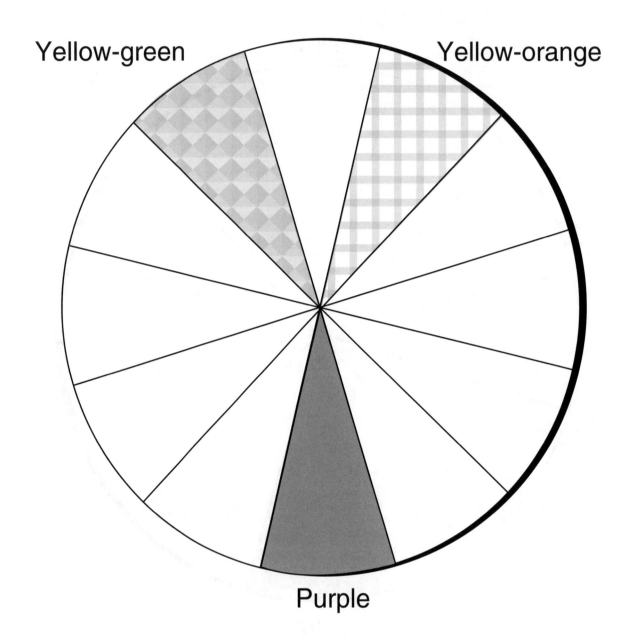

Yellow-green

Yellow-orange

Purple

Triadic Color Harmony Using Purple

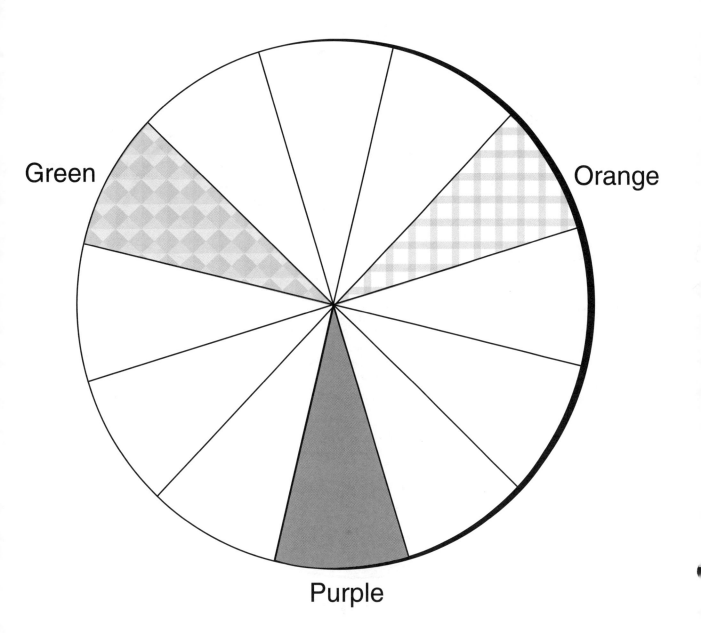

Green

Orange

Purple

Double-Complementary Color Harmony Using Purple

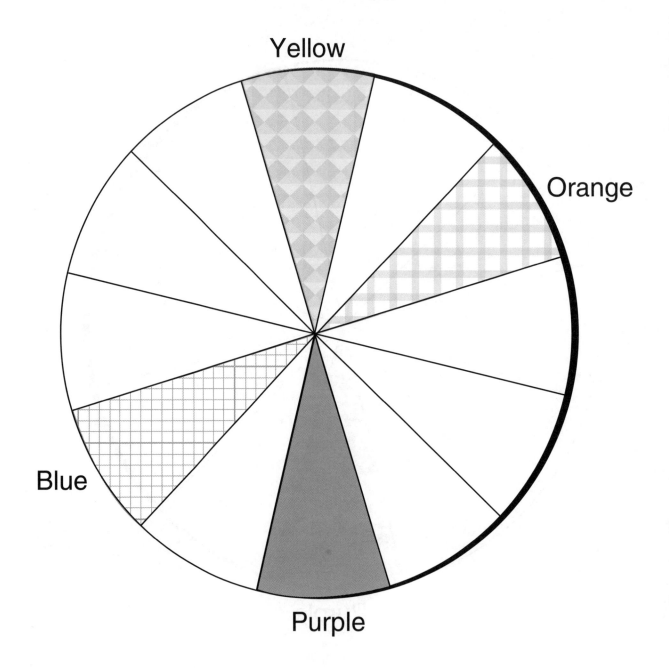

Note: Purple and yellow can be paired with any set of complements.

Color
Chapter 7
Mastery Test

Name _____

Date _____

Score _____

Multiple Choice: Select the best response and write the letter in the preceding blank.

_____ 1. The two colors that can make other colors look cleaner and livelier are _____.
A. blue and green
B. white and black
C. yellow and orange
D. violet and white

_____ 2. Intermediate colors are made by _____.
A. mixing a primary color with a secondary color
B. mixing two primary colors
C. mixing two secondary colors
D. mixing a neutral color with any color

_____ 3. The following group that contains only warm colors is _____.
A. violet, orange, and red
B. green, yellow, and orange
C. yellow, orange, and red
D. red, orange, and violet

_____ 4. The color harmony that is based on a single hue of the color wheel is _____.
A. monochromatic
B. analogous
C. complementary
D. triad

_____ 5. Among the following, _____ is *not* a guideline for planning color harmonies.
A. one color should dominate
B. dark values and warm hues make rooms appear smaller
C. rough textures make colors appear lighter
D. contrasting colors are emphasized when used side by side

_____ 6. The group of qualities that is most often linked to the color green is _____.
A. sympathy, prosperity, cowardice
B. hospitality, energy, hope
C. friendliness, coolness, peacefulness
D. serenity, tranquility, formality

_____ 7. The Greek word for *color* is _____.
A. hue
B. value
C. chroma
D. None of the above.

_____ 8. The color harmony made by combining two colors that are directly opposite each other on the standard color wheel is _____.
A. analogous
B. complementary
C. split complementary
D. double complementary

(continued)

Name _____

Completion: Complete the following sentences by writing the missing words in the preceding blanks.

_____   9. The color _____ has the reverse effect of red. It is cool, calm, and reserved, and communicates serenity, tranquility, and formality.

_____   10. The _____ _____ is the best tool for understanding color relationships in design.

_____   11. Yellow, blue, and red are called the _____ colors.

_____   12. The color _____ has the lightest normal value of the color wheel, and _____ has the darkest.

_____   13. The colors white, black, and gray are called _____ colors.

_____   14. _____ is cheerful, warm, and less aggressive than red. It expresses friendliness, courage, hospitality, energy, and hope.

_____   15. Royalty, dignity, and mystery are characteristics associated with the color _____.

_____   16. The _____ system is the best known and simplest of the color systems and is often called the Prang or standard color wheel.

_____   17. In the _____ color system, 24 hues can be created by mixing yellow, orange, red, purple, blue, turquoise, sea green, and leaf green plus white and black.

_____   18. Rooms that face south or west and receive sunlight will appear _____ if blues or greens are used.

Short Answer: Provide brief answers to the following questions or statements.

19. List the three ways that all other colors can be made from the primary colors. _____

_____

_____

_____

20. What are tints and shades? How are they produced? _____

_____

_____

_____

21. How is a complementary color harmony created? _____

_____

_____

22. Name the three secondary colors and the primary colors used to make each. _____

_____

_____

_____

(continued)

Name _____

23. In terms of color, what is meant by hue? _____

_____

_____

_____

24. In terms of color, what is meant by value? _____

_____

_____

25. In terms of color, what is meant by intensity? _____

_____

_____

26. Identify three sources of inspiration for determining the ideal color harmony for a room. _____

_____

_____

_____

_____

27. Explain how light gives an object its color. _____

_____

_____

_____

28. Some colors have a natural tendency to appear closer or farther away. Name three colors that
    appear to recede. _____

_____

_____

Chapter 8
Wood, Masonry, and Concrete

Objectives

After studying this chapter, students will be able to

- list the major characteristics and uses of hardwoods and softwoods.
- distinguish the various kinds of wood materials used in residential housing.
- list the main types of wood finishes and describe their characteristics and uses.
- list and describe the main types of masonry materials used in residential housing.
- describe the characteristics and uses of concrete and list types of decorative finishes that can be applied.

Teaching Materials

Text, pages 126–148

Student Activity Guide

Check Your Understanding
8-1, *Wood*
8-2, *Masonry*
8-3, *Concrete*

Instructor's Resources

Types of Wood Beams, transparency master 8-A
Masonry Materials, transparency master 8-B
Chapter 8 Mastery Test

Instructional Concepts and Student Activities

1. Have students read Chapter 8 in the text and complete the review questions.
2. Ask students to collect descriptions and specifications of wood, masonry, and concrete materials and products for their housing notebooks. A good source of these materials includes lumber and building-product distributors, housing-supply marketing companies, and related industry associations.

Wood

3. Lead a class discussion on wood classifications, materials, and finishes.
4. Ask students to define hardwoods and softwoods and give common examples of each category.
5. Provide samples of hardwoods and softwoods from your area of the country for students to examine and identify.
6. Review the terms *wood, lumber, seasoned, timber, millwork, plywood, laminated timber, composite board, hardboard,* and *particleboard,* which are defined in the wood materials section of the text.
7. *Wood,* Activity 8-1, SAG. Students are to demonstrate their understanding of common wood terms by matching them with their descriptions.
8. *Types of Wood Beams,* transparency master 8-A, IR. Introduce students to the types of beams used in traditional housing construction.
9. Ask students to distinguish between samples of various wood finishes.

Masonry

10. Show students illustrations, either photos or drawings, of masonry materials as they appear on the wall of a structure.
11. *Masonry,* Activity 8-2, SAG. Students are to illustrate four basic types of materials used in masonry construction using a specific scale.
12. Ask students to bring examples of masonry materials to class for examination by class members.
13. *Masonry Materials,* transparency master 8-B, IR. Use the transparency to lead a class discussion on the use of masonry materials in residential housing.

Concrete

14. Invite a local homebuilder to speak to the class about the appropriate use and cost of various wood, masonry, and concrete building materials.

15. *Concrete*, Activity 8-3, SAG. Students are to calculate the cost of the concrete required to form a driveway of specific dimensions.
16. Assign one or more tasks listed in the text's *Suggested Activities* section at the end of the chapter.

Suggested Evaluation Techniques

17. *Check Your Understanding*, SAG. Have students complete as many questions as possible without referring to the text. Then have them find answers to questions they do not know.
18. Administer the *Chapter 8 Mastery Test.*

Answer Key

Text

Review Questions, page 147

1. Hardwoods are deciduous trees whose wood: is usually harder, costs more, and accepts finishes well. Softwoods are coniferous trees whose wood: is usually less expensive and softer, scratches and dents more easily, and does not finish well.
2. Hardwoods are reserved for visible wood surfaces, such as on fine furniture and wood floors. Softwoods are used for house construction and unexposed furniture parts.
3. sawing, resawing, planing, crosscutting, and seasoning
4. for use in construction and making millwork
5. It removes water, which helps prevent wood from shrinking, warping, splitting, and rotting.
6. They are less expensive than solid wood, but can be laminated to have the same function and appearance.
7. Penetrating stain is more common on oak furniture, while pigmented stain is common on the pine siding.
8. Shellac is a special type of varnish that prevents stain from bleeding into the wood; varnish.
9. strength, durability, beauty, and low-maintenance requirements
10. bonds masonry units together, seals spaces between them, compensates for slight differences in sizes of masonry units, and provides a decorative effect
11. using decorative mortar, laying masonry in a decorative pattern, using decorative masonry units, and projecting some blocks from the surface
12. granite: tabletops, windowsills, building stones, steps, paving, and wall veneers

sandstone: fireplace hearths, decorative pieces, building stone, trim, and wall veneers
limestone: building stones, fireplaces, windowsills, trims, and ornamentation
marble: interior wall veneers, floors, tabletops, bath fixtures, sculpture, and landscape chips
slate: flooring stones and roofing shingles
manufactured stone: exterior and interior walls
terrazzo: interior floors, precast shower receptors, windowsills, stair treads, wall veneers, patios, and exterior pathways
13. color, exposed aggregate, textured finish, and geometric patterns

Student Activity Guide

Check Your Understanding, pages 69–72

1.	H	7.	K	13.	B
2.	A	8.	M	14.	N
3.	Q	9.	J	15.	D
4.	C	10.	L	16.	P
5.	O	11.	F	17.	G
6.	E	12.	I		

18. pigmented oil stains: contain insoluble pigments that are permanent and coat the wood's surface, are used to disguise irregular grain pattern of softwood and in covering trim to match stained siding
penetrating oil stains: contain soluble, organic dyes that penetrate the wood's surface; have a clean, transparent appearance; produce brighter colors, but fade more quickly than pigmented oil stains; should be sealed to prevent bleeding into succeeding coats of varnish or lacquer; are commonly used on furniture, cabinets, or any wood surface where clear, bright color is desired
19. to protect wood, enhance grain pattern, and give luster or gloss to wood's surface
20. oil
21. dries quickly; resists wear and abrasion well; and has high resistance to chemicals, alcohol, and grease
22. less expensive than brick, fairly lightweight, fire and weather resistant, and low maintenance
23. granite, limestone, and terrazzo
24. is economical, tough, weather resistant, long lasting, and able to be formed into unlimited patterns and textures
25. footings, foundations, exterior walls, floors, walks, and driveways
26. softwoods
27. particleboard
28. hardboard
29. bleaching
30. shellac
31. wax

32. paint
33. tile
34. mortar
35. manufactured
36. D
37. B
38. C
39. D
40. C
41. A
42. B

Wood, Activity 8-1

1. plywood
2. lumber
3. wood
4. softwoods
5. seasoned
6. timber
7. composite board
8. hardwoods
9. millwork
10. laminated timber

Masonry, Activity 8-2

Typical solution on page 134

Concrete, Activity 8-3

drive area = 1939.32 sq. ft.

total sq. ft. ÷ 3 = 646.4 cu. ft.

total cu. ft. ÷ 27 = 23.94 cu. yd.

total cu. yd. x $75 = $1,795.50

cost of concrete = $1,795.50

Instructor's Resources

Chapter 8 Mastery Test

1.	B	6.	C
2.	C	7.	C
3.	C	8.	B
4.	A	9.	D
5.	B	10.	D

11. California
12. plywood
13. timber
14. open
15. polyurethane
16. structural
17. glass blocks
18. concrete
19. terrazzo
20. a tree that sheds its leaves at the end of the growing season
21. (List one:) yellow pine, yew
22. laminated timber: all grain runs in the same direction
    plywood: grain of a ply runs at a right angle to the next ply
23. hardboard: made from refined wood fibers pressed together
    particleboard: made from wood flakes, chips, and shavings bonded with resins or adhesive
24. (List four:) varnish, shellac, lacquer, oil, wax, synthetic finishes
25. structural clay products, concrete masonry units, glass block, and stone
26. the adhesion of mortar to masonry
27. (List five:) concave or tooled, V-shaped, weathered, struck, flush or rough cut, raked, extruded
28. facing, veneer, and paving
29. economical, tough, weather resistant, and long lasting

Masonry
Activity 8-2

Typical Solution

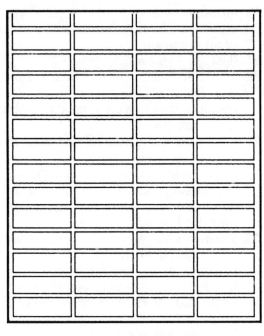

1. Brick

2. Concrete block

3. Glass block

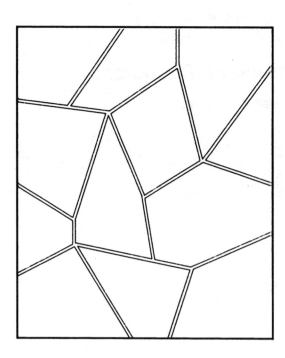

4. Stone

Scale: 1" = 1'-0"

Types of Wood Beams

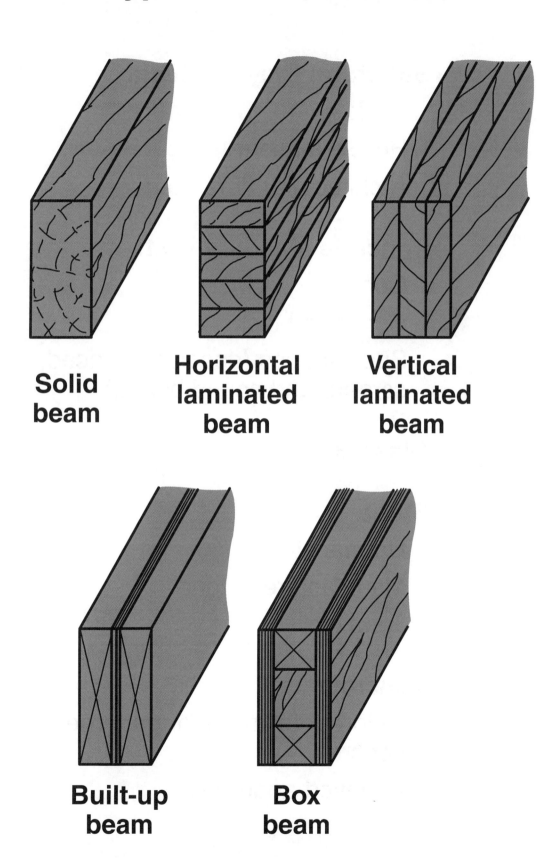

Solid beam

Horizontal laminated beam

Vertical laminated beam

Built-up beam

Box beam

Masonry Materials

Structural Clay Products
Brick

Hollow masonry

Architectural terra cotta

Concrete Masonry Units
Concrete brick

Concrete block

Special units (decorative, faced, screen, and sound blocks)

Glass Block

Stone
Natural stone

Manufactured stone

Terrazzo

Concrete
Colored, textured, or patterned concrete

Exposed aggregate

Wood, Masonry, and Concrete

Name _____

Date _____

Score _____

Chapter 8 Mastery Test

Multiple Choice: Select the best response and write the letter in the preceding blank.

_____ 1. An untrue statement about wood is: _____.
A. no other material is comparable to wood in its degree of workability, beauty, strength, durability, and versatility
B. wood is difficult to repair
C. wood has a higher strength to weight ratio than steel, concrete, or glass
D. wood is one of the few housing materials that is replenishable

_____ 2. The group that contains only hardwoods is _____.
A. black cherry, bald cypress, and American elm
B. white ash, American beech, and western cedar
C. black walnut, yellow poplar, and white oak
D. sugar maple, Douglas fir, and red oak

_____ 3. The actual dimensions of a "two-by-four" are _____.
A. 2 by 4 in.
B. 1⅝ by 3⅝ in.
C. 1½ by 3½ in.
D. None of the above.

_____ 4. Processed lumber such as doors, window frames, shutters, trim, panel work, and molding is called _____.
A. millwork
B. lumber
C. plywood
D. timber

_____ 5. If applied too heavily, _____ will obscure the wood grain.
A. penetrating oil stain
B. pigmented oil stain
C. alcohol-based stain
D. water-based stain

_____ 6. The four classes of brick most commonly used in residential construction are building or common brick, facing brick, paving brick, and _____.
A. glass brick
B. sand brick
C. firebrick
D. foundation brick

_____ 7. The most common size of concrete block is _____.
A. 4 by 8 by 8 in.
B. 8 by 8 by 8 in.
C. 8 by 8 by 16 in.
D. 8 by 16 by 16 in.

_____ 8. Blocks that are often used for outdoor fences and walls and have an open design to provide privacy and ventilation are called _____ blocks.
A. fluted
B. screen
C. ribbed
D. fence

(continued)

Name_____

_____ 9. Natural stone that is durable, white to black in color, able to be polished smooth, and used for tabletops and windowsills is _____.
A. sandstone
B. limestone
C. marble
D. granite

_____ 10. Concrete may be colored by _____.
A. mixing color into the dry batch
B. adding color to a top coating of concrete
C. adding color just before the concrete slab is smoothed
D. All of the above.

Completion: Complete the following sentences by writing the missing words in the preceding blanks.

_____ 11. Redwood is a softwood commonly found in the state of _____.

_____ 12. Wood can be processed to make lumber, _____, or other wood products used in construction.

_____ 13. Lumber that is five inches or larger in width and thickness, called _____, is used mainly for support posts or beams.

_____ 14. Fillers are used on _____-grained wood, such as walnut or oak, to fill open pores.

_____ 15. A clear, synthetic finish that is especially popular as a floor finish is _____.

_____ 16. The _____ bond is the way bricks are interlocked to provide support and strength.

_____ 17. Hollow units of clear, rippled, or frosted glass are called _____ _____.

_____ 18. Manufactured stone is a veneer made from a lightweight _____ or fiberglass to give the appearance of natural stone construction.

_____ 19. A very old material composed of marble chips bonded together with cement is called _____.

Short Answer: Provide brief responses to the following questions or statements.

20. What is a deciduous or broad-leaved tree? _____

_____

_____

21. Give one example of a softwood that is harder than many hardwoods. _____

_____

(continued)

Name _____

22. Explain how the construction of laminated timber differs from the construction of plywood.

_____

_____

_____

_____

_____

_____

23. Describe the difference between hardboard and particleboard. _____

_____

_____

_____

24. List four types of clear finishes used to protect wood, enhance the grain pattern, and give a luster or gloss to the wood surface. _____

_____

_____

_____

_____

25. Name the four categories of masonry materials. _____

_____

_____

_____

_____

26. What is mortar bond? _____

_____

_____

_____

_____

_____

(continued)

Name _____

27. List five styles of mortar joints. _____

_____

_____

_____

_____

_____

28. In what three nonstructural applications is stone used today? _____

_____

_____

_____

29. What are the four properties of hardened concrete as a building material? _____

_____

_____

_____

_____

Chapter 9
Metals, Glass, Ceramics, and Plastics

Objectives

After studying this chapter, students will be able to

- list the main properties and housing applications of iron, steel, aluminum, copper, brass, bronze, and lead.
- describe the main properties of glass and list the different types of glass products that are used in housing.
- list the main properties and housing applications of ceramics.
- identify plastic products used in housing.

Teaching Materials

Text, pages 149–164

Student Activity Guide

Check Your Understanding
9-1, *Metals*
9-2, *Types of Glass*
9-3, *Ceramics*
9-4, *Plastics*

Instructor's Resources

Metals Used in Housing, transparency master 9-A
Clay Roofing Tile, transparency master 9-B
Chapter 9 Mastery Test

Instructional Concepts and Student Activities

1. Have students read Chapter 9 in the text and complete the review questions.
2. Ask students to collect descriptions and specifications of metals, glass, ceramics, and plastic materials and products for their housing notebooks.

Metals

3. *Metals Used in Housing*, transparency master 9-A, IR. Introduce students to the common metals found in housing that are discussed in the text.

4. Lead a class discussion on the uses of iron, steel, aluminum, copper, brass, bronze, and lead in housing.
5. Have students examine and compare samples of metals commonly found in the home.
6. *Metals*, Activity 9-1, SAG. Students are to list the applications of the most commonly used metals in housing.

Glass

7. Lead a class discussion on the various types of glass, such as flat, decorative, tinted, reflective, insulating, handblown, molded, and leaded glass.
8. Have students examine and compare samples of the types of glass commonly found in the home.
9. *Types of Glass*, Activity 9-2, SAG. Students are to demonstrate their understanding of the types of glass used in residential housing by matching each with its description.

Ceramics

10. Ask students to describe ceramic products that are commonly used in housing, such as wall, floor, roofing, and drain tiles; chimney flue liners; dishes; and sculptured objects.
11. Help students identify examples of glazed tile, ceramic mosaic tile, quarry tile and pavers, roofing tile, and pottery.
12. *Clay Roofing Tile*, transparency master 9-B, IR. Introduce students to style varieties of clay roofing tiles and the way the roofing components are fitted together. Ask students to identify buildings that use a type of clay roofing tile.
13. *Ceramics*, Activity 9-3, SAG. Students are to list the typical sizes and applications of common ceramic tile as well as the firing temperatures and applications of three types of pottery.

Plastics

14. Review the important properties and applications of thermoplastics and thermosetting plastics by reviewing "A-16, Thermoplastics" and "A-17, Thermosetting Plastics" in the appendix of the text.
15. Lead a class discussion on thermoplastics and thermosetting plastics.

16. *Plastics*, Activity 9-4, SAG. Students are to demonstrate their understanding of various types of plastics by matching the appropriate plastic with its application or description.
17. Assign one or more tasks listed in the text's *Suggested Activities* section at the end of the chapter.

Suggested Evaluation Techniques

18. *Check Your Understanding*, SAG. Have students complete as many questions as possible without referring to the text. Then have them find answers to questions they do not know.
19. Administer the *Chapter 9 Mastery Test*.

Answer Key

Text

Review Questions, page 163

1. Cast iron has 2 to 3.75 percent carbon and is melted and cast into shapes, while wrought iron is almost pure iron and is worked into shapes.
2. cast iron: wood-burning stoves, bathtubs, sinks, skillets, sewer lines, waste disposal systems, and gas pipes
wrought iron: ornamental lawn furniture, lighting fixtures, fences, and railings
3. strong, ductile, less brittle than iron, malleable, and subject to corrosion
4. improves corrosion resistance; makes steel harder and more corrosion resistant over a wide range of temperatures
5. I-beams, appliances, cabinets, bathtubs, sinks, knife blades, siding, roofing products, flashing, gutters, downspouts, architectural trim, windowsills, railings, tubings, pipes, furniture, cooking and eating utensils, ranges and other appliances, countertops, and sinks
6. by extruding: window and door frames, louvers, railings, grilles, solar collectors, and builder's hardware such as door and window hinges
by casting: decorative panels, lamp bases, trivets, plant stands, electrical fittings, grilles, handles, and cookware
by rolling: pipes, air ducts, appliance cabinets, range hoods, suspended ceiling supports, awnings, garage doors, and grilles
7. Copper is a pure metal, brass is an alloy of copper and zinc, and bronze is an alloy of copper and tin.

8. copper: wiring, tubing, pipes, roof flashing, decorative nails and bolts, roofing materials, cookware, range hoods, lamps, and decorative pieces
brass: weatherstripping, screws, bolts, nails, wire, furniture, and decorative pieces
bronze: thresholds, glass sliding-door frames, windowsills, screens, screws, bolts, plumbing valves, and pipes
9. desirable qualities: allows passage of light, permits a view, does not conduct electricity, and is corrosion resistant
undesirable qualities: can break from too much force, can be scratched, and can break with rapid temperature change
10. more scratches and imperfections in one piece, improper production of one piece, and/or different heat conditions
11. flat glass: window and door panes, tabletops, shelves, and mirrors
decorative glass: partitions, decorative windows, and tub or shower enclosures
tinted glass: windows in warm climates
reflective glass: windows in warm climates
insulating glass: windows in cold climates
handblown glass: art pieces, vases, and fine drinking glasses
molded glass: storage containers, art pieces, and decorative dinnerware
leaded glass: doors, lampshades, and decorative windows
12. wall, floor, roofing, and drain tiles; chimney flue liners; dishes; and sculptured objects.
13. can have various shapes, finishes, and colors; and are resistant to heat, cold, moisture, acids, and salts
14. generally moisture and corrosion resistant, lightweight, tough, easily molded into complex shapes, and possess characteristics found in more expensive materials
15. (See A-16 and A-17 in the text's appendix.)

Student Activity Guide

Check Your Understanding, pages 77–79

1. F   5. K   9. A
2. H   6. D   10. I
3. C   7. G   11. J
4. E   8. B

12. (List four:) can be shaped by casting, rolling, extruding, machining, welding, bending, sawing, drilling, hammering, and spinning; available in a variety of natural colors; can be coated for a wider variety of colors and for added protection; strong; decorative; good conductor of heat and electricity

13. iron, steel, aluminum, copper, brass, bronze, lead
14. alloy of copper and tin; tin increases the hardness
15. float glass
16. tinted glass, reflective glass; reflective glass is more efficient
17. Handblown glass is made by dipping a hollow metal rod into molten glass, blowing it into a bubble, then rolling, twisting, or using a tool to shape it while hot and plastic. Molded glass is made by machine blowing molten glass into wood or cast iron molds. Handblown glass is made into art pieces, vases, and fine hollowware, while molded glass is made into storage containers, art pieces, and hollowware.
18. as high-quality, casual dinnerware

19. C	24. A
20. D	25. C
21. B	26. B
22. A	27. C
23. C	28. F

Metals, Activity 9-1

1. wood-burning stoves, bathtubs, sinks, skillets, sewer lines, waste disposal systems, gas pipes
2. ornamental lawn furniture, lighting fixtures, fences, porch railings
3. sheet metal products, such as siding, roofing products, flashing
4. siding on multi-family structures, rust-colored roof accents
5. gutters, downspouts, architectural trim, windowsills, railings, tubings, pipes, cooking utensils, eating utensils, sinks, appliances, countertops, furniture
6. window and door frames; louvers; railings; grilles; solar collectors; builder's hardware, such as door and window hinges
7. decorative panels, lamp bases, trivets, plant stands, electrical fittings, grilles, handles, cookware
8. pipes, air ducts, awnings, garage doors, appliance cabinets, range hoods, suspended-ceiling supports
9. wiring, tubing, pipes, roof flashing, decorative nails/bolts, roofing, cookware, range hoods, lamps, decorative pieces
10. weatherstripping, screws, bolts, nails, wire, furniture, decorative pieces
11. thresholds, glass sliding-door frames, windowsills, screens, screws, bolts, interior decorative pieces
12. under showers, pool liners, flashing, roofing, anchor bolts in concrete

Types of Glass, Activity 9-2

1. insulating glass
2. sheet glass
3. tinted glass
4. float glass
5. etched glass
6. reflective glass
7. cut glass
8. plate glass
9. handblown glass
10. leaded or stained glass
11. enameled glass
12. patterned glass
13. molded glass

Ceramics, Activity 9-3

1. 4¼ x 4¼ in., 4¼ x 6 in., 6 x 6 in.; wall and floor material
2. 1 x 1 in., 1 x 2 in., 2 x 2 in.; walls, floors, and countertops
3. 6-, 9-, and 12-in. squares; floor material
4. 2¾ x 6 in. and 4 x 8 in.; floor material
5. 1800 to 2100°F; casual pottery, porous, fragile, opaque; flower pots and casual dinnerware
6. 2100 to 2300°F; gray or light brown in color, not porous, more durable and waterproof than earthenware; a high-quality dinnerware
7. 2250 to 2500°F; white, finely textured finish, translucent and very hard; highest-quality pottery and dinnerware

Plastics, Activity 9-4

1.	F	6.	H
2.	I	7.	C
3.	A	8.	G
4.	B	9.	D
5.	J	10.	E

Instructor's Resources

Chapter 9 Mastery Test

1.	C	5.	A
2.	A	6.	B
3.	B	7.	A
4.	B	8.	C

9. alloy
10. wrought
11. extruding
12. zinc
13. tin
14. copper
15. translucent
16. thermosetting

17. (List five:) cast into complex shapes, rolled into sheets, extruded into standard shapes, machined, welded, bent, sawed, drilled, hammered, spun

18. iron, steel, aluminum, copper, brass, bronze, and lead

19. is lightweight, highly resistant to corrosion, excellent conductor of electricity, good reflector of heat and light, can be easily formed into many shapes, and is receptive to many finishes

20. Strength and ductility are affected. Copper is brittle when heated and cooled slowly, but malleable and ductile when heated and cooled rapidly.

21. Float glass and plate glass are distortion free, while sheet glass has ripples that cause distortion.

22. to reduce air-conditioning costs in warm climates and to reduce heat gains

23. advantages: durable and attractive; disadvantages: more porous and costly than other roofing materials and a waterproof membrane is needed underneath to prevent leaking

24. (List four:) moisture resistant, corrosion resistant, lightweight, tough, easily molded into complex shapes

Metals Used in Housing

Iron and Steel
Cast iron
Wrought iron
Copper-bearing steel
Weathering steel
Stainless steel

Aluminum
Extruded aluminum
Cast aluminum
Rolled aluminum

Copper

Brass

Bronze
Gunmetal bronze

Lead

Clay Roofing Tile

Spanish

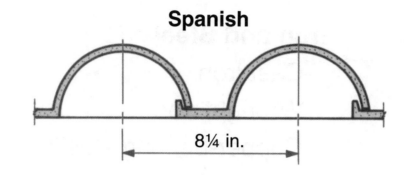

8¼ in.

Straight Barrel Mission

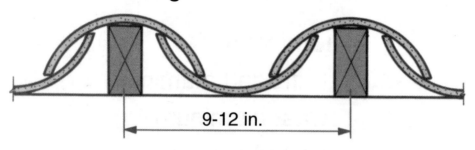

9-12 in.

Roman

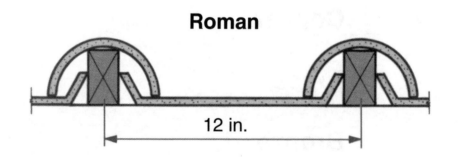

12 in.

Greek

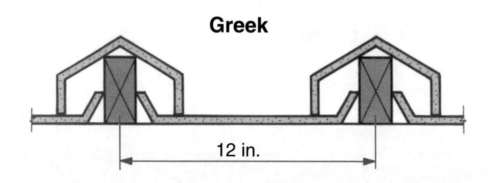

12 in.

Metals, Glass, Ceramics, and Plastics
Chapter 9 Mastery Test

Name _____

Date _____

Score _____

Multiple Choice: Select the best response and write the letter in the preceding blank.

_____ 1. Today's average "wood" home contains about _____ pounds of metal.
A. 1,000
B. 5,000
C. 8,000
D. 10,000

_____ 2. The group of products all made from cast iron is _____.
A. wood-burning stoves, bathtubs, and skillets
B. ornamental lawn furniture, sinks, and sewer lines
C. gas pipes, fences, and porch railings
D. lighting fixtures, waste disposal systems, and wire

_____ 3. The type of steel used for sheet-metal products, such as siding, roofing products, and flashing, is _____ steel.
A. stainless
B. copper-bearing
C. weathering
D. carbon

_____ 4. When copper is exposed to humid air, the thin coating of green carbonate that forms affects copper by _____.
A. slowly eating it away
B. protecting it against further corrosion
C. turning it into brass
D. removing its electrical conductivity

_____ 5. Patterned glass is used in residential structures for _____.
A. areas where privacy is desired
B. oven doors
C. fine mirrors
D. dinnerware

_____ 6. The smallest type of ceramic tile is _____ tile.
A. paver
B. ceramic mosaic
C. quarry
D. glazed

_____ 7. The most casual type of pottery is called _____.
A. earthenware
B. stoneware
C. porcelain
D. china

_____ 8. A plastic used for skylights, translucent panels, carpeting, draperies, and containers is _____.
A. polystyrene
B. nylon
C. acrylic
D. polyethylene

(continued)

Name _____

Completion: Complete the following sentences by writing the missing words in the preceding blanks.

_____   9. When several metals are mixed together, an _____ results.

_____   10. The two types of iron used in the housing industry are cast iron and _____ iron.

_____   11. The three main methods of processing aluminum are _____, casting, and rolling.

_____   12. Brass is an alloy of copper and _____.

_____   13. Bronze is an alloy of copper and _____.

_____   14. Leaded and stained glass are made by setting small pieces of clear or colored glass into strips of lead or _____ foil.

_____   15. While earthenware and stoneware are opaque, porcelain is _____.

_____   16. Plastics may be classified as thermoplastics and _____ plastics.

Short Answer: Provide brief answers to the following questions or statements.

17. Metals are versatile housing materials because they can be shaped in so many ways. List five common methods of shaping metals. _____

_____

_____

_____

_____

_____

18. List the seven metals most commonly used in housing. _____

_____

_____

_____

_____

_____

_____

19. Why is aluminum a good construction material? _____

_____

_____

_____

(continued)

Name _____

20. How is copper affected by the mechanical and heat treatment it receives? _____

_____

_____

_____

21. What are the three types of flat glass and how do they differ in distortion? _____

_____

_____

_____

22. Why is reflective glass used in windows?_____

_____

_____

23. What are the advantages and disadvantages of using clay roofing tile? _____

_____

_____

_____

24. List four common characteristics of plastics. _____

_____

_____

_____

_____

Chapter 10
Textiles

Objectives

After studying this chapter, students will be able to
- list the origins, qualities, and uses of natural and manufactured fibers.
- evaluate a yarn in terms of the method used to create it and its advantages, disadvantages, and uses.
- describe the various types of fabric construction in terms of their production, quality, and uses.
- evaluate the appropriateness of a fabric for a specific use within the home.

Teaching Materials

Text, pages 165–176

Student Activity Guide

Check Your Understanding
10-1, *Fibers*
10-2, *Weaves*
10-3, *Fabrics*
10-4, *Fabric Dyeing and Printing*

Instructor's Resources

Cotton Products, transparency master 10-A
Fiber Manufacturing Process, transparency master 10-B
Manufactured Fiber Production Worldwide, transparency master 10-C
Chapter 10 Mastery Test

Instructional Concepts and Student Activities

1. Have students read Chapter 10 in the text and complete the review questions.
2. Ask students to collect articles and manufacturer's descriptions about common textile materials and products. Have them label each as a natural fiber or a manufactured fiber and add these to their housing notebooks.

Fibers

3. Discuss the characteristics and uses of natural fibers and manufactured fibers with the class. Refer to Figures 10-2 and 10-4 in the text.
4. Show a video about fibers and fabrics. *What Everyone Should Know About Fabrics* from Learning Seed's catalog is suggested.
5. *Cotton Products*, transparency master 10-A, IR. Use the transparency to inspire students to independently research the importance of cotton production in this country. Cotton is the only natural fiber produced abundantly enough to cause the nation to rank near the top in world production. (The United States ranks number two, after China.)
6. *Fibers*, Activity 10-1, SAG. Students are to complete a diagram showing the categories of textile fibers.

Yarns

7. Lead a class discussion on how yarns are made and what types are produced.
8. *Fiber Manufacturing Process*, transparency master 10-B, IR. Show students the three possible ways to produce manufactured textile fibers.
9. Provide samples of various types of yarns and ask students to identify them as single, ply, or cord yarns. Then ask students to identify whether the yarns are made from staple fibers or filaments.
10. *Manufactured Fiber Production Worldwide*, transparency master 10-C, IR. Show students how production quantities of the five leading manufactured fibers have changed during a recent 20-year period.

Fabric Construction

11. Discuss with the class the various methods of creating fabrics: weaving, knitting, and tufting.
12. Show students examples of fabrics that were made by plain, twill, satin, jacquard, and leno weaving. Help them identify each type.
13. *Weaves*, Activity 10-2, SAG. Students are to demonstrate their understanding of common weaves by matching terms with their definitions or descriptions.

14. Ask students to collect samples of knitted, tufted, and felted fabrics. Have them make these samples available for class examination.
15. *Fabrics*, Activity 10-3, SAG. Students are to collect samples of fabrics made by methods other than weaving, knitting, or tufting, and identify each type of construction.

Dyeing and Printing Fabrics

16. Explain to the class the various processes of dyeing and printing fabrics. Show examples of the resulting fabrics.
17. Invite a speaker from a local fabric store to discuss fabrics and fabric finishes with the class. Involve students in a question and answer session following the presentation.
18. *Fabric Dyeing and Printing*, Activity 10-4, SAG. Students are to describe specific fabric dyeing and printing methods.
19. Assign one or more tasks listed in the text's *Suggested Activities* section at the end of the chapter.

Suggested Evaluation Techniques

20. *Check Your Understanding*, SAG. Have students complete as many questions as possible without referring to the text. Then have them find answers to questions they do not know.
21. Administer the *Chapter 10 Mastery Test*.

Answer Key

Text

Review Questions, page 175

1. plant: cotton, flax, hemp, jute, and ramie
   animal: silk, wool, cashmere, camel hair, mohair, and angora
   mineral: asbestos
2. no, because it fades in sunlight, yellows, is expensive, easily spots from contact with water, and is difficult to maintain
3. (Student response. See Figure 10-3 in the text.)
4. Spun yarns are made from staple fibers and have a fuzzy appearance, while monofilament yarns are made from a single filament and are very smooth.
5. They contain the best characteristics of each fiber used.
6. plain: passes a filling yarn over and under one warp yarn
   twill: passes a filling yarn over two or more warp yarns, forming a diagonal pattern

satin: passes a yarn over four or more intersecting yarns, forming long floats on the surface
jacquard: arranges the warp yarns differently, forming intricate patterns
leno: passes paired warp yarns over and under filling yarns in a figure-eight pattern
7. twill, because it is more durable and hides soil well
8. Yarn loops are punched into a material and one or two layers of latex coating are applied to the back to hold the loops in place to make carpeting.
9. felt, nonwovens, films, foams, and leather
10. fiber, yarn, and fabric stages; fiber dyeing
11. roller printing: Color is passed directly to fabric as it passes through a series of rollers.
    rotary screen printing: Dye is transferred to a fabric through a cylinder-shaped screen that rolls over the fabric.
    block printing: A design is carved into the surface of a block, dye is applied, and the block is stamped onto the fabric.
12. (Student response. See Figure 10-17 in the text.)

Student Activity Guide

Check Your Understanding, pages 85–88

1. fiber
2. mineral
3. wool
4. asbestos
5. noncellulosic
6. yarn
7. pilling
8. blend
9. combination
10. filaments
11. ply
12. filling
13. satin
14. jacquard
15. warp
16. felt
17. film
18. yarns
19. roller
20. block
21. B
22. C
23. A
24. D
25. D
26. B
27. A
28. B
29. C
30. B

31. A
32. Manufactured fibers are not fibrous in their natural form.
33. staple, filament
34. a fabric that has the best characteristics of both fibers
35. Two or more plies are twisted together into a cord yarn.
36. basket
37. plain, twill
38. tufting
39. (List five:) bedding, backing for quilts, coverings for box springs, carpet backing, upholstered fabric, draperies, mattress pads
40. by solution dyeing, which is adding dye to thick liquid before it is extruded into filaments
41. piece dyeing, because it allows manufacturers to store undyed fabric and dye to order as fashion dictates
42. Both sides are the same color for dyed fabrics, but one side appears much lighter for printed fabrics.

Fibers, Activity 10-1
Solution on page 154

Weaves, Activity 10-2
1. D
2. B
3. C
4. E
5. A

Fabrics, Activity 10-3
(Student response will be evaluated based on principles presented in the text.)

Fabric Dyeing and Printing, Activity 10-4
1. is the most common method of dyeing; which involves adding dye after the fabric is constructed
2. accounts for the majority of fabrics printed, involves transferring color directly to fabric as it passes between a series of rollers, and produces large quantities of printed fabrics inexpensively
3. is one of the fastest printing processes, which involves transferring dye to the fabric through a cylinder-shaped screen that rolls over the fabric to print a design
4. is a hand process, the oldest technique for decorating textiles, expensive, time-consuming, and seldom done commercially; and involves the following process: applying dye to a design carved on a block and stamping the block onto the fabric

Instructor's Resources

Chapter 10 Mastery Test
1. B
2. D
3. A
4. D
5. B
6. D
7. D
8. B
9. C
10. A
11. source
12. cellulosic
13. protein
14. petroleum
15. combination
16. weaving
17. warp
18. plain
19. knitted
20. solution
21. (Student response. See pages 165-167.)
22. (List one from each category:) cellulose: cotton, flax, hemp, jute, and ramie
protein: silk, wool, cashmere, camel hair, mohair, and angora
mineral: asbestos
23. They cannot be exactly duplicated by technology.
24. Through chemical engineering, they are first made into solutions. Then fibers are extruded from the liquid and solidified.
25. A blend is the result of two or more different staple fibers spun together into a single yarn. A combination is formed by twisting two different single yarns into one yarn.
26. to hold fibers or filaments together and to increase yarn strength
27. by passing the filling yarns over and under different numbers of warp yarns
28. plain, twill, satin, jacquard, leno (Descriptions are student response. See pages 167-170.)
29. damask, brocade, and tapestry; used for upholstery, tablecloths, and wall hangings
30. (Student response. See pages 173-174.)

Fibers
Activity 10-1

Solution

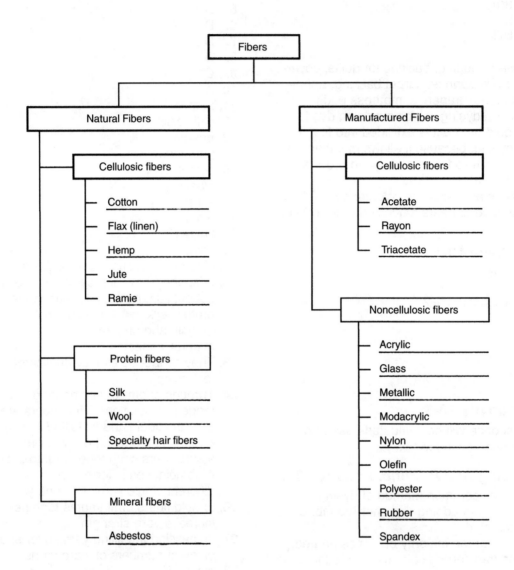

Cotton Products

A bale of cotton, which weighs about 480 pounds, can make

- 215 jeans

- 249 bedsheets

- 690 terry bath towels

- 765 men's dress shirts

- 1,256 pillowcases

- 3,085 diapers

- 313,600 pieces of U.S. "paper" currency (Dollar bills of all denominations are 75% cotton and 25% linen.)

Source: The National Cotton Council

Fiber Manufacturing Process

Wet Spinning
Filaments harden
in a chemical bath.

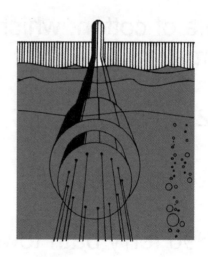

Dry Spinning
Filaments harden as
the liquefying agent
evaporates in a warm
airflow.

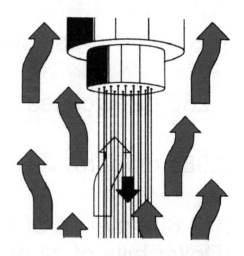

Melt Spinning
Filaments harden
in a cool airflow.

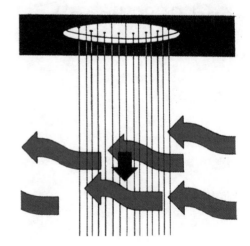

Manufactured Fiber Production Worldwide

2002

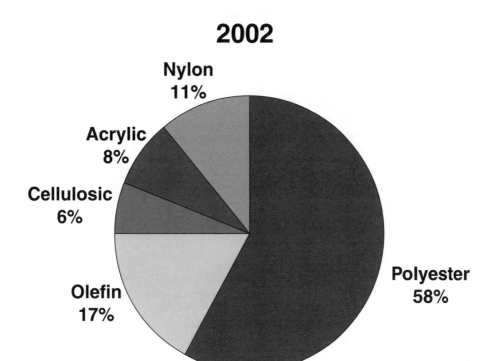

Nylon 11%
Acrylic 8%
Cellulosic 6%
Olefin 17%
Polyester 58%

1982

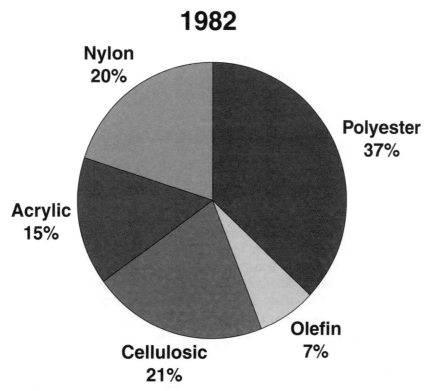

Nylon 20%
Polyester 37%
Acrylic 15%
Olefin 7%
Cellulosic 21%

Source: Fiber Economic Bureau

Textiles
Chapter 10
Mastery Test

Name _____

Date _____

Score _____

Multiple Choice: Select the best response and write the letter in the preceding blank.

_____ 1. Fibers are combined to form a continuous strand called a _____.
  A. filament
  B. yarn
  C. cord
  D. ply

_____ 2. Fibers determine a fabric's _____.
  A. strength and elasticity
  B. texture and shrinkage
  C. warmth, absorbency, and durability
  D. All of the above.

_____ 3. The natural fiber that is very absorbent, resists wrinkling, holds and retains shape well, and is expensive and warmer than all other fibers is _____.
  A. wool
  B. silk
  C. flax
  D. cotton

_____ 4. Because of the health problems linked to asbestos, the fiber that is replacing it is _____.
  A. vicuna
  B. ramie
  C. metallic
  D. novoloid

_____ 5. The element that is *not* found in noncellulosic fiber molecules is _____.
  A. carbon
  B. calcium
  C. nitrogen
  D. oxygen

_____ 6. The size and texture of a yarn depends on _____.
  A. the types of fibers from which it is made
  B. the tightness of the twist
  C. the number of plies it has
  D. All of the above.

_____ 7. Yarns can be classified as _____.
  A. single
  B. ply
  C. cord
  D. All of the above.

_____ 8. Fabrics woven in the twill weave have _____.
  A. long floats on the surface of the fabric
  B. diagonal lines called wales
  C. patterns created by different arrangements of the warp yarns
  D. paired warp yarns that are passed over and under the filling yarns in a figure-eight pattern

_____ 9. Tufting is a construction method used to make _____.
  A. backing for quilts
  B. upholstery
  C. carpeting
  D. pillow cushions

(continued)

Copyright Goodheart-Willcox

Name _____

_____ 10. The printing process that accounts for the majority of printed fabrics is _____.
   A. roller printing
   B. rotary screen printing
   C. block printing
   D. silk screening

Completion: Complete the following sentences by writing the missing words in the preceding blanks.

_____ 11. The properties of a fiber depend on its _____.

_____ 12. Fibers that come from plants are called _____ fibers.

_____ 13. Fibers that come from animals are called _____ fibers.

_____ 14. Manufactured fibers come from substances in nature, such as wood pulp and _____.

_____ 15. Twisting two different single yarns into one yarn forms a _____.

_____ 16. The method of fabric construction involving two sets of yarns interlaced at right angles is _____.

_____ 17. In weaving, _____ yarns run along the lengthwise grain.

_____ 18. The simplest form of weaving is the _____ weave.

_____ 19. Fabrics made by interlooping yarns are called _____ fabrics.

_____ 20. Natural fibers are stock dyed by adding dye to the loose fibers, while manufactured fibers are _____ dyed by adding dye to the thick liquid before it is extruded into filaments.

Short Answer: Provide brief answers to the following questions or statements.

21. Explain what *a fiber's properties depend on its source* means? _____

_____

_____

_____

22. Name the three naturally occurring sources of textile fibers and give an example of a fiber that derives from each . _____

_____

_____

_____

23. Why are natural fibers unique?_____

_____

24. How are substances such as wood pulp or petroleum transformed into manufactured fibers?

_____

_____

_____

_____

(continued)

Name _____

25. What is the difference between a blend and a combination? _____

_____

_____

26. Why is twist needed in yarn? _____

_____

27. How are different weaves created? _____

_____

28. List and describe the five weaves often used for the construction of fabrics used in the home.

_____

_____

_____

_____

_____

_____

_____

_____

_____

_____

29. List the three fabrics made on the Jacquard loom and give examples of how they can be used
    in the home. _____

_____

_____

_____

30. List two fabric finishes and their purposes. _____

_____

_____

_____

Chapter 11
Furniture Styles

Objectives

After studying this chapter, students will be able to
- list the distinguishing features of furniture from the Late Renaissance, Baroque, Regence, Rococo, Neoclassic, Directoire, and Empire periods in France.
- describe furniture of various styles from the Early, Middle, and Late Renaissance periods in England.
- cite the distinguishing features of the furniture of Chippendale, Hepplewhite, Sheraton, and the Adam brothers.
- differentiate the features of Early American, American Georgian, and Federal furniture styles.
- name and describe the regional styles of furniture found in early America.
- identify the main features of Twentieth-Century furniture styles.
- describe the features of Contemporary, Traditional, Casual, Country, and Eclectic furniture styles.

Teaching Materials

Text, pages 178–210

Student Activity Guide

Check Your Understanding
11-1, *Furniture Terms*
11-2, *Traditional French Furniture*
11-3, *Traditional English Furniture*
11-4, *English Furniture*
11-5, *Traditional American Furniture*

Instructor's Resources

Traditional Furniture Styles from France, transparency master 11-A

Traditional Furniture Styles from England, transparency master 11-B

Traditional Furniture Styles in America, transparency master 11-C

Twentieth-Century Furniture Styles, transparency master 11-D

Twenty-First Century Furniture Styles, transparency master 11-E

Chapter 11 Mastery Test

Instructional Concepts and Student Activities

1. Have students read Chapter 11 in the text and complete the review questions.
2. Ask students to collect pictures of furniture pieces that represent as many of the furniture styles discussed in the text as possible. They should identify each style and add it to their housing notebooks.

Traditional Styles

3. Review the terms that are used to describe furniture styles in Figure 11-1 in the text.
4. *Furniture Terms,* Activity 11-1, SAG. Students are to demonstrate their understanding of furniture terms by matching them with their definitions or descriptions.
5. Provide an overview of the time frames during which the Traditional furniture styles discussed in Figure 11-2 in the text were popular.

Traditional Furniture from France

6. *Traditional Furniture Styles from France,* transparency master 11-A, IR. Use the transparency to lead a class discussion on French furniture styles including the Late Renaissance, Baroque, Regence, Rococo, Neoclassic, Directoire, and Empire periods.
7. Plan a field trip to a nearby museum to view its collection of Traditional French furniture. If this is not possible, show photos, slides, or drawings of Traditional French furniture styles to the class.
8. *Traditional French Furniture,* Activity 11-2, SAG. Students are to describe the dominant features of each of the Traditional furniture styles from France.
9. Divide the class into two teams. Have the teams compete to list on the board the most features or qualities of Traditional French furniture styles.

Traditional Furniture from England

10. *Traditional Furniture Styles from England*, transparency master 11-B, IR. Use the transparency to lead a class discussion on English furniture styles from the Early, Middle, and Late Renaissance periods.
11. Ask students to list as many furniture styles as they can from each of the three periods discussed in Item 10.
12. Define for the class each Traditional English furniture style in terms of features and qualities.
13. Show slides, photos, or drawings of Traditional furniture from England. Have students point out the primary characteristics of each style.
14. *Traditional English Furniture*, Activity 11-3, SAG. Students are to identify English furniture pieces, architectural details, and designs of the Early and Middle Renaissance periods.
15. *English Furniture*, Activity 11-4, SAG. Students are to identify Late Georgian furniture pieces by identifying the cabinetmaker or designer and key features about each item.

Traditional American Styles

16. *Traditional Furniture Styles in America*, transparency master 11-C, IR. Use the transparency to lead a class discussion on American furniture styles including the Early American, American Georgian, Federal, and Post Federal periods.
17. Show students a video about traditional American styles of furniture. *Styles of American Furniture* from Learning Seed's catalog is suggested.
18. Plan a field trip to a local furniture store or antique shop that deals in Traditional American furniture styles. Ask the students to keep a list of the various pieces they see.
19. *Traditional American Furniture*, Activity 11-5, SAG. Students are to match Traditional American furniture pieces with their descriptions.

Twentieth-Century Styles

20. *Twentieth-Century Furniture Styles*, transparency master 11-D, IR. Use the transparency to lead a class discussion on modern furniture styles including the Art Nouveau, Frank Lloyd Wright, Bauhaus, Scandinavian, and Contemporary periods.
21. Ask students to share photos, pictures, or drawings of Twentieth-Century furniture styles from their housing notebook with other members of the class.
22. Have the class discuss the characteristics they believe caused Twentieth-Century styles to become popular.

Twenty-First Century Styles

23. *Twenty-First Century Furniture Styles*, transparency master 11-E, IR. Use the transparency to lead a class discussion on current furniture styles, which include Contemporary, Traditional, Casual, Country, and Eclectic.
24. Assign one or more tasks listed in the texts *Suggested Activities* section at the end of the chapter.

Suggested Evaluation Techniques

25. *Check Your Understanding*, SAG. Have students complete as many questions as possible without referring to the text. Then have them find answers to questions they do not know.
26. Administer the *Chapter 11 Mastery Test*.

Answer Key

Text

Review Questions, page 209

1. ormolu
2. elaborate moldings; carvings; and marquetry with inlays of ormolu, pewter, brass, and semitransparent tortoiseshell
3. cabriole leg
4. Curves, flowing lines, asymmetry, and a scale closer to human proportions replaced the massive, rectangular Baroque shapes.
5. Neoclassic motifs focused on romantic themes, such as roses, garlands, ribbons, and Cupid's bows and darts. Directoire motifs focused on military and agricultural themes, such as arrows, spears, drums, stars, and wheat.
6. Egyptian, Greek, and Roman
7. Jacobean furniture was smaller, lighter, and less ornate.
8. japanning
9. curved lines, cabriole legs, claw-and-ball feet, oriental designs, spooned-back splats
10. Chippendale's furniture was heavier and typically in mahogany. Hepplewhite's furniture was typically in satinwood, with slender lines, subtle curves, and little ornamentation. Sheraton's furniture was dominated by straight lines and sometimes incorporated porcelain plaques.
11. furnishings: chests, a table, one or few chairs, stools, a cupboard, beds, and a cradle furniture decorations: split-spindles, turnings, bun feet, geometric or floral carvings in low relief, and painted decorations

12. American Queen Anne, American Chippendale, Hepplewhite, and Sheraton
13. eagle, cornucopia, fruit, flowers, spiral turnings, lion heads, acanthus leaves, lyres, swags, and festoons
14. simple lines, functional designs
15. Quality was lower, the look was awkward and poorly designed, and several styles were combined into one piece of furniture.
16. simpler lines and forms, more attention to function
17. Contemporary
18. Casual

Student Activity Guide

Check Your Understanding, pages 93–95

1. Regence period furniture was large, but curves and lighter motifs were used more often; cabriole legs were introduced; and lighter woods began replacing walnut and ebony. Baroque period furniture was massive, rectangular, and heavy; elaborate carvings and rich tapestries, brocades, and silks were used; and boulle work was introduced.
2. Symbols reminiscent of the French monarchy were replaced with military and agricultural forms such as arrows, spears, drums, stars, and wheat.
3. The William and Mary style used highly polished wood; marquetry; squared leg forms; mushroom, bell, or inverted cup turnings; and bun feet. The Jacobean style used slender bulbous forms; less pronounced carvings; split balusters; pronounced turnings and flutings; acanthus leaves, intertwined circles, palmettes, and ionic capital motifs; and caricatures of human heads.
4. (List four:) slender lines; delicate proportions; subtle curves; straight, tapered legs that were round or square; straight, spade, or thimble feet; heart, oval, camel, wheel, and shield designs for chair backs; satinwood with some mahogany; little ornamentation; wheat, oval, ribbon, and fluted carvings; painted motifs of the three-feathered crest of the Prince of Wales and floral designs
5. European cabinetmakers traveled to America, based their early creations on European designs, and later varied their styles.

6. A	11. B
7. C	12. C
8. B	13. B
9. C	14. B
10. A	15. A

16. marquetry
17. ormolu
18. boulle

19. cabriole
20. Gothic
21. arabesque
22. bulbous
23. wainscot
24. romayne
25. split balusters
26. japanning
27. ribband
28. slatback
29. Prairie
30. eclectic
31. wicker
32. Country

Furniture Terms, Activity 11-1

1. B	6. G
2. I	7. E
3. C	8. D
4. F	9. H
5. A	10. J

Traditional French Furniture, Activity 11-2

1. Furniture showed strong Italian and Flemish influence and was large and upright. Walnut, oak, and ebony were the primary woods. Marquetry, tortoiseshell, and gilded bronze were used for ornamentation. Tall, slender columns and spiral turnings were used for supports and decoration. Bun feet and Flemish feet were typical.
2. Furniture was massive, rectangular, and heavy in proportion. Marble tops rested on elaborately carved, square legs. Upholstered chairs and sofas were covered in rich tapestries, brocades, and silks. Boulle work was typical.
3. Furniture was large, but with more curves and lighter motifs. The cabriole leg was introduced. Lighter woods replaced walnut and ebony.
4. Furniture was scaled down and better sized to human proportions. Curves, flowing lines, and asymmetry replaced the rectangular Baroque shapes. The scroll foot was used. Ornamentation was based on shapes of shells, foliage, shepherd's crooks, and musical instruments. Inlaying and marquetry were used as well as marble and leather tops.
5. Furniture kept the intimacy of Rococo, but returned to the straight lines of earlier styles. Straight lines, geometric curves, and symmetry were incorporated. Straight, tapered legs were emphasized with fluting and grooving.
6. Furniture retained the graceful lines and proportions of the Neoclassic style. Motifs included military and agricultural forms such as arrows, spears, drums, stars, and wheat. Native fruitwood, walnut, and oak were primarily used.

7. Furniture was masculine with geometric shapes, absolute symmetry, and heavy, solid proportions. Large surfaces featured plain, highly polished veneers. Ornamentation was mainly bronze and ormolu. Motifs included military symbols; ancient Egyptian, Roman, and Greek symbols; and Napoleon's initial.

Traditional English Furniture, Activity 11-3
1. Tudor arch (1500-1588)
2. Elizabethan table (1558-1603)
3. Jacobean chair (1603-1649)
4. Restoration Charles II chair (1660-1689)
5. William and Mary highboy (1689-1702)
6. Queen Anne chair (1702-1714)
7. Early Georgian chair (1714-1750)
8. Early English stool (1558-1603)

English Furniture, Activity 11-4
1. developed by George Hepplewhite; contains slender lines, delicate proportions, and subtle curves; includes straight, tapered legs ending in straight, spade, or thimble feet; uses satinwood or mahogany; and has fluting and carvings of wheat, oval patterns, and ribbons
2. developed by Thomas Chippendale; has an elaborately carved back that is available in many styles; uses mahogany exclusively; and is best remembered for his chairs, which were some of his most characteristic pieces
3. designed by the Adam brothers; uses symmetrical styles inspired by Greek and Pompeiian designs; and aided the transition from mahogany to satinwood as the preferred furniture wood
4. designed by Thomas Sheraton; emphasizes straight lines; uses porcelain plaques for decoration; and includes motifs consisting of urns, swags, and leaves

Traditional American Furniture, Activity 11-5
1. C
2. D
3. A
4. B

Instructor's Resources

Chapter 11 Mastery Test
1. B	5. C	9. C
2. A	6. D	10. D
3. D	7. B	11. B
4. B	8. B	12. C

13. traditional
14. Late Renaissance
15. Regence
16. Jacobean
17. japanning
18. Late Renaissance
19. satinwood
20. Thomas Sheraton
21. Jacobean
22. lowboys
23. American Empire
24. Prairie
25. content: an alloy of copper and zinc; appearance: goldlike; use: furniture decoration
26. The Italian influence of the Renaissance and Baroque styles was lost during this period.
27. Ornamentation was of simpler carvings and marquetry; motifs included roses, garlands, ribbons, and Cupid's bows and darts; and some Greek and Roman influences were seen toward the end of the period.
28. Furniture became masculine with geometric shapes, absolute symmetry, and heavy proportions; and motifs included military symbols and Napoleon's initial.
29. Restoration, William and Mary, Queen Anne, and Early Georgian
30. The Oriental influence was evident in gracefully curved lines, cabriole legs, and the lion mask and claw-and-ball foot motifs.
31. Georgian, Regency, and Victorian
32. the mixture of styles brought to America by the colonists from their many homelands
33. Early American, American Georgian, Federal, and Post Federal
34. Boston, Newport, New York, and Philadelphia
35. Almost no ornamentation was used, inexpensive woods replaced mahogany and satinwood, and furniture was designed to be mass-produced rather than custom made.
36. are the very latest designs; have no design rules or guidelines to follow; and display the new, the unclassified, and the experimental
37. ideal for comfort and informality, and uses less expensive woods and durable fabrics

Traditional Furniture Styles from France

Late Renaissance, 1589-1643

Baroque, 1643-1700

Regence, 1700-1730

Rococo, 1730-1760

Neoclassic, 1760-1789

Directoire, 1789-1804

Empire, 1804-1820

Traditional Furniture Styles from England

Early Renaissance Period
- Tudor, 1500-1558
- Elizabethan, 1558-1603
- Jacobean, 1603-1649
- Cromwellian, 1649-1660

Middle Renaissance Period
- Restoration, 1660-1689
- William and Mary, 1689-1702
- Queen Anne, 1702-1714
- Early Georgian, 1714-1750

Late Renaissance Period
- Late Georgian, 1750-1810
  - Thomas Chippendale
  - George Hepplewhite
  - Thomas Sheraton
  - The Adam Brothers
- Regency, 1810-1837
- Victorian, 1837-1901

Traditional Furniture Styles in America

Early American, 1630-1770

American Georgian, 1720-1790

Federal, 1790-1820
- Regional Styles
  - Pennsylvania Dutch
  - Scandinavian
  - Shaker

Post Federal, 1820-1880

Twentieth-Century Furniture Styles

Art Nouveau

Frank Lloyd Wright

Bauhaus

Scandinavian

Art Deco

Twenty-First Century Furniture Styles

Contemporary

Traditional

Casual

Country

Eclectic

Furniture Styles

Chapter 11 Mastery Test

Name _____

Date _____

Score _____

Multiple Choice: Select the best response and write the letter in the preceding blank.

_____ 1.   A furniture support that is the shape of a flattened ball is a _____.
A. thimble foot
B. bun foot
C. Flemish foot
D. None of the above.

_____ 2.   A term used to describe the arts of the Middle Ages is _____.
A. Gothic
B. Arabesque
C. Neoclassic
D. Empire

_____ 3.   Traditional furniture styles from France are often associated with _____.
A. the reigns of Louis XIII, XIV, XV, and XVI
B. the French Revolution
C. the reign of Napoleon
D. All of the above.

_____ 4.   The Baroque period (1643-1700) is roughly associated with the French king, _____.
A. Louis XIII
B. Louis XIV
C. Louis XV
D. Louis XVI

_____ 5.   Turned chairs and wainscot chairs were common during the _____ period.
A. Tudor
B. Cromwellian
C. Elizabethan
D. Jacobean

_____ 6.   Of the following, _____ is *not* an English furniture style of the Middle Renaissance period.
A. Restoration
B. William and Mary
C. Queen Anne
D. Queen Elizabeth

_____ 7.   Among the prominent English furniture designers or master cabinetmakers of the Late Georgian period, _____ was (were) best known for heart, oval, camel, wheel, and shield shapes on chair backs.
A. Thomas Chippendale
B. George Hepplewhite
C. Thomas Sheraton
D. the Adam brothers

_____ 8.   Furniture produced for the middleclass market is linked to the _____ period.
A. Regency
B. Victorian
C. Queen Anne
D. Late Georgian

_____ 9.   The most common item of furniture during the Early American period was the _____.
A. ladder-back chair
B. cradle
C. chest
D. chair table

(continued)

Name _____

_____ 10. Furniture of the Federal period commonly included _____.
   A. ornamentation that was patriotic in nature
   B. the widely used eagle motif
   C. symbols such as cornucopias, fruit, flowers, and spiral turnings
   D. All of the above.

_____ 11. From 1840 to 1880, American designs were patterned after _____ furniture styles.
   A. French Regence
   B. English Victorian
   C. English Georgian
   D. Shaker

_____ 12. The founder of a school, known as the Bauhaus, in Germany in 1919 was _____.
   A. Mies Van der Rohe
   B. Marcel Brewer
   C. Walter Gropius
   D. Charles Eames

Completion: Complete the following sentences by writing the missing words in the preceding blanks.

_____ 13. All furniture styles may be classified into the broad categories of _____ (or period), Twentieth Century, and Twenty-First Century.

_____ 14. Furniture of the _____ _____ period in France, which spanned the reigns of Henry IV and Louis XIII, had both Italian and Flemish influence.

_____ 15. The transition style between Baroque and Rococo was _____.

_____ 16. Traditional English furniture during the Early Renaissance period includes Tudor, Elizabethan, _____, and Cromwellian.

_____ 17. During the reign of William and Mary, the technique known as _____became popular.

_____ 18. The last of the three main periods of traditional furniture from England was the _____ _____ period (1750-1901).

_____ 19. The age of walnut and the age of _____ occurred during the Late Renaissance period in England.

_____ 20. The *Cabinetmaker and Upholsterers Drawing Book* was published in 1791 by _____ _____.

_____ 21. Most Early American furniture was patterned after English Gothic and _____ styles.

_____ 22. During the American Georgian period, highboys and _____ became the most elegant storage pieces built in America.

_____ 23. From 1820 to 1840, the _____ _____ style was popular in America.

_____ 24. In the early twentieth century, Frank Lloyd Wright designed and built a series of homes called _____ style.

Short Answer: Provide brief answers to the following questions or statements.

25. Describe the content, appearance, and use of ormolu. _____

_____

_____

(continued)

Name _____

26. Why was the Rococo style the first traditional style that was truly French in origin? _____

27. Identify the ornamentation used on Neoclassic furniture. _____

_____

_____

28. How did Napoleon influence furniture during the Empire period? _____

_____

_____

_____

29. Which furniture styles were included in the English Middle Renaissance period? _____

_____

_____

30. What strong outside influence was seen in Queen Anne style furniture and how was it displayed?

_____

_____

_____

31. Identify the three English furniture styles included in the Late Renaissance period. _____

_____

_____

_____

32. What influenced the furniture styles of early America? _____

_____

_____

33. List the four traditional American styles of furniture. _____

_____

_____

_____

_____

34. List the four design centers of the American Georgian period. _____

_____

_____

_____

_____

(continued)

Name _____

35. The Art Nouveau furniture style was based on a rebellion against the ornamentation of the Victorian style. How was this executed? _____

_____

_____

36. Describe Contemporary furniture styles. _____

_____

_____

37. Describe the main characteristics of Casual style furniture. _____

_____

_____

Chapter 12
Furniture Construction and Selection

Objectives

After studying this chapter, students will be able to
- list and describe the types of woods used in furniture construction.
- evaluate the type and quality of a furniture joint.
- describe the methods and materials used in the construction of upholstered furniture.
- list ways in which metals and plastics are used in furniture.
- evaluate the usability of furniture according to its quality, cost, style, size, fabric, ergonomics, and maintenance requirements.

Teaching Materials

Text, pages 211–230

Student Activity Guide

Check Your Understanding
12-1, *Woods*
12-2, *Furniture Wood*
12-3, *Wood-Joint Identification*
12-4, *Wood Joints*
12-5, *Furniture-Piece Identification*

Instructor's Resources

Indoor Furniture Care, reproducible master 12-A
Outdoor Furniture Care, reproducible master 12-B
Furniture-Shopping Guidelines, transparency master 12-C
Furniture Safety, reproducible master 12-D
Chapter 12 Mastery Test

Instructional Concepts and Student Activities

1. Have students read Chapter 12 in the text and complete the review questions.
2. Ask each student to find an article in a book or magazine that discusses quality furniture wood, furniture construction, or furniture selection. Have students write a summary of the main points of their articles and add the material to their housing notebooks.

Wood Furniture

3. Lead a class discussion on wood furniture. Be sure to include wood types, wood finishes, and wood furniture construction.
4. Provide samples of as many furniture woods as possible for students to examine. Have students identify the samples by comparing them to the photos and descriptions in the text.
5. Assign each student a different wood to research. Then have students share their findings with the class.
6. *Woods*, Activity 12-1, SAG. Students are to match each type of hardwood or softwood with its description.
7. Show students examples of wood veneer, solid wood, and composite board. Explain the advantages and disadvantages of each for furniture construction.
8. Invite a local cabinetmaker to speak to the class about the considerations in building quality case goods.
9. *Furniture Wood*, Activity 12-2, SAG. Students are to explain why they would or would not use the specified materials for the exposed parts of a piece of furniture.
10. Lead a class discussion on wood finishes while showing examples.
11. Provide examples of the common construction joints in wood furniture for students to identify. Then have students explain where each joint might be used on a piece of furniture.
12. *Wood-Joint Identification*, Activity 12-3, SAG. Students are to identify illustrations of common wood joints used in furniture construction.
13. *Wood Joints*, Activity 12-4, SAG. Students are to demonstrate their understanding of wood joints by matching each name with its description.
14. Show the *Furniture: A Buyer's Guide* video from Learning Seed's catalog and have the class discuss it.

Upholstered Furniture

15. Lead a class discussion on upholstery fabrics, construction, and bedding.
16. *Indoor Furniture Care*, reproducible master 12-A, IR. Use the master as a handout to help students learn how to properly care for indoor furniture. Review key points in class.

17. Plan a field trip to a local upholstery shop to
    see how upholstered furniture is constructed
    and covered.

Metal and Plastic Furniture

18. Describe the advantages and disadvantages
    of metal and plastic furniture. Ask students to
    describe where they encounter such furniture.
19. *Outdoor Furniture Care,* reproducible master
    12-B, IR. Use the master as a handout to
    help students learn how to properly care for
    outdoor furniture. Review key points in class.

Furniture Selection

20. Lead a class discussion on the basic consid-
    erations of selecting good furniture, such as
    quality, cost, style, size, and maintenance
    requirements.
21. *Furniture-Shopping Guidelines,* transparency
    master 12-C, IR. Lead a class discussion on
    how to make satisfactory furniture purchases.
22. Invite a salesperson from a quality furniture
    store to speak to the class about shopping
    for well-constructed furniture.
23. *Furniture-Piece Identification,* Activity 12-5,
    SAG. Students are to give descriptions of
    several standard pieces of furniture.
24. *Furniture Safety,* reproducible master 12-D,
    IR. Use the master as a handout to help
    students learn to avoid unsafe practices
    with furniture. Ask students what additional
    guidelines could be added to this list.
25. Assign one or more tasks listed in the text's
    Suggested Activities section at the end of the
    chapter.

Suggested Evaluation Techniques

26. *Check Your Understanding,* SAG. Have students
    complete as many questions as possible
    without referring to the text. Then have them
    find answers to questions they do not know.
27. Administer the *Chapter 12 Mastery Test.*

Answer Key

Text

Review Questions, page 229

1. Hardwoods are hard and durable; have
   greater dimensional stability, less pitch, more
   durability; hold screws better; and are less
   likely to dent than softwoods.
2. rotary cut: bold, variegated ripple pattern
   flat slicing: variegated, wavy figure
   quarter slicing: series of stripes

half-round slicing: variegated and striped
rift-cut: radiating, ray-cell pattern
3. Furniture made of solid wood is usually more
   expensive than veneered wood and has a
   greater tendency to crack, warp, and swell.
4. for furniture and drawer parts, tabletops,
   backs of bookcases, cabinets, chests, and
   core wood for lower-quality cabinets
5. butt, rabbet, dado, lap, dowel, mortise-and-tenon,
   tongue-and-groove, spline, and dovetail joints,
   and blocking (Descriptions are student
   response.)
6. butt joint
7. plain or twill weaves
8. the seat-base construction and type of
   cushioning used
9. steel: used for framework, strong, lightweight,
   fairly inexpensive, but may be considered
   unattractive without plating
   aluminum: used for lawn furniture framework;
   lighter and less expensive than steel, but
   tends to bend and dent
   cast metal: used for decorative and outdoor
   furniture, considered attractive for some
   uses, is heavy, but sometimes corrodes
   chrome, brass, nickel, copper, and zinc: used
   for plating, are attractive and expensive, but
   may tarnish
10. prohibition of furniture manufacturers and
    dealers from providing false or misleading
    information, manufacturer tags and labels
    that identify furniture content and construction,
    and standardization of furniture terms
11. paint chips, fabric swatches, color samples,
    room measurements, and door and hallway
    measurements
12. comfort, durability, attractiveness, soil
    resistance

Student Activity Guide

Check Your Understanding, pages 101–104

1. case goods
2. hardwood
3. softwood
4. pitch
5. veneer
6. hardboard
7. particleboard
8. patina
9. frame
10. serpentine
11. helical
12. coil
13. welting
14. innerspring
15. air-chamber
16. plating

17. solid
18. genuine
19. plywood
20. B
21. C
22. D
23. D
24. A
25. B
26. D
27. wood, metals, plastics, and fabrics
28. greater dimensional stability; less pitch; more durability; and harder, so they hold nails and screws better and are less likely to dent
29. have checks and cracks that are considered attractive, are less expensive, and weather well
30. is cheaper than expensive solid woods and lighter in weight
31. more likely to crack, warp, and swell; and are more expensive
32. A. hardboard
    B. hardboard
    C. particleboard
33. dovetail joint
34. (List three:) steel, aluminum, wrought iron, cast iron
35. (List five:) can be made to imitate almost any other material, may display a unique character of its own, lightweight, durable, inexpensive, easily cleaned
36. Federal Trade Commission
37. strength; shrinkage; warmth; durability; and resistance to stains, fire, sunlight, mildew, and abrasion

Woods, Activity 12-1

1. black cherry
2. cypress
3. rosewood (Brazilian)
4. teak
5. white oak
6. redwood
7. black walnut
8. eastern red cedar
9. mahogany
10. sugar maple

Furniture Wood, Activity 12-2

1. permits the use of rare and expensive woods in furniture that might otherwise be too expensive or impractical; produces beautiful grain patterns that may be arranged in interesting designs; and is used for a wide variety of quality furniture pieces

2. have a tendency to crack, warp, and swell; develop checks and cracks with changing moisture conditions; are less expensive than hardwoods and wood veneer; are often preferred for rustic and outdoor furniture; and are used to make processed wood

3. are generally preferred over softwood for quality furniture because of greater dimensional stability, less pitch, and more durability; hold nails, screws, and other fasteners better than softwoods; are less likely to dent; and are very expensive

4. is exceptionally strong and resistant to splits, cracks, splinters, abrasion, and moisture; can have a smooth surface or one that is textured to imitate the look of wood grain; and is considered an excellent material for furniture door and drawer parts, tabletops, and backs of chests

5. is sturdy and versatile; is often used as the core wood for cabinets and other furniture of lower quality; may have the surface covered with laminated plastic or wood veneer; and is identified by an irregular crystallized pattern

Wood-Joint Identification, Activity 12-3

1. edge spline
2. through dovetail
3. edge butt
4. cross-lap
5. rabbet joint
6. tongue-and-groove
7. end-lap
8. mortise-and-tenon
9. dowel joint
10. blind dado
11. half-blind dovetail
12. corner spline

Wood Joints, Activity 12-4

1. A		6. F	
2. G		7. I	
3. B		8. H	
4. E		9. C	
5. D			

Furniture-Piece Identification, Activity 12-5

1. a large piece, usually of wood, with doors to use in place of a closet for storing clothing or household linens
2. a furniture piece made from wood that has been steam-bent into soft, curved shapes
3. chair or sofa that has a curved hump along the back
4. comfortable, heavily upholstered chair with a cushioned seat

5. a low chest of drawers that is generally set against a wall
6. upholstered sofa that may be made into a bed
7. chest or cabinet on legs with an open shelf above
8. small sofa for two people
9. classic, square or rectangular table with an apron and legs of the same width
10. bed with four decorative posts
11. armless dining chair
12. a low bed on casters that may be rolled under a full-height bed
13. overstuffed chair that has projecting sides on the high, upholstered back

Instructor's Resources

Chapter 12 Mastery Test

1. C
2. A
3. C
4. D
5. D
6. A
7. C
8. B
9. D
10. B
11. D

12. wood
13. case goods
14. veneer
15. figure patterns
16. plywood
17. solid
18. patina
19. dovetail
20. welting
21. plastic
22. stains
23. Materials and construction determine furniture quality. Well-built pieces from appropriate materials will provide years of useful service, but if either is shortchanged, the results will be less than satisfactory.
24. wood, metals, plastics, and fabrics (Advantages and disadvantages are student response.)
25. solid woods, veneers, and composite board *or* processed woods (Descriptions are student response.)
26. Hardwoods have greater dimensional stability, less pitch, more durability, and better fastener-holding capabilities than softwoods.
27. book match: the back of one veneer sheet meets the front of the adjacent veneer, which produces a matching joint design with a mirrored image
slip match: adjacent sheets are joined side by side, without turning, to repeat the same grain pattern
special match: may be used to produce a variety of patterns, such as diamond, reverse, V, herringbone, checkerboard, and others
28. by using a different wood for unexposed parts
29. hardboard and particleboard, because these processed woods are less expensive and often more durable than solid woods or veneered plywood
30. frame, cushioning material, and covering
31. kiln-dried hardwood, because it has been properly dried and will be less likely to split and buckle
32. plain and twill weaves: are recommended for frequently used furniture
pile weaves: show wear more quickly
brocades and tapestry: are beautiful, but have surface threads that catch and snag easily
leathers and vinyls: are sturdy and easily cleaned
33. to prohibit furniture manufacturers and dealers from giving false or misleading information about furniture
34. to produce furnishings that are comfortable for their function

Indoor Furniture Care

Cleaning	Never use soap and water on wood furniture.
	Always dust with a soft, lint-free cloth moistened with polish since dust can be abrasive. Wipe in a circular motion to loosen old polish and buff until it's dry for a perfect finish.
	Use the same type of furniture polish consistently, as furniture can appear streaky if oil and wax-based polishes are mixed.
	Use a natural-bristle paintbrush to dust intricate designs in wood.
	Vacuum upholstery and rotate cushions once weekly to avoid fabric problems. (The round brush attachment can be used to clean wood furniture.)
	Always follow the manufacturer's care instructions. Keep them handy for future reference.
Longevity	Do not expose wood furniture and upholstery to continuous direct sunlight, which can cause fading and other damage.
	Protect wood furniture from humidity by using an air conditioner in the summer and a humidifier in winter. Place furniture at least a foot away from temperature extremes such as heaters and air conditioners.
	Use coasters, pads, and other protection against spills and stains.
	Gently lift, open, and close furniture doors, lids, and drawers.
	Keep cats and dogs off furniture, as they can be extremely abrasive.
Everyday Use	Sit only on structures designed for that purpose.
	Do not place hot items on a finish that will melt or stain.
	Beware of spills and condensation on drink glasses that can damage furniture coatings.
	Do not drag furniture when moving it. Instead, move the item from its strongest part.

Source: American Furniture Manufacturers Association

Outdoor Furniture Care

Aluminum Frames	Clean with mild soap and water. Apply an automotive wax to nontextured surfaces every few months. On textured finishes, periodically apply baby or mineral oil. Spray oil lubricant on chair swivels or glides occasionally.
Tempered-Glass Tabletops	Clean regularly with a soft cloth, mild detergent, and warm water. Buff dry with a clean, lint-free cloth. Commercial glass cleaners may also be used.
Outdoor Wicker	Vacuum gently or brush with a soft bristle brush. Hose off every few weeks and clean periodically with mild detergent and water. Rinse thoroughly and air dry.
Vinyl Straps	Wash with mild detergent and warm water, using a soft sponge or cloth. Rinse thoroughly. Apply vinyl protector to the straps after cleaning. To remove scuff marks, apply toothpaste or gentle abrasive, and rub gently with a dry cloth. To remove mildew, use a solution of warm water, mild detergent, and bleach (no more than ¼ cup to 3 gallons of water).
Sling Furniture	Wash with mild soap and water, rinse thoroughly, and air dry.

Cushions	Vacuum as needed to remove organic material and prevent decay.
	Clean by sponging with mild detergent and warm water. Then rinse thoroughly and air dry.
	To remove mildew, use a solution of 1 cup bleach and a squirt of detergent per gallon of water. Scrub with a sponge or soft brush, rinse thoroughly with clean water, and air dry. (Always test an inconspicuous spot first to make sure the color won't fade. Bleach may not be suitable for some fabrics.)
Wrought Iron and Steel	Clean with warm, soapy water.
	To maintain the gloss, apply automotive wax on nontextured surfaces. On textured finishes, periodically apply mineral or baby oil.
	To remove rust, clean by sanding lightly. Then wipe thoroughly and apply touch-up paint (usually provided by the manufacturer).
Hardwoods	Clean with mild detergent and water. Rinse well. (Some manufacturers recommend an occasional application of oil.)
	Store furniture made of pine, oak, and cedar for the winter. Teak can stay outdoors year-round.
	Repaint painted woods every year or so.
Umbrellas	Wash covers with mild soap and water by using a long-handled brush. Spray silicone on the joints of wire frames. Use wax or furniture polish on wooden umbrellas.

Source: American Furniture Manufacturers Association

Furniture-Shopping Guidelines

- Identify your favorite style.

- Examine your color, texture, and pattern preferences.

- Keep a scrapbook of favorite interiors.

- Consider your lifestyle.

- Prioritize your purchases.

- Determine your budget.

- Plan your time to suit your shopping style.

- Explore available resources.

- Take advantage of free services.

- Trust your judgment and buy what you like.

Source: American Furniture Manufacturers Association

Furniture Safety

General Guidelines

- Furniture surfaces should be smooth and free of splinters or rough edges.

- Nails, screws, and other joiners should be tight and unexposed.

- Be wary of older pieces of furniture that may contain lead paint.

Bunk Beds

- The top bunk should have guardrails on each side, with no more than a 15 in. open at each end. Rails should be secure, sturdy, and extending at least 5 in. above the top surface of the mattress.

- The mattress should be the proper size, as stated by the manufacturer.

- Always use a sturdy ladder to access the top bunk, and only one person should be on the top bunk at a time.

- These are not recommended for children under age six.

New Upholstery

- Make sure upholstered furniture displays the gold UFAC tag, which means the manufacturer has met the construction criteria outlined by the Upholstered Furniture Action Council.

Cribs

- Crib slats or spindles should be spaced no more than 2⅜ in. apart, and none should be loose or missing.

- Make sure all screws, brackets, and other hardware are properly installed and intact.

- The mattress should fit snugly, with no more than two-fingers width between the edge of the mattress and the crib.

Dressers and Chests of Drawers

- Open only one drawer at a time. Drawers should slide in and out easily.

- Never allow children to stand in open drawers, which can cause furniture to tip.

- Check for automatic drawer-stops when purchasing children's furniture to prevent children from accidentally pulling drawers onto themselves.

(continued)

Bookcases

- Be careful not to overload shelves.

- Consider securing the top portion of a bookcase to the wall to prevent tipping, especially with children around.

- Always be sure that any shelf unit attached to a desk or chest, which is common in children's furniture, is secure.

Entertainment Centers and TV Stands

- Use correctly sized furniture to house the television, especially larger models that can fall forward if not properly supported.

Storage and Toy Chests

- Lids should feature safety latches that prevent tops from falling freely or slamming shut. (For older chests without safety latches, contact the manufacturer for a replacement latch or remove the lid.)

- Lids should not lock automatically.

Reclining Chairs

- Never allow children to play on recliners, particularly when in the reclined position.

Source: American Furniture Manufacturers Association

Furniture Construction and Selection

Name _____

Date _____

Chapter 12 Mastery Test

Score _____

Multiple Choice: Select the best response and write the letter in the preceding blank.

_____ 1. Wood from trees that bear cones and needles and remain green all year is classified as _____.
   A. pines and firs
   B. hardwoods
   C. softwoods
   D. construction grades

_____ 2. The native hardwoods most commonly used for fine furniture are _____.
   A. cherry, maple, oak, pecan, and walnut
   B. cherry, mahogany, maple, oak, and walnut
   C. maple, oak, pecan, teak, and walnut
   D. mahogany, maple, walnut, and white pine

_____ 3. The four softwoods most popular for furniture construction are _____.
   A. pine, teak, cypress, and cocobola
   B. pine, redwood, cedar, and teak
   C. pine, cypress, cedar, and redwood
   D. pine, redwood, fir, and sugar maple

_____ 4. The method of cutting veneer that is most commonly used for softwood veneers is _____.
   A. quarter slicing
   B. rift cut
   C. flat slicing
   D. rotary cut

_____ 5. Some of the most interesting and valuable veneer patterns are cut from the _____ of the tree.
   A. crotch
   B. burl
   C. stump
   D. All of the above.

_____ 6. The simplest type of wood joint to construct is the _____ joint.
   A. butt
   B. rabbet
   C. lap
   D. spline

_____ 7. The type of wood joint used with other joints when extra strength is desired is the _____ joint.
   A. dado
   B. tongue-and-groove
   C. dowel
   D. mortise-and-tenon

_____ 8. The joint formed by cutting a recess along an edge or on the end of one or both pieces to be joined is the _____ joint.
   A. dado
   B. rabbet
   C. lap
   D. tongue-and-groove

(continued)

Name _____

_____ 9. The main disadvantage of leather as an upholstery material is _____.
A. fading
B. lack of stain resistance
C. lack of wear resistance
D. the expensive cost

_____ 10. Aluminum tubing is used frequently for lawn furniture because it _____.
A. is less resistant to corrosion and may be cast into shapes
B. is lighter in weight and less expensive than steel
C. is more attractive than steel or plastic
D. requires no plating, but will readily accept paint finishes

_____ 11. Factors that add to the cost of a piece of furniture include _____.
A. curved construction
B. deep patinas
C. intricate carvings
D. All of the above.

Completion: Complete the following sentences by writing the missing words in the preceding blanks.

_____ 12. The most common material used in furniture is _____.

_____ 13. Furniture pieces that include chests, dressers, tables, and desks are called _____ _____.

_____ 14. Wood _____ permits the use of rare and expensive woods in furniture that would otherwise be impractical or too costly.

_____ 15. The _____ _____ of a veneer is greatly affected by the part of the tree used.

_____ 16. Veneered furniture is made by gluing together layers, or plies, of wood to make _____.

_____ 17. When comparing solid wood and veneered wood, the one most likely to crack, warp, and swell is _____ wood.

_____ 18. Polishing, sanding, and rubbing wood will produce a _____.

_____ 19. To fasten corners together when maximum strength is required, _____ joints are used.

_____ 20. The function of _____ in the covering of an upholstered piece is to add strength.

_____ 21. The material used in furniture production that will probably replace many traditional materials is _____.

_____ 22. Plastic, metal, and vinyl furniture surfaces are easily cleaned and are generally resistant to _____.

Short Answer: Provide brief answers to the following questions or statements.

23. What two critical factors determine the quality of furniture and why is quality important?

_____

_____

_____

(continued)

Name _____

24. What are the four primary groups of materials used to make furniture and the advantages and disadvantages of each? _____

_____

_____

_____

_____

_____

_____

_____

_____

_____

25. Name and describe the three types of wood products used to produce furniture of different construction quality. _____

_____

_____

_____

_____

_____

_____

26. Why are hardwoods generally preferred over softwoods for quality furniture? _____

_____

_____

27. List the most common veneered patterns and the characteristics of each. _____

_____

_____

_____

_____

_____

28. If a case good is made from an expensive solid wood, how is the amount of this wood reduced in a given piece of furniture? _____

_____

(continued)

Name _____

29. Name the two main types of processed woods that are more frequently used as furniture
construction materials and explain why. _____

_____

_____

_____

30. What are the three principal parts of a piece of upholstered furniture?_____

_____

_____

_____

31. From what type of wood is the frame of an upholstered piece of furniture generally made? Why?

_____

_____

32. Identify an important care factor regarding each of the following upholstery fabrics:

plain or twill weaves: _____

pile weave: _____

brocades and tapestry: _____

leathers and vinyls:_____

33. The Federal Trade Commission has instituted *Guidelines for the Household Furniture Industry* for
what purpose? _____

_____

_____

34. What is the purpose of ergonomics in furniture design? _____

_____

_____

Chapter 13
Walls

Objectives

After studying this chapter, students will be able to

- describe the basic construction techniques used in building frame, masonry veneer, and masonry walls.
- evaluate the appropriateness of an exterior wall in relationship to its style, maintenance requirements, and ability to withstand weather conditions.
- list and describe various types of wall treatments.
- choose a wall treatment that is appropriate for both the function and design of a setting.

Teaching Materials

Text, pages 232–251

Student Activity Guide

Check Your Understanding
13-1, *Frame Walls*
13-2, *Brick Veneer Walls*
13-3, *Basement Walls*
13-4, *Exterior Wall Materials*
13-5, *Interior Walls*
13-6, *Interior Wall Treatments*
13-7, *Wall Decoration*

Instructor's Resources

Common Brick Bonds, transparency master 13-A
Exterior Masonry Walls, transparency master 13-B
Common Wall Treatments, transparency master 13-C
Chapter 13 Mastery Test

Instructional Concepts and Student Activities

1. Have students read Chapter 13 in the text and complete the review questions.

2. Ask students to clip illustrations, pictures, and articles from magazines or sales literature about wall construction, materials, and treatments. Have them add this material to their housing notebooks for future reference.

Wall Types

3. Lead a class discussion on frame walls and masonry walls, the main types of walls used in residential housing construction.
4. Ask students to describe the difference between interior and exterior frame walls.
5. Invite a local carpenter to explain to the class the process of constructing a frame wall.
6. Show the *Walls: Framing and Removal* video from Hobar Publications and have the class discuss it.
7. *Frame Walls*, Activity 13-1, SAG. Students are to label the components of frame walls.
8. Lead a class discussion on the components of brick veneer walls.
9. *Common Brick Bonds*, transparency master 13-A, IR. Have students examine and discuss the differences among typical brick bonds used in wall construction.
10. *Brick Veneer Walls*, Activity 13-2, SAG. Students are to label the components in the brick veneer of a frame wall.
11. Hold a class discussion about the construction of masonry walls. Be sure to include exterior, interior, and basement/foundation walls.
12. *Exterior Masonry Walls*, transparency master 13-B, IR. Have students examine and discuss typical masonry materials used for constructing exterior walls.
13. Invite a brick mason to speak to the class about building masonry walls.
14. *Basement Walls*, Activity 13-3, SAG. Students are to label the components of a basement/foundation wall and floor system.

Wall Treatments

15. *Common Wall Treatments,* transparency master 13-C, IR. Discuss common exterior and interior wall treatments for residential structures.
16. Provide wall-material samples for students to examine.

17. *Exterior Wall Materials*, Activity 13-4, SAG. Students are to sketch elevation views of eight exterior wall materials using the proper scale.

Selection of Wall Treatments

18. Lead a class discussion on the function of wall treatments in a room.
19. Explain how the principles of design can be used to decorate the interior walls of a home.
20. Invite a professional interior designer to speak to the class on guidelines for decorating residential walls.
21. *Interior Walls*, Activity 13-5, SAG. Students are to plan the interior wall treatment and trim for a family room.
22. *Interior Wall Treatments*, Activity 13-6, SAG. Students are to analyze the cost of four interior wall treatments: clear redwood boards, hardwood paneling, ceramic tile, and wallpaper.
23. *Wall Decoration*, Activity 13-7, SAG. Students are to select a picture from a magazine that displays good wall design, and identify the design principles and elements used.
24. Assign one or more tasks listed in the text's *Suggested Activities* section at the end of the chapter.

Suggested Evaluation Techniques

25. *Check Your Understanding*, SAG. Have students complete as many questions as possible without referring to the text. Then have them find answers to questions they do not know.
26. Administer the *Chapter 13 Mastery Test*.

Answer Key

Text

Review Questions, page 250

1. bearing wall: for most exterior walls and some main partitions; nonbearing wall: for most partitions
2. Besides drywall, several weatherproofing materials are applied to the exterior wall such as insulation, sheathing, felt, and siding.
3. A brick veneer wall is a frame wall with brick attached to the front, so it supports only its own structural weight. A masonry wall is constructed entirely of masonry and may support other weight from the structure.
4. brick veneer
5. Furring strips must be applied before paneling or drywall is attached.

6. A footing is made at the bottom of the wall. Concrete is then cast in forms or concrete blocks are laid to form a wall generally 10 in. thick (depending on type of structure, height of wall, and ground pressure), sometimes with pilasters placed along the wall for extra support.
7. coating the wall with hot tar, cement-based paint, commercially prepared material, or cement mortar; and providing good drainage by placing a drain tile surrounded by a bed of gravel at the bottom of the wall
8. manufactured siding: made of aluminum, vinyl, or fiberglass; requires less maintenance than wood siding; more durable than wood siding; provides more insulative value than wood siding; and appeals to people who want or need to eliminate maintenance concerns wood siding: appeals to people who want the natural look of wood and are willing to handle maintenance
9. wood shingles, decorative masonry, stucco/plaster, texture paint, wallpaper, fabric, carpeting, paneling, boards, and ceramic tile
10. categories: latex and alkyd; finishes: matte, gloss, and textured
11. The paint develops a chalky surface at a controlled rate that washes away with surface dirt when it rains, leaving the paint looking fresh.
12. economical; can be used in any room; available in many colors, patterns, and textures; completely covers old wall treatments; ideal for disguising odd-shaped architectural details; available in a wide price range; can make a room appear formal or informal, larger or smaller, and quiet or vibrant; can be used as a foundation for period furnishings; a quick, easy way to remodel or change a room's decor; provides continuity to a basic design theme; and can be used to establish the scale of an interior space.
13. formality level, amount of visual interest, texture, and light-absorbency level
14. light colors, small-scale patterns, mirrors, or a wall scene in perspective

Student Activity Guide

Check Your Understanding, pages 111–120

1.	N	9.	E
2.	M	10.	C
3.	B	11.	F
4.	A	12.	J
5.	H	13.	G
6.	O	14.	I
7.	K	15.	L
8.	D	16.	C

17. D
18. B
19. C
20. A
21. C
22. D

23. B
24. C
25. C
26. B
27. A

28. nonbearing
29. header
30. foundation
31. horizontal
32. cedar
33. Portland
34. oil
35. flat
36. mirrors
37. wainscot
38. active
39. passive

Frame Walls, Activity 13-1

Solution on page 188

Brick Veneer Walls, Activity 13-2

Solution on page 189

Basement Walls, Activity 13-3

Solution on page 190

Exterior Wall Materials, Activity 13-4

Typical solution on page 191

Instructor's Resources

Chapter 13 Mastery Test

1. B
2. C
3. C
4. A
5. B
6. C
7. C

8. B
9. B
10. C
11. D
12. D
13. B

14. bearing
15. partitions
16. studs
17. gypsum
18. sheathing

19. masonry
20. furring strips
21. pilasters
22. grounded
23. stucco
24. alkyd
25. glazed
26. wainscot
27. by defining space, assuring privacy, keeping out the elements, and providing protection
28. (List four:) Douglas fir, southern yellow pine, hemlock, spruce, larch
29. ¼, ⅜, ½, and ⅝ in.; ½ in.
30. to provide extra support over door and window openings
31. ½ in. plywood, ½ in. weatherboard, and ¾ in. rigid foam insulation
32. to provide insulation and allow moisture to collect and escape at the bottom of the wall
33. to distribute the load of the wall's weight to a wider area
34. (Student response. See page 238 in the text.)
35. aluminum, vinyl, and fiberglass—imitate wood but offer low maintenance and high durability
36. roofing: over 50 years; exterior siding: indefinitely
37. (List three:) gluing, tacking, using double-faced carpet tape, fastening to a frame that is mounted on a wall
38. durability and low maintenance
39. using small-scale patterns in light colors, mirrors to create an illusion of more space, or scenes in perspective that lead the eye beyond the wall to create the illusion of more space
40. (List five:) available in a wide price range; free samples available to help decision making; can be used in most areas of the house; produced in many colors, patterns, and textures; can make a room appear larger, smaller, or more or less formal or active; can be used as a foundation for period furnishings; provides a quick, easy way to remodel or change decor; provides continuity to a design theme; can be used to establish the scale of an interior space

Frame Walls
Activity 13-1

Solution

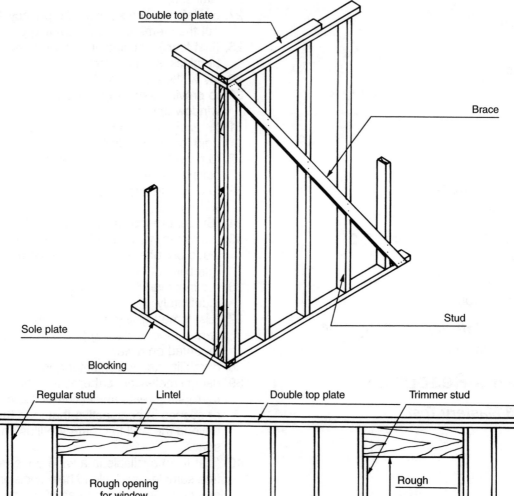

Double top plate

Brace

Sole plate

Stud

Blocking

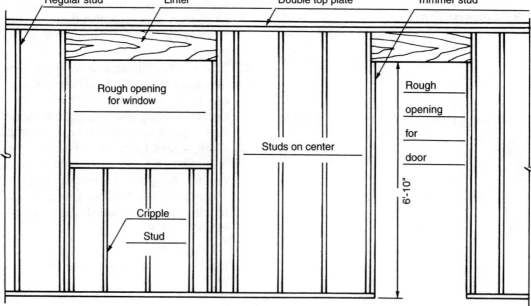

Regular stud   Lintel   Double top plate   Trimmer stud

Rough opening for window

Rough opening for door

Studs on center

6'-10"

Cripple
Stud

Brick Veneer Walls
Activity 13-2

Solution

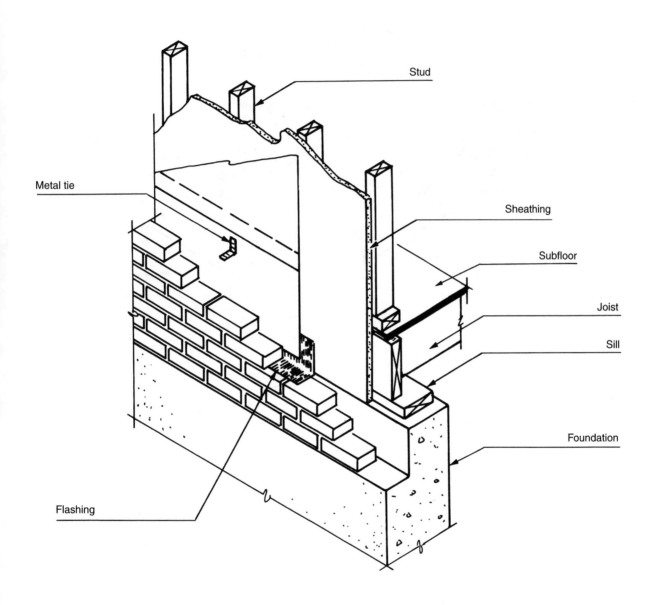

Stud

Metal tie

Sheathing

Subfloor

Joist

Sill

Foundation

Flashing

Basement Walls
Activity 13-3

Solution

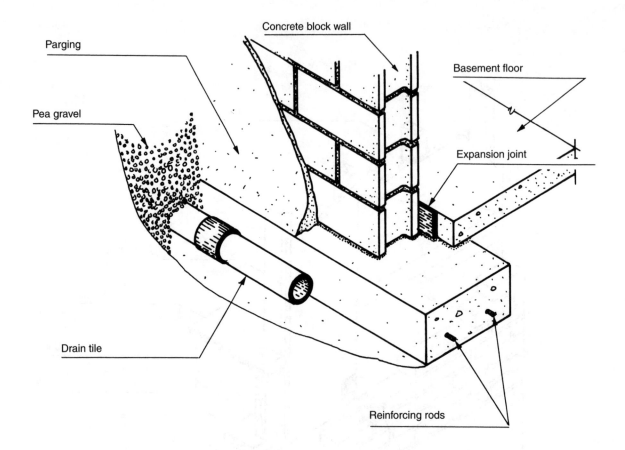

Parging

Pea gravel

Concrete block wall

Basement floor

Expansion joint

Drain tile

Reinforcing rods

Exterior Wall Materials
Activity 13-4

Typical Solution

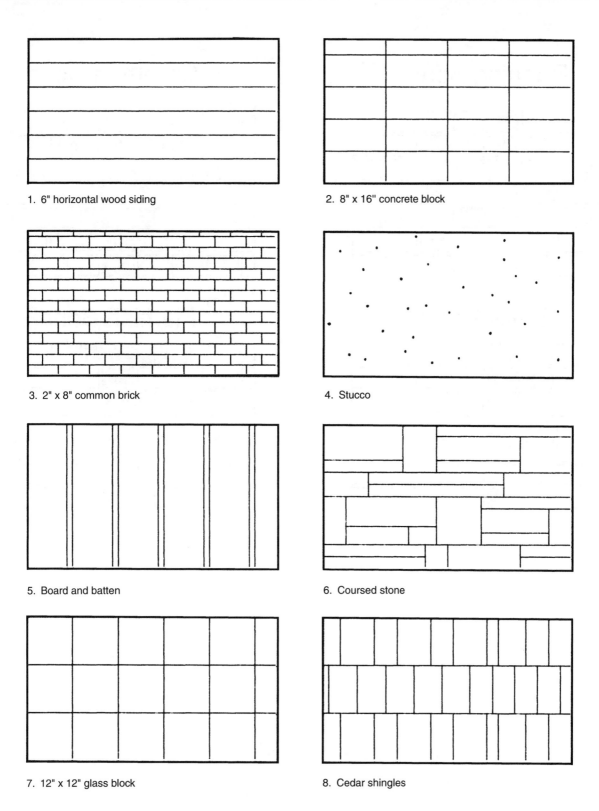

1. 6" horizontal wood siding

2. 8" x 16" concrete block

3. 2" x 8" common brick

4. Stucco

5. Board and batten

6. Coursed stone

7. 12" x 12" glass block

8. Cedar shingles

Scale: $1/2$" = 1'-0"

Common Brick Bonds

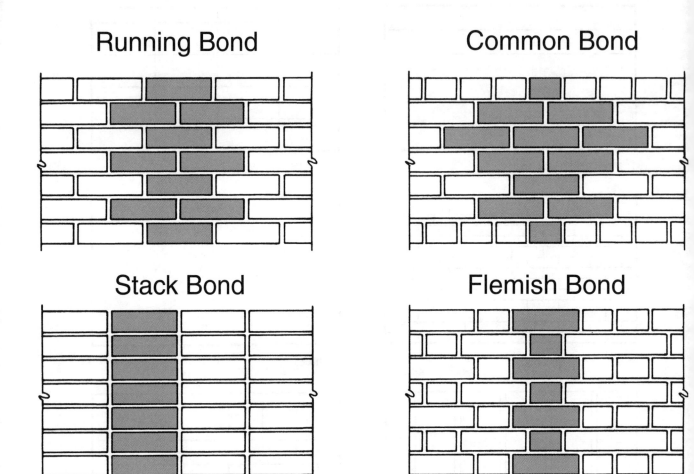

Running Bond

Common Bond

Stack Bond

Flemish Bond

Exterior Masonry Walls

Concrete Block

Brick

Ashlar Stone

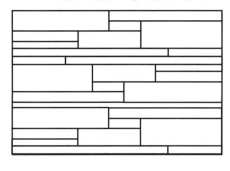

Random Rubble Stone

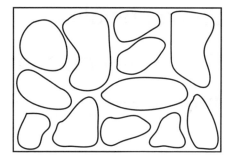

Stucco

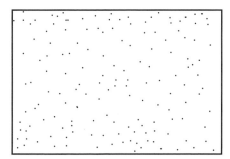

Uncoursed Cobweb

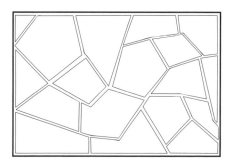

Common Wall Treatments

Exterior Walls

Wood siding

Manufactured siding

- aluminum
- vinyl
- fiberglass

Mineral fiber shingles

Wood shingles

Decorative masonry

Stucco (or plaster)

Interior Walls

Paint

Wallpaper

Fabric

Paneling and boards

Ceramic tile

Mirrors

Walls
Chapter 13
Mastery Test

Name _____

Date _____

Score _____

Multiple Choice: Select the best response and write the letter in the preceding blank.

_____ 1. The most typical spacing is _____ in. for wall studs.
   A. 12
   B. 16
   C. 18
   D. 24

_____ 2. Frame walls made from kiln-dried lumber have a moisture content of _____ percent.
   A. less than 10
   B. 10 to 14
   C. 15 to 19
   D. more than 19

_____ 3. A typical interior frame wall with drywall on both sides is _____ in. thick.
   A. 3½
   B. 4
   C. 4½
   D. 5

_____ 4. An exterior wall that uses brick or other masonry as a covering for a frame wall is a _____ wall.
   A. veneer
   B. composite
   C. masonry
   D. sandwich

_____ 5. The type of material generally used for wood foundations is _____.
   A. a moisture-resistant species
   B. pressure-treated construction lumber
   C. composite-board products
   D. manufactured wood

_____ 6. Of the following, the true statement about wood foundations is: they _____.
   A. are most common in warm climates
   B. have a life span of 10 to 15 years
   C. are less expensive than typical masonry or concrete foundations
   D. are recognized as an accepted method of building residential foundations

_____ 7. Exterior masonry walls for residential construction are generally _____ in. thick.
   A. 4
   B. 6
   C. 8
   D. 10

_____ 8. The materials recommended for both interior and exterior wall coverings are _____.
   A. mineral fiber shingles, wood siding, and wood shingles
   B. wood shingles, decorative masonry, and stucco or plaster
   C. paint, wood shingles, and fabric
   D. tile, paneling, and decorative masonry

_____ 9. Mineral fiber shingles are made from _____.
   A. wood cellulose and concrete
   B. asbestos and concrete
   C. asbestos and asphalt
   D. None of the above.

(continued)

Name _____

_____ 10. The most popular type of exterior house paint is _____.
    A. enamel
    B. water based
    C. oil based
    D. cement based

_____ 11. The ideal wall finish for disguising odd-shaped architectural details is _____.
    A. brightly colored paint
    B. paneling
    C. textured paint
    D. wallpaper

_____ 12. Mirrors are frequently used as a wall treatment to _____.
    A. increase the light in a room
    B. make a small room appear larger
    C. produce a dramatic effect
    D. All of the above.

_____ 13. The treatment most appropriate for a passive wall is _____.
    A. a wall mural
    B. wallpaper with a fine pattern
    C. wallpaper with random patterns or graphic designs
    D. wallpaper with a large pattern

Completion: Complete the following sentences by writing the missing words in the preceding blanks.

_____ 14. A _____ wall supports weight from the ceiling or roof of the structure.

_____ 15. Interior frame walls are called _____ to distinguish them from exterior walls.

_____ 16. Frame-wall construction consists of regularly spaced _____ attached to a sole plate at the bottom and a double plate at the top.

_____ 17. The material most frequently used to cover a frame partition is _____ wallboard, more commonly called drywall.

_____ 18. The outside face of a frame wall has a protective layer called _____, which is nailed to the studs to help weatherproof the wall.

_____ 19. A true _____ wall is constructed entirely of brick, concrete block, stone, clay tile, or a combination of these materials.

_____ 20. If the inside of a masonry wall is to be covered, _____ _____ are required.

_____ 21. Thickened sections built into the wall from the footing to the top of the wall are _____.

_____ 22. Aluminum conducts electricity, so homes with aluminum siding must be properly _____.

_____ 23. The term _____ has traditionally been applied to exterior plastering.

_____ 24. Paints are categorized as latex (water based) or _____ (oil based).

_____ 25. The most practical type of tile for walls in kitchens and bathrooms is _____ tile because it has a smooth, hard surface that is easily cleaned.

_____ 26. The lower 3 or 4 ft. of a wall finished differently from the rest of the wall is called _____.

(continued)

Name _____

Short Answer: Provide brief answers to the following questions or statements.

27. How do walls serve both aesthetic and practical functions as one of the three basic elements of a room? _____

_____

_____

28. List four species of construction grade lumber that are most generally used for residential frame-wall construction. _____

_____

_____

_____

29. What are the available choices in drywall thicknesses? Which is most common? _____

_____

_____

30. What is the purpose of lintels in frame-wall construction? _____

_____

31. What three sheathing materials are generally used on exterior frame walls? _____

_____

_____

_____

32. Why is 1 in. of air space left between the sheathing of the frame wall and the masonry?

_____

_____

33. What is the purpose of the footing below a foundation wall? _____

_____

34. Compare horizontal and vertical siding, listing the advantages and disadvantages of each.

_____

_____

_____

_____

_____

(continued)

Name_____

35. What three manufactured materials are produced as alternatives to traditional wood siding? What are the advantages of using a manufactured siding?_____

_____

_____

_____

_____

36. What is the expected longevity of red cedar shingles used as roofing versus exterior siding?

_____

_____

37. Identify three methods of attaching fabric to a wall._____

_____

_____

_____

38. What qualities make paneling popular for family rooms, game rooms, and kitchens? _____

_____

_____

39. What can be done to make a small wall appear larger? _____

_____

_____

40. Name five advantages of wallpaper as a wall covering._____

_____

_____

_____

_____

_____

_____

_____

Chapter 14
Floors

Objectives

After studying this chapter, students will be able to

- differentiate the materials and construction methods used to make concrete floors and wood-frame floors.
- describe the construction methods used in laying flooring materials and floor coverings.
- compare the appearance, texture, and maintenance requirements of various flooring materials and floor coverings.
- evaluate the appropriateness of a floor treatment for a room according to principles of function and design.

Teaching Materials

Text, pages 252–273

Student Activity Guide

Check Your Understanding
14-1, *Wood-Floor Construction*
14-2, *Concrete-Floor Construction*
14-3, *Wood Flooring Materials*
14-4, *Wood-Floor Patterns*
14-5, *Flooring Materials*
14-6, *Carpet Fibers and Construction*
14-7, *Resilient Floor Coverings*
14-8, *Floor-Area Design*

Instructor's Resources

Types of Flooring Materials, transparency master 14-A

Suitable Locations for Wood Flooring, transparency master 14-B

Types of Floor Coverings, transparency master 14-C

Cleaning Carpet Stains, reproducible master 14-D

Choosing Floor Treatments, reproducible master 14-E

Chapter 14 Mastery Test

Instructional Concepts and Student Activities

1. Have students read Chapter 14 in the text and complete the review questions.
2. Ask students to clip illustrations, pictures, and articles from magazines or sales literature about floor construction, materials, and coverings. Have them add this material to their housing notebooks for future reference.

Floor Systems

3. Lead a class discussion on wood-floor construction based on the illustrations in the text. Identify the structural components, framing methods, spans, and loads.
4. Show the *Framing* video from Hobar Publications and have the class discuss it.
5. *Wood-Floor Construction*, Activity 14-1, SAG. Students are to label the components of the two typical wood-floor systems.
6. Describe the types of concrete-floor systems commonly used for residential structures. Be sure to distinguish the thickened-edge slab from the floating slab.
7. Involve students in a discussion on the advantages and disadvantages of concrete-floor systems.
8. *Concrete-Floor Construction*, Activity 14-2, SAG. Students are to label the components of the three typical concrete-floor systems.

Floor Treatments

9. *Types of Flooring Materials*, transparency master 14-A, IR. Acquaint students with the many types of flooring materials covered in the text.
10. Explain to students the difference between flooring materials and floor coverings.
11. Plan a field trip to a local building materials store to examine various types of flooring materials. Examine the range of choices available and compare prices per square foot.
12. Show the *Wood Flooring* video from Hobar Publications and have the class discuss it.

13. *Wood Flooring Materials*, Activity 14-3, SAG.
Students are to prepare a reference chart for
standard wood flooring materials.
14. *Wood-Floor Patterns*, Activity 14-4, SAG.
Students are to plan four wood-floor patterns
with any combination of standard, modular,
wood flooring materials.
15. *Suitable Locations for Wood Flooring*, transparency master 14-B, IR. Show students
what basic types of wood flooring are recommended for the various levels in a home.
16. Lead a class discussion on ceramic tile,
concrete, masonry, and terrazzo flooring
materials.
17. *Flooring Materials*, Activity 14-5, SAG.
Students are to draw plan views of six
different flooring materials.
18. *Types of Floor Coverings*, transparency
master 14-C, IR. Acquaint students with
the many types of floor coverings
discussed in the text.
19. Lead a class discussion on soft floor
coverings.
20. Show the *Vinyl Flooring* video from Hobar
Publications and have the class discuss it.
21. Provide carpet samples of different fibers and
construction methods for students to examine.
22. *Carpet Fibers and Construction*, Activity 14-6,
SAG. Students are to demonstrate their
knowledge of carpet fibers and construction
by matching common terms with their
descriptions.
23. *Cleaning Carpet Stains*, reproducible master
14-D, IR. Use the master as a handout on
stain-removal guidelines for carpeting.
Review key points in class.
24. *Resilient Floor Coverings*, Activity 14-7, SAG.
Students are to list qualities of various
materials for resilient floor coverings.

Selection of Floor Treatments

25. Ask students to bring pictures of floor
treatments they like to class. Have the
class discuss the pictures in terms of design,
wearability, and cost.
26. *Floor-Area Design*, Activity 14-8, SAG.
Students are to individually select a picture
from a magazine that applies the principles of
good design to an interior floor and explain
how good the floor contributes to good design.
27. *Choosing Floor Treatments*, reproducible
master 14-E, IR. Students are to select
suitable floor treatments, based on principles
presented in the text, for all the areas of a
given floor plan.
28. Assign one or more tasks listed in the text's
Suggested Activities section at the end of the
chapter.

Suggested Evaluation Techniques

29. *Check Your Understanding*, SAG. Have students
complete as many questions as possible
without referring to the text. Then have them
find answers to questions they do not know.
30. Administer the *Chapter 14 Mastery Test.*

Answer Key

Text

Review Questions, page 272

1. Joists or trusses, possibly resting on a support
beam, are fastened to a sill plate on the
foundation. Covering them is a plywood
subfloor, which is covered by plywood or
particleboard underlayment.
2. A thickened-edge slab combines slab and
foundation into one unit, while a floating slab
is separate from the foundation wall.
3. Most strip flooring has tongue-and-groove edges
that are fitted together. The strips are nailed to a
wood subfloor. On a concrete floor, the strips are
nailed over a vapor barrier to imbedded furring
strips, or the strips are installed as a floating floor
using a unique clip system underneath.
4. advantages: durable, long lasting, and
requires little maintenance
disadvantages: expensive and cool to the touch
5. bathrooms, kitchens, and possibly living
rooms and patio areas
6. concrete, brick, slate, and flagstone
7. reinforced concrete
8. nylon: long-lasting wear, highly resistant to
crushing, may pill, conducts static electricity,
easy to clean, and fades with sunlight exposure
acrylic: looks and feels like wool, good color
retention, soft, does not resist crushing as well
as wool, and conducts little static electricity
polyester: feels somewhat like wool, resists
wear, does not resist crushing well, is
economical for heavy-duty carpets, and
generates little static electricity
olefin: very tough, water resistant, fade
resistant, stain resistant, difficult to dye,
and reduces static electricity
9. type of fiber, type of construction, pile density,
and the strength of the backing
10. room size rugs: to cover the room's floor
except for a small perimeter
area rugs: to define the different areas of a
room, emphasize separate functions, and
unify furniture groupings
scatter rugs: to reduce wear in high-traffic
areas and protect an area from dirt and spills

11. easiest: vinyl floor covering with a no-wax finish, which simply needs damp mopping
    most difficult: cork tile, which damages and stains easily, and requires careful wax maintenance
12. smaller: with dark colors, deep textures, bold patterns, or more than one kind of floor treatment in a room
    larger: with light colors, smooth textures, or the same treatment for the entire room
    warmer: with textured treatments or warm colors
    cooler: with smooth treatments or cool colors

Student Activity Guide

Check Your Understanding, pages 121–123

1.	E	8.	K
2.	J	9.	M
3.	D	10.	H
4.	A	11.	L
5.	C	12.	G
6.	I	13.	F
7.	B		

14. 40
15. bearing
16. slat
17. quarry
18. concrete
19. sedimentary
20. axminster
21. sheet
22. slab is enlarged to allow heating ducts, conduits, and water pipes cast into the structure's floor, making them inaccessible
23. even coloring and few knotholes or other imperfections
24. Strip flooring is narrower than wood planks and more likely to be used in formal settings. Wood planks are more rustic and generally used in casual settings.
25. The thinset method has no mortar bed, so equal thicknesses of slate must be used. With the thickbed method, different thicknesses of slate can be used since the mortar is used to help level the slate.
26. olefin
27. A room-size rug leaves a border of the floor's perimeter exposed, frames the floor, and defines the space. An area rug unifies furniture groupings, serves as a focal point, defines an area of the room, and does not cover the entire floor.
28. paver tile, quarry tile, brick, slate, flagstone, terrazzo, olefin carpeting, tile, and sheet floor coverings

Wood-Floor Construction, Activity 14-1
Solution on page 207

Concrete-Floor Construction, Activity 14-2
Solution on page 208

Wood Flooring Materials, Activity 14-3
Solution on page 209

Wood-Floor Patterns, Activity 14-4
Typical solution on page 210

Flooring Materials, Activity 14-5
Typical solution on page 211

Carpet Fibers and Construction, Activity 14-6

1.	E	6.	G
2.	B	7.	F
3.	A	8.	I
4.	D	9.	J
5.	C	10.	H

Resilient Floor Coverings, Activity 14-7
1. durable and moisture resistant; may be damaged by grease; does not recover well from indentation; good for concrete floors below grade; least expensive of all permanent, smooth floor coverings; slippery when wet; and moderately hard
2. luxury floor covering, for light traffic areas, quiet and comfortable, damages easily, not resistant to grease or stains, requires careful wax maintenance, and moderately expensive
3. quiet and comfortable, very resilient, good resistance to denting and staining, requires moderate maintenance, but more commonly used commercially
4. made of solid vinyl; resists damage from alcohol, petroleum products, ammonia, bleaches, household cleaners, stains, and grease; very durable; suitable for high traffic areas; often has no-wax finish for easy care; and moderately expensive
5. very durable, has a clear urethane coating that provides high shine without waxing, resists scuffs, can be cleaned with a damp mop, and is the most popular resilient floor covering material today
6. made by sealing cork under a clear plastic covering, more resistant than cork to dents and dirt, easy to maintain, not strong enough for heavy traffic areas, but may be used at any grade level

Instructor's Resources

Chapter 14 Mastery Test

1. B   8. D
2. A   9. B
3. C   10. A
4. D   11. B
5. B   12. D
6. C   13. B
7. C

14. concrete
15. foundation
16. 16
17. slabs
18. utilities
19. strip
20. planks
21. bathroom
22. blue-gray
23. ¼
24. marble
25. nylon
26. asphalt
27. light (or neutral)
28. support a home's furnishings and occupants and provide decoration, supply space for movement within the structure
29. platform framing: floor is placed on sill connected to top of wall below it, floor acts as platform, and walls above floor are constructed separately and placed on platform
    balloon framing: wall is continuous from sill to top of wall and floor joists are attached to studs
30. by using beams, bearing walls, or engineered-wood floor trusses for extra support
31. by nailing and gluing ¾ in. tongue-and-groove plywood to joists or trusses
32. materials used as the wearing surface of a floor that are structurally part of the floor and usually are more permanent than floor coverings
33. (List four:) wood, ceramic tile, concrete, masonry, terrazzo
34. length, general appearance, and number of imperfections
35. unit, laminated, and slat blocks
36. paver and quarry tile
37. (List three): high resistance to abrasion; suitable for indoor and outdoor floors; may be designed with various patterns, textures, and colors; may be waxed for a polished look indoors
38. soft coverings and resilient coverings
39. when it leaves a 3 to 12 in. border of the floor exposed
40. Resilient floor coverings are smooth, hard materials that return to their original shape.
41. ceramic tile and resilient floor covering

Wood-Floor Construction
Activity 14-1

Solution

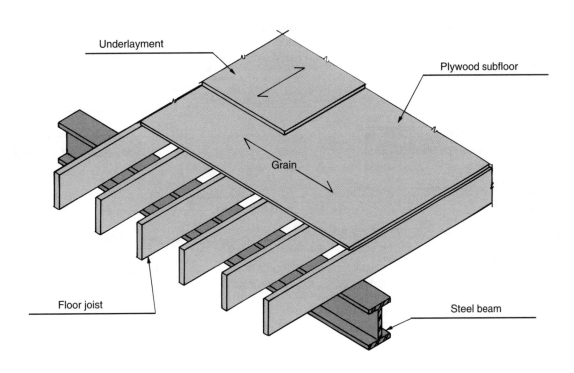

Underlayment

Plywood subfloor

Grain

Floor joist

Steel beam

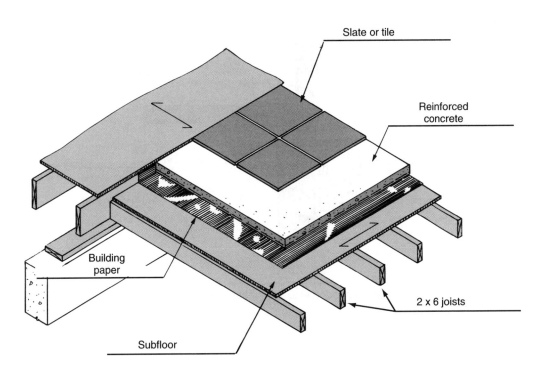

Slate or tile

Reinforced concrete

Building paper

2 x 6 joists

Subfloor

Concrete-Floor Construction
Activity 14-2

Solution

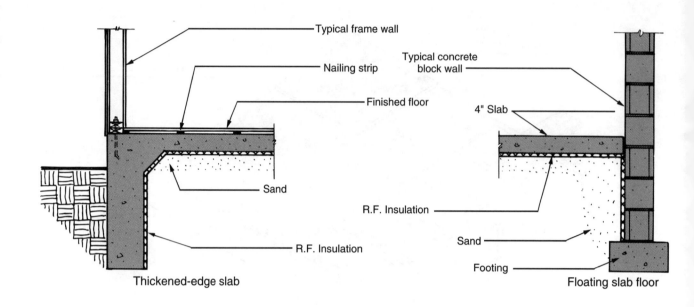

Typical frame wall

Nailing strip

Finished floor

Typical concrete block wall

4" Slab

Sand

R.F. Insulation

Sand

R.F. Insulation

Footing

Thickened-edge slab

Floating slab floor

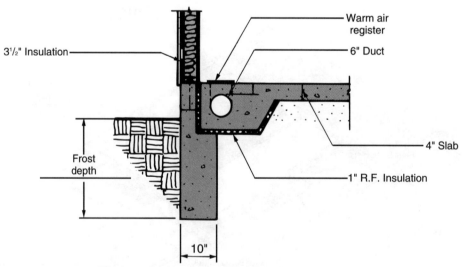

3½" Insulation

Warm air register

6" Duct

Frost depth

4" Slab

1" R.F. Insulation

10"

Thickened-edge slab with heating duct

Wood Flooring Materials
Activity 14-3

Solution

Wood Flooring Materials

Strip Flooring	Wood Planks	Wood Blocks
Width: $1^1/_2$" Thickness: $^3/_8$", $^1/_2$", $^3/_4$"	Width: 3", 5", 7" Thickness: $^3/_8$", $^1/_2$"	Unit Blocks Size: 6, 8, 9, or 12" sq. Thickness: $^3/_4$"
Width: $2^1/_2$" Thickness: $^3/_8$", $^1/_2$", $^3/_4$"	Width: 4" Thickness: $^{25}/_{32}$", $^{33}/_{32}$"	Laminated Blocks Size: 6, 8, 9, or 12" sq. Thickness: $^5/_{16}$", $^1/_2$"
Width: $3^1/_4$" Thickness: $^3/_8$", $^1/_2$", $^3/_4$"	Width: 3", 4", 6" Thickness: $^3/_8$", $^3/_4$"	Slat Blocks Width: $^3/_4$" to 3" Length: 4" to 7"
	Width: $2^1/_4$", $3^1/_4$" Thickness: $^3/_4$"	Thickness: $^3/_8$", $^3/_4$"

Wood-Floor Patterns
Activity 14-4

Typical Solution

Flooring Materials
Activity 14-5

Typical Solution

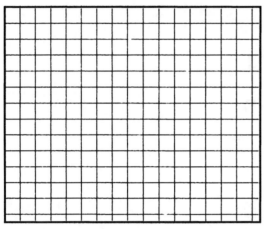

1. 2" x 2" ceramic mosaic tile

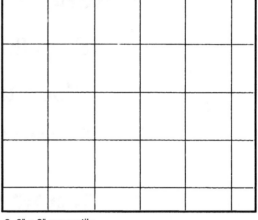

2. 6" x 6" quarry tile

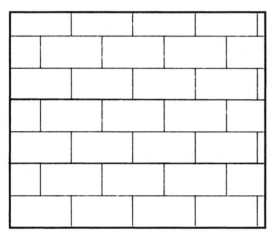

3. 4" x 6" brick pavers

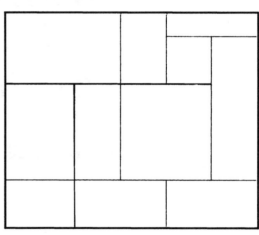

4. Random rectangle slate

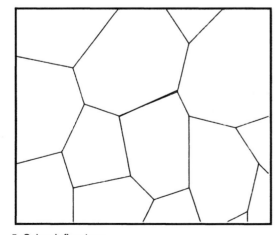

5. Cobweb flagstone

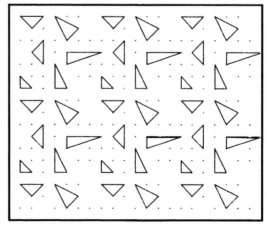

6. Terrazzo

Scale: 1" = 1'-0"

Types of Flooring Materials

Wood

Strip flooring

Wood planks

Parquet

Ceramic tile

Glazed

Ceramic mosaic

Quarry and paver

Concrete and masonry

Concrete (poured cement)

Brick

Slate

Flagstone

Terrazzo

Suitable Locations for Wood Flooring

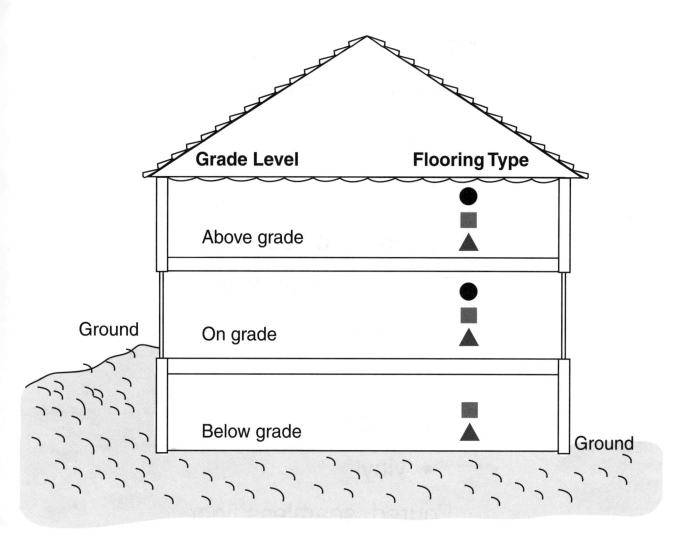

● Solid Wood (wood pieces, regardless of length or width)

■ Engineered floor (layers of wood pressed together)

▲ Floating floor with underlying fasteners

Source: National Wood Flooring Association

Types of Floor Coverings

Soft floor coverings

Wall-to-wall carpet

Room-size carpet

Area rug

Resilient floor covering

Tiles and sheet flooring

- asphalt

- cork

- rubber

- vinyl

Poured, seamless floor

Cleaning Carpet Stains

1.   **Act quickly.** Stains can become permanent.

2.   **Blot liquids.** Use a dry, white, absorbent cloth or a plain white paper towel.

3.   **Avoid scrubbing.** Scrubbing can distort the pile. Scrape up or vacuum solids. Continue blotting till dry.

> If you know the cause of the stain, check a spot-removal guide and follow its directions carefully. If not, use a commercial spot-removal agent.

4.   **Pretest the spot remover.** Find an inconspicuous area of the rug, apply several drops, and press a white cloth to the test area for 10 seconds. Examine the carpet for color change or other carpet damage. If damage occurs, try another agent. If no damage occurs, proceed to the next steps.

5.   **Apply remover to a white cloth.** Use a small amount and wait 10 minutes. Then gently work the agent into the stain.

6.   **Work in from the edges.** Blot the stained area, working toward the center to prevent spreading the stain. Avoid scrubbing. Blot the area, absorbing as much of the agent as possible.

7.   **Be patient.** If any color transfers to the white cloth, the spot remover is working. Repeat steps, several times if needed. If no color is removed from the carpet, try another agent.

8.   **Rinse thoroughly with cold water** after the stain is gone. Blot with a dry cloth until completely dry. Some cleaning solutions cause rapid soiling unless completely removed.

Source: Carpet and Rug Institute

Choosing Floor Treatments

Name _____

Date _____

Study the floor plan and determine what floor treatments you would recommend for various rooms and areas indoors as well as all outdoor areas shown. Use a different color for each type of floor treatment chosen and color the floor plan accordingly. Make a color key at the bottom of the page that identifies the various floor treatments used.

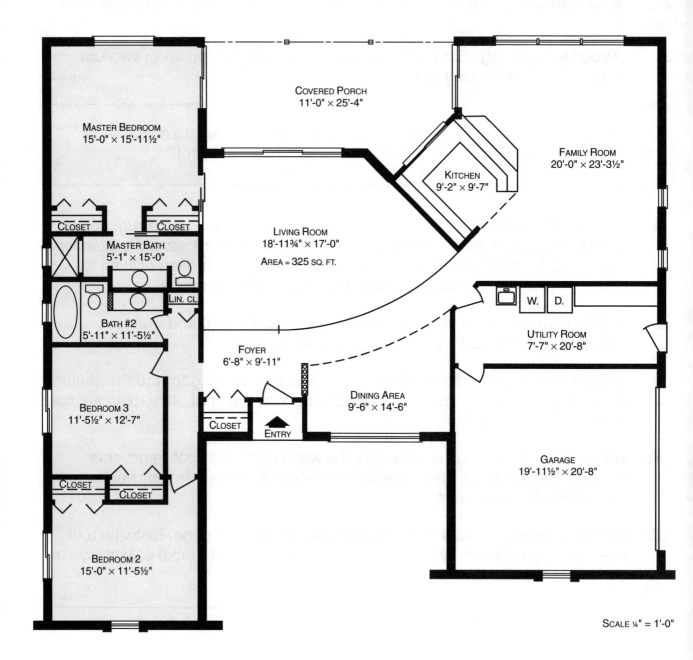

Floors
Chapter 14
Mastery Test

Name _____

Date _____

Score _____

Multiple Choice: Select the best response and write the letter in the preceding blank.

_____ 1. The two types of floor framing used in residential construction are _____.
A. platform and solid-floor framing
B. platform and balloon framing
C. balloon and solid-floor framing
D. balloon and built-up floor framing

_____ 2. The function of the sill plate in wood-floor construction is to _____.
A. form the connection between the foundation wall and the floor
B. level the foundation wall
C. reduce air infiltration between the joists
D. level the structure

_____ 3. A span of 15 ft. supporting a live load of 40 lbs./ft.^{2} needs floor joists that have a _____ in. size and are spaced 16 in. apart.
A. 2 by 4
B. 2 by 6
C. 2 by 10
D. 2 by 12

_____ 4. The typical spacing of 12 in. engineered-wood floor trusses is _____ in. apart.
A. 12
B. 16
C. 18
D. 24

_____ 5. The accurate description of a thickened-edge slab is _____.
A. a slab separate from the foundation wall
B. a slab and foundation combined into a single unit
C. a slab supported only by the soil below
D. a slab used only for garages

_____ 6. Of the following species of hardwoods, _____ are commonly used for wood flooring.
A. oak, birch, and red cedar
B. oak, hemlock, and beech
C. oak, beech, and hard maple
D. larch, hemlock, and southern pine

_____ 7. Ceramic tile is a popular flooring material because it _____.
A. is cool to the touch
B. requires little maintenance and is inexpensive to install
C. lasts indefinitely and requires little maintenance
D. is quick to install and is economical

_____ 8. The grout used to fill the joints between ceramic tiles is _____.
A. cementitious
B. resinous
C. a combination of cementitious and resinous
D. All of the above.

_____ 9. The basic difference between special pavers and regular brick is pavers are _____.
A. larger than brick
B. thinner than brick
C. less expensive than brick
D. identical to brick

(continued)

Name _____

_____ 10. About 90 percent of the carpets and rugs produced today are made of the following
synthetic fibers: _____.
A. nylon, acrylic, polyester, and olefin
B. polyester, olefin, wool, and nylon
C. nylon, acrylic, cotton, jute
D. acrylic, acetate, polyester, and lastrile

_____ 11. The key factor in determining the quality of a carpet is the _____.
A. length of the pile
B. density of the pile
C. texture of the pile
D. backing of the carpet

_____ 12. Vinyl tile is one of the most popular resilient floor coverings for residential use because it
_____.
A. often has an easy-care, no-wax finish
B. resists damage from alcohol, petroleum products, ammonia, bleaches, household
cleaners, stains, and grease
C. is very durable and attractive in most traffic areas of the home
D. All of the above.

_____ 13. The type of carpeting that camouflages dirt best is a _____.
A. light brown velvet plush
B. tweed carpet
C. light gray saxony plush
D. flocked carpet

Completion: Complete the following sentences by writing the missing words in the preceding blanks.

_____ 14. Floor systems for housing structures are classified as wood or _____
floors.

_____ 15. All floor systems are supported by a _____ wall that may also be a
basement wall.

_____ 16. Floor joists are spaced 12, 16, or 24 in., but _____ in. is the most common
spacing.

_____ 17. The use of concrete _____ for floors in homes and garages is common
throughout the United States.

_____ 18. A major disadvantage of concrete-floor systems is that _____ are
inaccessible.

_____ 19. The three main types of wood flooring used in housing structures are
_____ flooring, planks, and parquet.

_____ 20. Floor boards wider than 3¼ in. are called _____.

_____ 21. Glazed tile is especially popular for _____ floors.

_____ 22. Slate frequently has a _____-_____ color, but it is also available in
green, red, brown, or black.

_____ 23. A thin mortar joint of _____ in. is best with slate and should be consistent
throughout the floor area.

_____ 24. Modern terrazzo generally combines _____ chips with a Portland cement
binder.

_____ 25. Unless an antistatic finish is applied, _____ carpet fiber conducts static
electricity.

(continued)

Name _____

_____ 26. The least expensive of all permanent, smooth, floor coverings is _____ tile.

_____ 27. Floor treatments with simple patterns and _____ colors are most appropriate for rooms with dominant furnishings or accessories.

Short Answer: Provide brief answers to the following questions or statements.

28. Identify three functions floors perform in a home. _____

_____

_____

_____

29. How does platform framing differ from balloon framing? _____

_____

_____

_____

_____

30. If the span required for a floor is greater than the joists can support, how can the floor be supported?

_____

_____

_____

31. In modern residential construction, the subfloor and underlayment are combined into a single thickness to save labor costs. How is this accomplished? _____

_____

32. Floor treatments are categorized as flooring materials and floor coverings. What is meant by flooring materials? _____

_____

_____

33. List four flooring materials commonly used in residential housing. _____

_____

_____

_____

_____

34. The grading of wood flooring boards is based on what three criteria? _____

_____

_____

_____

(continued)

Name _____

35. Wood-block flooring, more commonly called parquet, is produced in what three types? _____

_____

_____

_____

36. What types of ceramic tile are designed for high-traffic areas and are frostproof for outdoor use?

_____

37. List three advantages of using concrete and masonry floors. _____

_____

_____

_____

38. What are the two main types of floor coverings used in residential housing? _____

_____

_____

39. When is a rug considered room size? _____

_____

40. What distinguishes resilient floor coverings from soft floor coverings? _____

_____

41. What two types of floor treatments are most functional for high-traffic areas where dirt and moisture are prevalent? _____

_____

_____

Chapter 15
Ceilings and Roofs

Objectives

After studying this chapter, students will be able to

- describe the construction methods and materials used to build a roof.
- evaluate ceiling-surface materials according to their ease of placement, cost, and treatment requirements.
- explain how a roof is constructed and identify its major parts.
- identify common roof styles.
- list and describe various types of roofing materials.

Teaching Materials

Text, pages 274–287

Student Activity Guide

Check Your Understanding
15-1, *Ceiling Types*
15-2, *Ceiling Treatments*
15-3, *Roofs*
15-4, *Roofing Materials*

Instructor's Resources

Painting Guidelines for Ceilings, reproducible master 15-A

Cost of Roofing Materials, reproducible master 15-B

Chapter 15 Mastery Test

Instructional Concepts and Student Activities

1. Have students read Chapter 15 in the text and complete the review questions.
2. Ask students to clip illustrations, pictures, and articles from magazines or sales literature about roof construction, materials, and ceiling treatments. Have them add this material to their housing notebooks for future reference.

Ceilings

3. Lead a class discussion on ceiling construction and the function of ceilings.
4. Involve the class in a discussion about various ceiling-surface materials such as gypsum board, plaster, wood boards, and suspended-ceiling materials.
5. *Ceiling Types*, Activity 15-1, SAG. Students are to identify the primary qualities and considerations involved with four common types of ceiling surfaces.
6. Explain why paint and ceiling tiles are the most common types of ceiling treatments.
7. *Painting Guidelines for Ceilings*, reproducible master 15-A, IR. Use the master as a hand-out to acquaint students with procedures for painting ceilings.
8. Show the *Ceilings* video from Hobar Publications and have the class discuss it.
9. *Ceiling Treatments*, Activity 15-2, SAG. Students are to plan the ceiling treatment for a specific family room and calculate the cost of materials required.

Roofs

10. Lead a class discussion on roof construction, roof styles, and roofing materials based on the illustrations in the text.
11. *Roofs*, Activity 15-3, SAG. Students are to match common roof styles with their descriptions.
12. Ask students to bring in photos or pictures of dwellings that display various roof styles. Then have the class discuss them.
13. *Roofing Materials*, Activity 15-4, SAG. Students are to describe four specific roofing materials.
14. *Cost of Roofing Materials*, reproducible master 15-B, IR. Have students compare the costs of various roofing materials. Note that average prices do not take into account the costs involved in reinforcing structures for unusually heavy loads.
15. Assign one or more tasks listed in the text's *Suggested Activities* section at the end of the chapter.

Suggested Evaluation Techniques

16. *Check Your Understanding*, SAG. Have students complete as many questions as possible without referring to the text. Then have them find answers to questions they do not know.
17. Administer the *Chapter 15 Mastery Test*.

Answer Key

Text

Review Questions, page 286

1. Ceiling joists are lighter than floor joists, but their construction and spacing are generally the same.
2. gypsum board, plaster
3. A hanging metal framework forms a grid that supports the ceiling panels.
4. kitchens, bathrooms, basements
5. paint
6. by joining the rafters of two sections of roof to a ridge board
7. by finding the ratio between the rise and the run of the roof
8. around chimneys, at valleys, and where the roof intersects a wall
9. gable
10. Flat and shed roofs use layers of roofing felt and tar covered with gravel, while other roofs use traditional roofing materials.
11. asphalt roofing, copper

Student Activity Guide

Check Your Understanding, pages 133–135

1. lower construction costs and heating costs
2. Ceiling joists are lighter because they do not support much weight.
3. Translucent panels with fluorescent lighting above can be used to provide ample lighting.
4. (List two:) sound absorption, softened light reflection, coverage of cracks or imperfections, surface interest
5. acoustical ceiling tiles
6. open cornice
7. (List four:) particleboard, waferboard, oriented strand board, shiplap, plywood composite
8. a wide metal strip of galvanized sheet metal, aluminum, or copper; to prevent the roof from leaking
9. They prevent water from running directly off the eaves, splashing onto the house, and settling around the foundation.

10. to allow air circulation in the attic and prevent moisture from forming on the underside of the sheathing, on the underside of the roof overhang or extended through the roof
11. With a flat roof, there is a buildup of roofing-felt layers and tar, which are covered with gravel. Other roofs use traditional roofing materials such as asphalt roofing, wood shingles and shakes, tile, slate, concrete materials, and metal.
12. Heavy materials, such as tile and slate, require special roof construction to support the weight.
13. cathedral
14. gypsum
15. lath
16. scratch
17. brown
18. paint
19. rafters
20. ridge
21. valley
22. rise
23. run
24. span
25. cornice
26. soffit
27. gable
28. gambrel
29. roll

Ceiling Types, Activity 15-1

1. most common ceiling material, less expensive than plaster, can be installed quicker than plaster, can be finished with several types of treatments, is fire resistant, is attached with nails and adhesive, and provides a smooth surface
2. a traditional ceiling material, durable, economical, fire resistant, structurally rigid, good sound insulator, can be applied to curved surfaces and molded into shapes, requires a lath base for attachment, and is often painted
3. available as boards or sheet products, is often prefinished, can be nailed directly to joists or trusses, durable, and needs little maintenance
4. popular for kitchens, baths, and basements; requires a metal grid suspended from joists or trusses by wires to support ceiling panels; and is available in a wide variety of styles

Ceiling Treatments, Activity 15-2

total area of ceiling = 295.625 sq. ft.
(Remaining answers are student response.)

Roofs, Activity 15-3

1. gable
2. Dutch hip

3. gambrel
4. flat
5. Mansard
6. shed
7. hip
8. B
9. F
10. E
11. C
12. A
13. G
14. D

Roofing Materials, Activity 15-4

1. lasts about 20 years and is available in saturated felts for built-up roofs, shingles, and roll roofing
2. resist decay and may last as long as 50 years; more fire resistant than older wood roofing products; commonly made of redwood, cypress, and western red cedar; and are more expensive than asphalt materials
3. expensive, can enhance the architectural style of a home, heavy, require special roof construction to support the weight, and are durable enough to last the life of the structure
4. is the most durable roofing material used, very expensive, seldom covers an entire roof, and copper is the most popular

Instructor's Resources

Chapter 15 Mastery Test

1. B
2. C
3. D
4. C
5. A
6. C
7. B
8. A
9. D
10. C

11. roof trusses
12. 24
13. lath
14. wires
15. luminous
16. textured
17. ridge
18. slope
19. drip edge
20. copper
21. defines the height of a room, provides support for lighting fixtures, and adds to the decoration of a room or area
22. gypsum board (drywall), plaster, wood boards, and suspended ceiling materials
23. is structurally rigid, a good sound insulator, and can be applied to curved walls and molded into shapes
24. kitchens, bathrooms, basements; because they need ample light, which is best provided by fluorescent lighting above translucent ceiling panels to form a luminous ceiling
25. enamel or semi-gloss paint
26. to cover cracks or other imperfections, absorb sound, soften light reflection, or add interest
27. The rafters of open cornices are exposed, while the rafters of boxed cornices are enclosed by soffit board.
28. particleboard, waferboard, oriented strand board, plywood composite, and shiplap; to make the roof stronger and more rigid and serve as a base for nailing the roof-covering material
29. to prevent moisture from forming on the underside of the sheathing
30. (List five:) gable, gambrel, shed, hip, flat, Mansard, Dutch hip

Painting Guidelines for Ceilings

1. **Prepare the surface.** Remove peeled or blistered spots and lightly sand their edges. Wash ceilings that show dirt or stains, such as in kitchens. Let the ceiling dry completely and prime any new or patched areas.

2. **Use quality applicators.** Inexpensive brushes do not spread paint evenly, leaving unsightly marks. Cheap roller covers often leave fuzz on the painted surface. Roller covers range in thickness from thin pile (for painting flat surfaces) to deep pile (for getting paint into the crevices of highly textured surfaces).

3. **Work from top to bottom**. Do the ceiling first, followed by walls, trimwork, cabinets, and finally doors. Use a drop cloth to catch drips.

4. **Prepare the paint.** Always follow label directions. Recently purchased paint is ready for use if it was mixed ("machine shaken") at the store. Paint must be stirred smooth if left unused since solids can settle, and this can take considerable time when done by hand. If using more than one can of the same color, mix them to ensure a uniform color.

5. **Paint the ceiling's perimeter first.** Use a brush to carefully paint a few inches all along the edge of the ceiling. This helps prevent accidental paint streaks on walls later.

6. **Use a roller in the "N" technique.** Load the roller with paint and apply it in an N-shape on a 3 by 3 ft. area. To even the paint across the area, use long back-and-forth strokes. Finally, smooth the painted area with long, light, straight strokes. Continue across the ceiling, working from a dry area into an adjoining wet area.

7. **Keep working so adjacent areas do not dry.** Try to keep painting until the ceiling is done. Applying paint next to an area where fresh paint has dried causes lap lines. (Glossier paints have a tendency to show lap lines.) If the ceiling is very large, plan your break so the lap lines that may result will be in a less conspicuous place.

8. **Do not leave brushes and rollers sitting in paint or exposed to the air.** When taking a break, wrap them tightly in a plastic bag or foil. Cover open containers and paint trays with damp cloths.

9. **Clean up after each use.** Clean and store brushes and rollers according to label directions. Clean paint trays and tightly seal cans.

10. **Let the ceiling thoroughly dry.** Avoid touching, wiping, or wetting a newly painted surface for 30 days to allow paint to cure.

Cost of Roofing Materials

Estimates are per 100 sq. ft. and do not include the costs of reinforcing structures for unusually heavy loads.

	Materials	Installation
Asphalt shingles	$25-30	$36
Wood shakes or shingles	$100-165	$75
Clay tile	$300	$140
Slate	$550	$134
Slate composite	$275	$75
Steel	$250-275	$105

Source: Better Homes and Gardens, 2004

Ceilings and Roofs
Chapter 15
Mastery Test

Name _____

Date _____

Score _____

Multiple Choice: Select the best response and write the letter in the preceding blank.

_____ 1. Today, the standard ceiling height in first and second floor areas of typical residences is _____ ft.
A. 7
B. 8
C. 9
D. 12 to 14

_____ 2. A key property of gypsum board, the ceiling-surface material, is its _____.
A. installation ease because of light weight
B. low cost compared to other ceiling surface materials
C. ability to be finished with several types of treatments
D. ability to hide loose nails or shrinkage cracks

_____ 3. A common lath used with gypsum plaster is _____.
A. perforated gypsum
B. insulating fireboard
C. expanded metal
D. All of the above.

_____ 4. The most common size for ceiling panels used with suspended ceilings is _____.
A. 1 by 1 or 2 by 2 ft.
B. 1 by 2 or 2 by 4 ft.
C. 2 by 2 or 2 by 4 ft.
D. 2 by 2 or 4 by 4 in.

_____ 5. White and light paint colors make a ceiling appear _____.
A. higher
B. lower
C. active
D. None of the above.

_____ 6. A size of _____ in. is most common for ceiling tiles.
A. 6 by 6
B. 9 by 9
C. 12 by 12
D. 16 by 16

_____ 7. The type of ceiling tile generally used to contain sound in noisy areas such as recreation rooms and music rooms is _____ tile.
A. gypsum cement
B. acoustical
C. vinyl coated
D. rigid foam

_____ 8. The overhanging area of the roof is called the _____.
A. cornice
B. soffit
C. rake
D. gable

_____ 9. Flashing is generally used on a roof _____.
A. around chimneys
B. at valleys
C. where the roof intersects the wall
D. All of the above.

(continued)

Name _____

_____ 10. The most common roofing material for residential structures is _____.
    A. roll roofing
    B. tile and slate
    C. asphalt shingles
    D. wood shingles and shakes

Completion: Complete the following sentences by writing the missing words in the preceding blanks.

_____ 11. If a ceiling spans a very large distance, a beam or bearing wall may be needed for extra support, or _____ _____ may be used as a ceiling frame.

_____ 12. Ceiling-joist spacing is typically 16 in., but trusses are usually spaced _____ in. apart.

_____ 13. The base material for gypsum plaster is called a _____.

_____ 14. Suspended ceilings use a metal framework designed to support the ceiling panels. The grid is suspended from joists or trusses by _____.

_____ 15. With suspended ceilings, translucent panels can be used to form _____ ceilings.

_____ 16. To add interest to a ceiling, _____ paints can be swirled, stippled, or troweled.

_____ 17. Rafters are arranged to form sections of roof that extend from the top of exterior walls to the _____.

_____ 18. The _____ of the roof represents the ratio between the rise and run of the roof.

_____ 19. A plastic or metal _____ _____ is usually used at the eave line and the rakes to preserve the soffit boards and prevent water from getting under the roofing materials.

_____ 20. The most popular metal used for roofing is _____.

Short Answer: Provide brief answers to the following questions or statements.

21. What are the functions of a ceiling? _____

_____

22. Name four materials commonly used to form the ceiling surface of a residence. _____

_____

_____

_____

_____

23. What qualities does gypsum plaster have that other ceiling surface materials do not?_____

_____

_____

_____

(continued)

Name _____

24. What three areas of the home are popular locations for suspended ceilings? Why? _____

_____

_____

_____

_____

25. What type of ceiling treatment may be used on kitchen and bathroom ceilings to make cleaning easier? _____

_____

26. Why might textured paint be desirable as a ceiling treatment material? _____

_____

_____

27. What makes open cornices different from boxed cornices?_____

_____

_____

_____

28. List five typical roof sheathing materials and explain why sheathing is used. _____

_____

_____

_____

_____

_____

_____

_____

29. Why must roofs be ventilated? _____

_____

_____

_____

30. List five popular roof styles used on residential structures. _____

_____

_____

_____

_____

Chapter 16
Windows and Doors

Objectives

After studying this chapter, students will be able to

- list standard types of windows available for residential use and cite their advantages and disadvantages.
- evaluate the quality of a window's construction in terms of appearance, function, and insulative value.
- select and place windows in a home so optimum lighting, ventilation, privacy, and appearance are achieved.
- list and describe various types of window treatments.
- distinguish among various types of doors by their appearance and method of operation.
- describe the construction of a door.
- list possible treatments for interior and exterior doors.

Teaching Materials

Text, pages 288–313

Student Activity Guide

Check Your Understanding
16-1, *Window Types*
16-2, *Window Sizes*
16-3, *Window Features*
16-4, *Window Placement*
16-5, *Interior Window Treatments*
16-6, *Door Symbols*
16-7, *Door Applications*

Instructor's Resources

Types of Windows and Treatments, transparency master 16-A

Window Decisions, reproducible master 16-B

Selecting Window Treatments, reproducible master 16-C

Types of Doors, transparency master 16-D

Adding Doors to a Floor Plan, reproducible master 16-E

Chapter 16 Mastery Test

Instructional Concepts and Student Activities

1. Have students read Chapter 16 in the text and complete the review questions.
2. Ask students to collect pictures, articles, and technical literature about residential windows and doors. Have them add this material to their housing notebooks.

Windows

3. *Types of Windows and Treatments*, transparency master 16-A, IR. Provide students an overview of the types of windows and window treatments they will cover in the text.
4. Lead a class discussion on window types. Be sure to include sliding windows, swinging windows, fixed windows, combination windows, skylights, and clerestory windows. Show students illustrations of each type of window as it is discussed.
5. *Window Types*, Activity 16-1, SAG. Students are to identify illustrations of basic window types.
6. Have students read window manufacturers' technical literature to find out information about sizes and variations in window construction.
7. *Window Sizes*, Activity 16-2, SAG. Students are to select a window style in a typical housing situation and specify common rough-opening sizes.
8. Lead a class discussion on the advantages, disadvantages, maintenance, and cost of window construction. Be sure to include frames made of wood, metal, vinyl, and metal- or vinyl-clad wood in the discussion.
9. *Window Features*, Activity, 16-3, SAG. Students are to describe features, materials, or considerations that would interest a housing designer regarding common types of windows.
10. Involve the class in a discussion of window selection and placement. Using a stock floor plan will help focus this discussion on real-life designs.
11. *Window Decisions*, reproducible master 16-B, IR. Students are to incorporate windows in a dining room.

12. *Window Placement*, Activity 16-4, SAG. Students are to redesign the window size and placement in a bedroom to gain better airflow and room use.

Window Treatments

13. Lead a class discussion on the various types of interior window treatments. Be sure to include draperies, cornices, valances, lambrequins, curtains, shades, blinds, and sliding panels and screens. Show students pictures of each type of window treatment as it is discussed.
14. *Interior Window Treatments*, Activity 16-5, SAG. Students are to sketch specific window treatments, using proper proportion and placement.
15. *Selecting Window Treatments*, reproducible master 16-C, IR. Students are to work with six given window styles, determining an appropriate room and window treatment for each.
16. Lead a class discussion on exterior window treatments. Be sure to include awnings, shutters, trellises, and grilles.
17. Have students bring pictures of exterior window treatments to class for discussion and comparison.

Doors

18. *Types of Doors*, transparency master 16-D, IR. Provide students an overview of the types of windows and window treatments they will cover in the text.
19. Explain the differences and similarities among various types of residential doors, such as flush, panel, swinging, sliding, folding, and garage doors.
20. *Door Symbols*, Activity 16-6, SAG. Students are to draw the proper plan view symbol for specified residential door types.
21. Involve the class in a discussion on door construction. Define and explain terms, such as door jamb, rough opening, threshold, and lockset.
22. *Adding Doors to a Floor Plan*, reproducible master 16-E, IR. Students are to determine appropriate doors for a given floor plan, sketch the correct symbols on the plan, and label them.
23. *Door Applications*, Activity 16-7, SAG. Students are to sketch symbols of specific types of doors on a given floor plan.
24. Assign one or more tasks listed in the text's *Suggested Activities* section at the end of the chapter.

Suggested Evaluation Techniques

25. *Check Your Understanding*, SAG. Have students complete as many questions as possible without referring to the text. Then have them find answers to questions they do not know.
26. Administer the *Chapter 16 Mastery Test*.

Answer Key

Text

Review Questions, page 312

1. provide natural light and ventilation, contribute to the atmosphere of a room, and add details to the decorative scheme
2. give balance and design
3. (Student response. See pages 288-292.)
4. hopper windows with fixed windows, fixed glass with casements on both sides, bay windows, and bow windows
   uses: for obtaining an unobstructed view plus ventilation
5. wood-frame advantages: good insulator, attractive, and blends well with most interiors
   wood-frame disadvantages: expands and contracts with temperature and moisture changes, and needs protective coating that must be maintained
   metal-frame advantages: less expensive than wood, needs less maintenance, thinner and lighter than wood frames
   metal-frame disadvantages: poor insulator and prone to condensation formation
6. Add another pane to a single-pane or double-pane window to produce insulating glass. Apply reflective coating to the glass.
7. Draperies are pleated panels that can be drawn across the glass area or placed at one or both sides. Curtains are lighter, less formal, and generally opened by hand.
8. to prevent fading, protect against sun deterioration, reduce any incoming dust or drafts, provide extra insulation, add fullness to the drapery, and provide a uniform appearance to the building's exterior
9. for blocked sunlight: opaque draperies, shades, blinds, sliding panels, and screens; for filtered sunlight: sheer draperies, curtains, lightweight shades, blinds, and shutters
10. to increase security and protect windows during bad weather
11. awnings, shutters, trellises, and grilles

12. Flush doors are hollow or solid core covered by a flat, plain veneer. Stile-and-rail doors have a heavier frame around the perimeter with glass or wood panels inserted.
13. Interior doors are usually thinner, smaller, lighter in weight, and have a hollow-core, while exterior doors are thicker, larger, heavier, and have a solid core.
14. a type of sliding door because no clearance space is needed to open it
15. wallpaper, paint, and fabric

Student Activity Guide

Check Your Understanding, pages 141–143

1.	D	7.	A
2.	C	8.	C
3.	A	9.	B
4.	B	10.	A
5.	C	11.	C
6.	A	12.	B

13. sash
14. hopper
15. bow
16. clerestory
17. 20
18. 10
19. cornices
20. lambrequin
21. Roman
22. awning
23. flush
24. rails
25. louver
26. Dutch
27. accordion
28. 16
29. jamb
30. advantages: great ventilators, can be opened easily, and screens and storm sashes are easily installed
disadvantages: project outward and may interfere with outside activities, collect dirt easily, do not keep out rain when opened, and vertical lines may be distracting
31. wood window frame
32. A. single glazing
B. welded-edge insulating glass
33. one large window
34. 2 in. Venetian blinds, 1 in. miniblinds, and ½ in. microblinds

35. solid-core doors: made of solid particleboard or tightly fitted wood blocks covered with a veneer, heavy and strong, good insulators, expensive, and used on exteriors
hollow-core doors: framework made of wood and covered with wood, metal, or vinyl veneer; lightweight; relatively inexpensive; low strength and insulation value; and used indoors

Window Types, Activity 16-1

1. bow
2. bay
3. trapezoid
4. awning
5. hopper
6. picture
7. casement
8. horizontal sliding
9. combination
10. double-hung

Window Features, Activity 16-3

1. good insulator; attractive and blends well with most interiors; expands and contracts with different moisture conditions, causing gaps and stickiness; needs protective coating; and requires considerable maintenance
2. less expensive than wood; requires less maintenance; lighter, thinner frame than is possible with wood; not a good insulator; and may have condensation form on the inside
3. increased cost, reduces maintenance on the exterior, and maintains advantages of wood frame windows
4. more expensive than wood alone, reduces maintenance on the exterior, maintains advantages of wood frame windows
5. similar to metal frames, but better insulators than metal
6. poor insulator, but insulation value can be doubled by adding a storm window
7. has two or three panes of glass with a sealed space between, greatly reduces heat loss or gain, and is expensive
8. reduces heat gain or loss and may be transparent or tinted

Window Placement, Activity 16-4

Typical solution on page 229

Interior Window Treatments, Activity 16-5

Typical solution on page 230

Door Symbols, **Activity 16-6**

Solution on page 231

Door Applications, **Activity 16-7**

Typical solution on page 232

Instructor's Resources

Chapter 16 Mastery Test

1. D   7. B
2. B   8. D
3. C   9. D
4. B   10. C
5. A   11. B
6. D

12. friction
13. casement
14. awning
15. fixed
16. double-hung
17. muntins
18. aluminum
19. textured
20. cafe
21. interior
22. main entry
23. provide natural light, ventilation, and privacy; contribute to the atmosphere of a room; add detail to a decorative scheme; and give balance and design to the exterior of a structure
24. (List three:) swinging, fixed, sliding, combination, overhead
25. consist of a series of narrow glass slats that are held by a metal frame and operate in unison, similar to Venetian blinds
26. to admit light into areas of the structure that have little or no natural light
27. to serve as an insulator; dry gases
28. to reduce heat loss or gain
29. by individually controlling each tier in tier draperies
30. need a series of tracks at top and bottom of screen and space beside the door or window to open them fully
31. enhanced exterior appearance of a house, no interference with interior wall space or furniture
32. are made of slats that would admit outdoor air
33. overhead sectional and one-piece overhead
34. as architectural design elements
35. Accordion pleated shades have a single layer of fabric folded into thin, horizontal pleats, while honeycomb shades have smaller pleats, heavier fabric, and two pleated shades bonded together to form a cross-section with a series of airspaces resembling a honeycomb.

Window Placement
Activity 16-4

Typical Solution

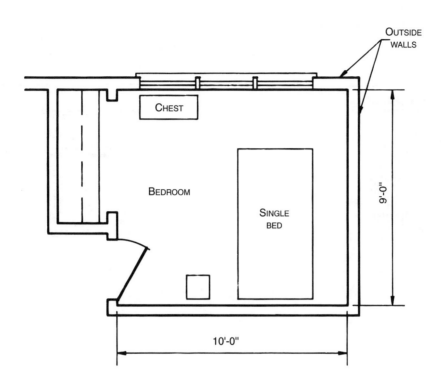

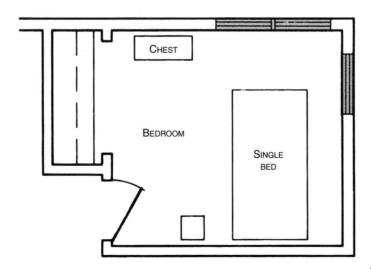

Scale: $^{1}/_{4}$" = 1'-0"

Interior Window Treatments
Activity 16-5

Typical Solution

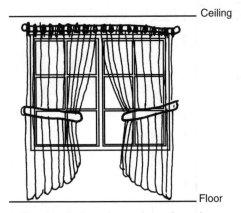

1. Floor length draperies on decorative rod

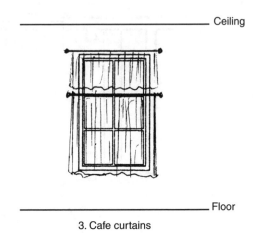

3. Cafe curtains

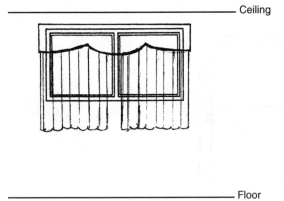

2. Draperies with a cornice or valance

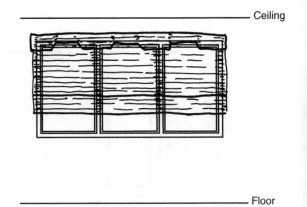

4. Roman Shades

Door Symbols
Activity 16-6

Solution

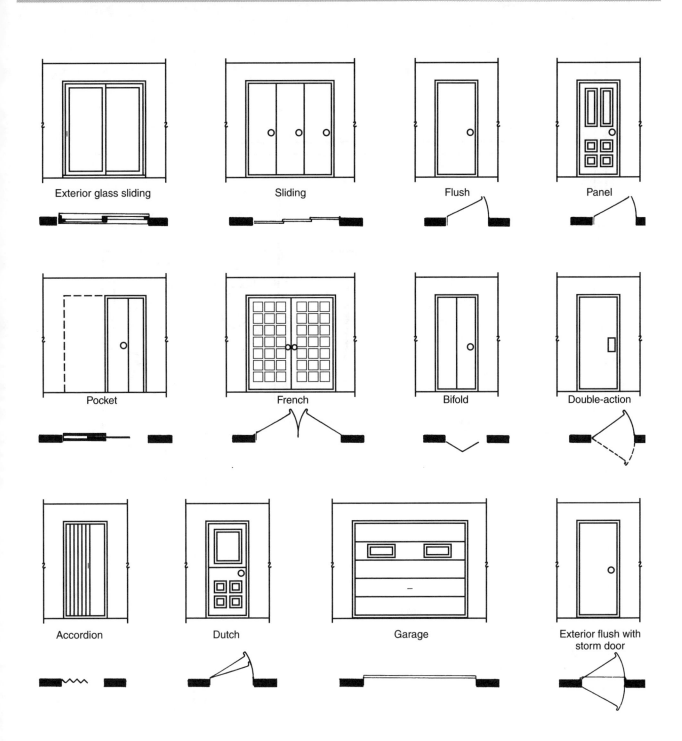

Exterior glass sliding

Sliding

Flush

Panel

Pocket

French

Bifold

Double-action

Accordion

Dutch

Garage

Exterior flush with
storm door

Door Applications
Activity 16-7

Typical Solution

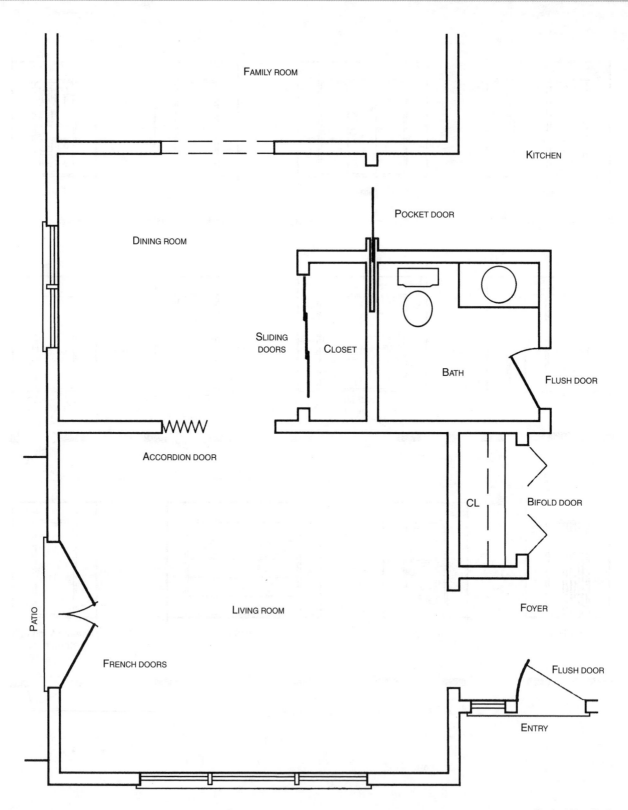

FAMILY ROOM

KITCHEN

POCKET DOOR

DINING ROOM

SLIDING DOORS

CLOSET

BATH

FLUSH DOOR

ACCORDION DOOR

CL

BIFOLD DOOR

PATIO

LIVING ROOM

FOYER

FRENCH DOORS

FLUSH DOOR

ENTRY

Scale: ¼" = 1'-0"

Types of Windows and Treatments

Windows

Sliding

Swinging

Fixed and special-shaped

Combination

Skylights and clerestory

Interior Window Treatments

Draperies

Curtains

Shades

Blinds

Shutters

Sliding panels and screens

Others

Exterior Window Treatments

Awnings

Shutters

Trellises

Grilles

Window
Decisions

Name _____

Date _____

Examine the dining room plan and determine what type and size of windows to place along one or both exterior walls. Explain your decisions below. Use a colored pen to mark the size and location of your window(s), using *¼ in. = 1 ft.* as your guide.

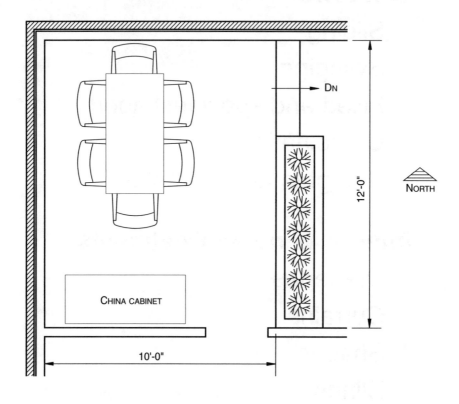

Indicate type, number, and number of window(s) selected: _____

_____

_____

_____

_____

Summarize the factors that influenced your decision: _____

_____

_____

_____

Describe the overall effect that the new window(s) will achieve: _____

_____

_____

_____

Selecting Window Treatments

Name _____

Date _____

Select one window style shown here for each of the following rooms: the kitchen, dining room, bathroom, child's bedroom, master bedroom, family room, or living room. Sketch compatible treatments for the windows using the principles covered in your text. Summarize the suggested window treatments.

1. Awning Window

_____Ceiling

_____Floor

Location (room): _____

Suggested window treatment: _____

_____

_____

_____

_____

_____

_____

2. Sliding Window

_____Ceiling

_____Floor

Location (room): _____

Suggested window treatment: _____

_____

_____

_____

_____

_____

_____

3. Picture Window

_____Ceiling

_____Floor

Location (room): _____

Suggested window treatment: _____

_____

_____

_____

_____

_____

_____

(continued)

Name _____

4. Bay Window

_____Ceiling

_____Floor

Location (room): _____

_____

Suggested window treatment: _____

_____

_____

_____

_____

_____

_____

5.   Casement Window

_____Ceiling

_____Floor

Location (room): _____

_____

Suggested window treatment: _____

_____

_____

_____

_____

_____

_____

6. Combination Window

_____Ceiling

_____Floor

Location (room): _____

_____

Suggested window treatment: _____

_____

_____

_____

_____

_____

Types of Doors

Flush

Hollow core

Solid core

Stile-and-Rail

Panel

Louver

Swinging

Single-action

Double-action

Dutch door

Sliding

Bypass

Pocket

Surface-sliding

Folding

Bifold

Accordion

Garage Door

Adding Doors to a Floor Plan

Name _____

Date _____

On the floor plan below, sketch door symbols in appropriate locations for the following types of doors: accordion, bifold, flush, French, pocket, sliding, and garage. Label each sketch. Identify the total number of doors used in your plan.

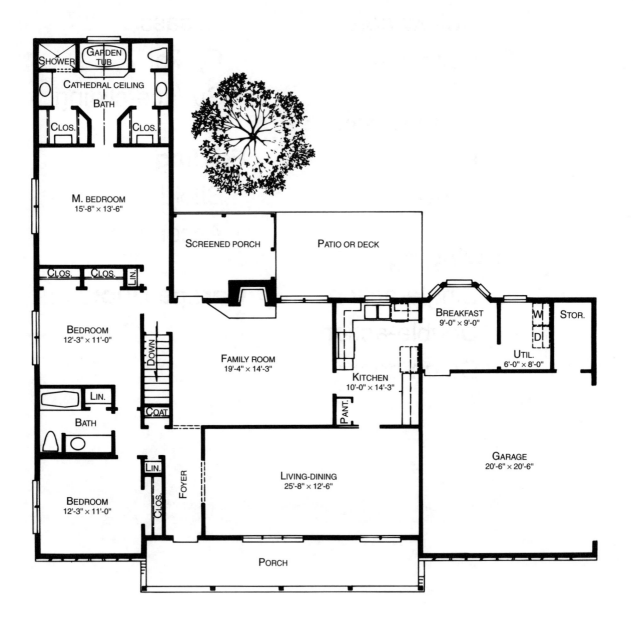

Total number of interior doors: _____

Total number of exterior doors: _____

Windows and Doors
Chapter 16
Mastery Test

Name _____

Date _____

Score _____

Multiple Choice: Select the best response and write the letter in the preceding blank.

_____   1.   Factors to consider when selecting a type of window for a specific application include _____.
A. the architectural style of the structure
B. specific functions to be performed
C. personal taste
D. All of the above.

_____   2.   The type of window that moves on tracks at the bottom and top of the window is _____.
A. double-hung
B. horizontal sliding
C. casement
D. jalousie

_____   3.   The _____ window is the best ventilator.
A. double-hung
B. horizontal sliding
C. casement
D. awning

_____   4.   The type of window most frequently used as a basement window is the _____ window.
A. awning
B. hopper
C. combination
D. clerestory

_____   5.   A window that contains four to seven units and forms an arc extending beyond the outside wall is a _____ window.
A. bow
B. clerestory
C. bay
D. fixed

_____   6.   Of the following types of window glazing, _____ allows the least amount of heat loss.
A. single glazing
B. single glazing with storm glazing
C. metal-edge insulating glass
D. welded-edge insulating glass

_____   7.   The common spacing between two panes of glass in a double-glazed window is _____ in.
A. ⅛ to ¼
B. ¼ to ⅝
C. ½ to ¾
D. ¾ to 1

_____   8.   Before an individual selects a window treatment for a room, he or she should consider _____.
A. the style of living in that room or area
B. whether to make the outdoor view a focal point
C. what direction the window faces
D. All of the above.

(continued)

Name_____

_____ 9. Draperies can be topped with _____.
A. cornices
B. valances
C. lambrequins
D. All of the above.

_____ 10. The size most common for an interior flush or panel door is _____.
A. 1⅜ in. thick, 6 ft. 6 in. high, and 30 in. wide
B. 2¼ in. thick, 6 ft. 8 in. high, and 34 in. wide
C. 1⅜ in. thick, 6 ft. 8 in. high, and 32 in. wide
D. 2¼ in. thick, 6 ft. 8 in. high, and 36 in. wide

_____ 11. The type of door used to close large openings where other types of doors would be impractical is the _____ door.
A. bifold
B. accordion
C. pocket
D. bypass

Completion: Complete the following sentences by writing the missing words in the preceding blanks.

_____ 12. When double-hung windows are moved up or down, each sash is held in place by _____ , springs, or weights.

_____ 13. Common types of swinging windows include _____, awning, hopper, and jalousie windows.

_____ 14. Like casement windows, _____ windows should *not* be located where they might interfere with pedestrian traffic, such as between the house and carport.

_____ 15. The purpose of _____ windows is to admit light and provide a view.

_____ 16. Bay windows generally use two _____-_____ windows with a fixed window in the center.

_____ 17. Window sashes may have dividers called _____ and bars across them to separate the glass into several rectangular panes.

_____ 18. Metal window frames are usually made from _____, although steel, brass, and bronze frames are also made.

_____ 19. _____ window glass increases privacy in bedrooms and bathrooms.

_____ 20. Popular types of curtains include shirred, ruffled, and _____.

_____ 21. Hollow-core flush doors are used almost exclusively as _____ doors.

_____ 22. _____-_____ doors should be attractive on both the inside and the outside.

Short Answer: Provide brief answers to the following questions or statements.

23. What functions do windows serve? _____

_____

_____

_____

_____

(continued)

Name _____

24. List three basic types of windows used in housing construction._____

_____

_____

_____

25. Describe jalousie windows and how they operate._____

_____

_____

_____

26. What is the purpose of skylights? _____

_____

27. What is the function of dead airspace between storm and regular windows? What can be used
    instead of air in insulated glass windows? _____

_____

_____

28. What is the function of reflective coatings on window glass? _____

_____

29. How can the level of natural light in a room with draperies be varied? _____

_____

30. What are the requirements of sliding screens used to cover sliding glass doors and windows?

_____

_____

31. What are the two advantages of exterior window treatments?_____

_____

_____

32. Why are louver doors *not* practical for exterior use? _____

_____

_____

33. What two basic types of doors account for most garage doors used today?_____

_____

34. How are special-shaped windows used? _____

_____

(continued)

Name _____

35. How does a honeycomb shade differ from an accordion pleated shade? _____

_____

_____

_____

_____

_____

Chapter 17
Stairs and Halls

Objectives

After studying this chapter, students will be able to

- describe the seven basic design shapes used for stairways and evaluate their appropriateness for various applications.
- evaluate a stairway in terms of comfort and safety.
- identify stairway requirements for individuals with special needs.
- apply basic design principles to the choice of stairway treatments.
- evaluate a hallway in terms of function, durability, and decoration.

Teaching Materials

Text, pages 314–323

Student Activity Guide

Check Your Understanding
17-1, *Stair Designs*
17-2, *Stair Specifications*
17-3, *Hall Space*

Instructor's Resources

Examining Stair Design, transparency master 17-A
Stair Plan View and Elevation,
    transparency/reproducible master 17-B
Evaluating Hall Space, reproducible master 17-C
Hallway Modification, reproducible master 17-D
Chapter 17 Mastery Test

Instructional Concepts and Student Activities

1. Have students read Chapter 17 in the text and complete the review questions.
2. Ask students to collect pictures and technical information about stairs and hallways. Have them add this material to their housing notebooks.

Stairways

3. Review with the class the basic stairway terms in Figure 17-1 in the text.
4. Explain to students the difference between main and service stairways.
5. Discuss with the class the seven basic stair designs: straight-run, L, double-L, U, winder, spiral, and circular stairs.
6. *Examining Stair Design*, transparency master 17-A, IR. Have students review stair designs based on the number of turns and landings in each.
7. *Stair Designs*, Activity 17-1, SAG. Students are to identify illustrations of common types of stairways.
8. Lead a class discussion on stairway comfort and safety.
9. *Stair Plan View and Elevation*, transparency/reproducible master 17-B, IR. Have students examine a detailed set of straight-run stairs that will connect the first and second floors of a residence. Ask students if sufficient headroom is planned.
10. Invite a local carpenter to speak to the class about the procedure involved in building residential stairs, the materials locally available, and code requirements.
11. *Stair Specifications*, Activity 17-2, SAG. Students are to analyze data from four main stairways in terms of recommended design principles.

Stairway Treatment

12. Lead a class discussion on stairway treatments. Be sure to cover the important considerations regarding decorating, selecting carpeting and padding, and designing for safety.
13. Ask students to share with the class any unsafe stair conditions they have encountered.

Adaptations for Special Needs

14. Lead a class discussion on considerations in stairs and stairways for people with special physical needs.

15. Have students determine the minimum length of ramps built at a 1:15 ratio that connect floor levels separated by the following vertical distances: 16 in., 2 ft., and 39 in. (Answers: 20 ft. ramp, 30 ft. ramp, and two ramps equaling 48 ft. 9 in. connected by a 5 ft. sq. landing)

Halls

16. Lead a class discussion on halls. Be sure to include the function of halls, proper widths, and good placement.
17. *Hall Space*, Activity 17-3, SAG. Students are to evaluate the amount, configuration, and location of circulation space in a given floor plan.
18. Have students identify areas in homes that serve as hallways, but technically are not.
19. *Evaluating Hall Space*, reproducible master 17-C, IR. Students are to evaluate the amount, configuration, and location of circulation space in a given floor plan.
20. *Hallway Modification*, reproducible master 17-D, IR. Students are to recommend ways to blend a service hallway into kitchen space after removing an awkward kitchen door. (Note: At minimum, student plans should call for the installation of a door at the top of the stairs to block transfer of airflow between the living space and unheated basement.)
21. Assign one or more tasks listed in the text's *Suggested Activities* section at the end of the chapter.

Suggested Evaluation Techniques

22. *Check Your Understanding*, SAG. Have students complete as many questions as possible without referring to the text. Then have them find answers to questions they do not know.
23. Administer the *Chapter 17 Mastery Test*.

Answer Key

Text

Review Questions, page 322

1. Main stairways are a focal point, usually visible from a living area, and decorated attractively. Service stairways are not visible to guests and are usually built of typical construction materials.
2. straight run, L, double-L, U, winder, spiral, and circular
3. spiral stairs or one straight-run stairway directly above another

4. proper stair slope, uniform height and tread width of steps, minimum stairway width of 36 in., good lighting, sturdy handrails, nonskid treads, and adequate headroom
5. The rise of a step is less, treads are wider, handrails are placed on both sides of the stairs, and for comfortable wheelchair use, handrails are lowered to 30 in. from the floor.
6. 1:12
7. frequency of use, ability to accommodate the moving of large pieces of furniture, and the presence of turns in the stairway

Student Activity Guide

Check Your Understanding, pages 151–153

1. J
2. D
3. I
4. K
5. G
6. F
7. E
8. H
9. B
10. A
11. C

12. main stairway: connects first and second floors or upper and lower levels; assembled with prefabricated parts; and made of durable, quality materials such as hardwoods, terrazzo, stone, or tile
service stairway: connects the first level to the basement and is constructed on site, usually with softwoods
13. straight run
14. winder
15. spiral
16. circular
17. consistent height and width for each step and nonskid covering on each tread
18. Main stairways are generally wider than service stairways, and stairs with turns must be wider to permit the same accessibility as straight stairways.
19. as long as the length of the stairway plus the landing, 30 in. above the nosing of each step and 34 in. above the floor on landings
20. Measure the vertical distance from the nosing of each step to the ceiling, and look for minimum headroom of 6 ft. 6 in.
21. The decorating scheme of the room or area where the stairway is most visible should be the guide. If a stairway is very attractive or unique, it can become a focal point.
22. carpeting with short, tight pile
23. 36 to 42 in.
24. the tan carpet because it is durable and less likely to show soil
25. durability and easy maintenance

Stair Designs, Activity 17-1

1. straight-run stairs
2. U stairs
3. L stairs
4. winder stairs
5. double-L stairs
6. spiral stairs

Stair Specifications, Activity 17-2

1. width of stairs and handrail height
2. riser height and slope of the stairs
3. width of the stairs, handrail height, and headroom of stairs
4. run of a step and slope of the stairs

Hall Space, Activity 17-3

amount: typical for a ranch style home

configuration: a logical flow from main entrance to foyer to living area, from family room to sleeping area, and from service entrance to breakfast/kitchen area

location: generally convenient and practical except for the family room serving as a large hall for kitchen-to-bedroom traffic and living room-to-porch/patio traffic

Instructor's Resources

Chapter 17 Mastery Test

1. C
2. D
3. A
4. B
5. C
6. C
7. D

8. main
9. service
10. U
11. 7¼, 10½
12. handrail
13. 6 ft. 6 in.
14. 36, 42
15. 1:12
16. the shortest clear vertical distance measured between the nosing of the treads and the ceiling
17. stairs that have no wall on one or both sides
18. straight-run, L, double-L, U, winder, spiral, and circular stairs
19. Stairs should be wide enough to permit passage of individuals and movement of large furniture, and turns should be wider than straight stairs.
20. (List four:) stride of the person using the stairway, stair width, amount of lighting, presence of handrail(s), use of nonskid treads, amount of headroom
21. when one stairway is located directly above another as in a two-story building with a basement
22. when the stairway is particularly attractive or unique in design or workmanship
23. a lower rise, wider treads, and handrails on both sides of stairs

Examining Stair Designs

Stairway	Number and Type of Turns	Number of Landings
Straight-run	none	none
L	one, 90°	one
Double-L	two, 90°	two
U	one, 180°	two
Winder	usually one, 90° or 180°	none
Spiral	tightly circular	none
Circular	irregular curve	none

Stair Plan View and Elevation

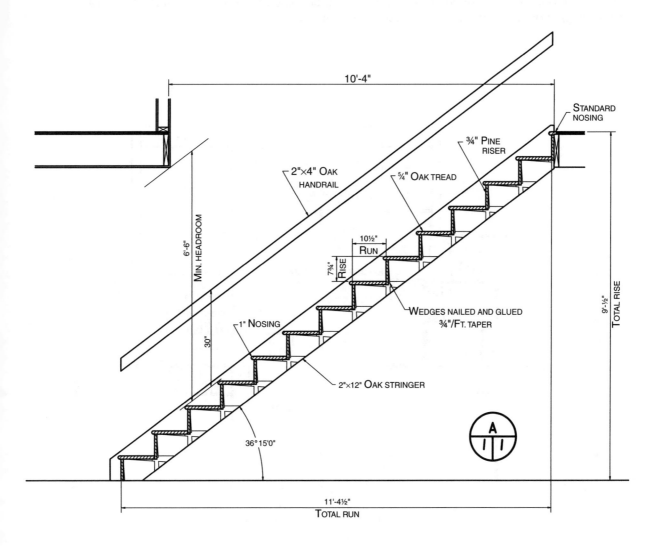

10'-4"

STANDARD
NOSING

¾" PINE
RISER

2"×4" OAK
HANDRAIL

⁵⁄₄" OAK TREAD

MIN. HEADROOM

6'-6"

10½"
RUN

7¾"
RISE

WEDGES NAILED AND GLUED
¾"/FT. TAPER

30"

1" NOSING

TOTAL RISE

9'-½"

2"×12" OAK STRINGER

36° 15'0"

A

11'-4½"
TOTAL RUN

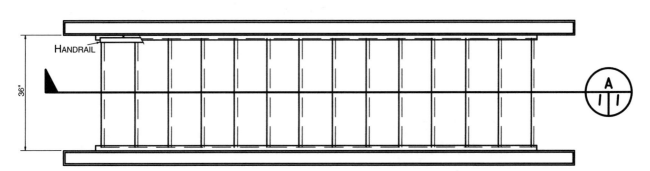

HANDRAIL

36"

A

Evaluating Hall Space

Name _____

Date _____

Study the floor plan below and shade the hallway and any other circulation space with a colored pencil. Evaluate the amount, configuration, and location of the circulation space in this plan. Write your recommendations on a separate sheet of paper and attach it to this page.

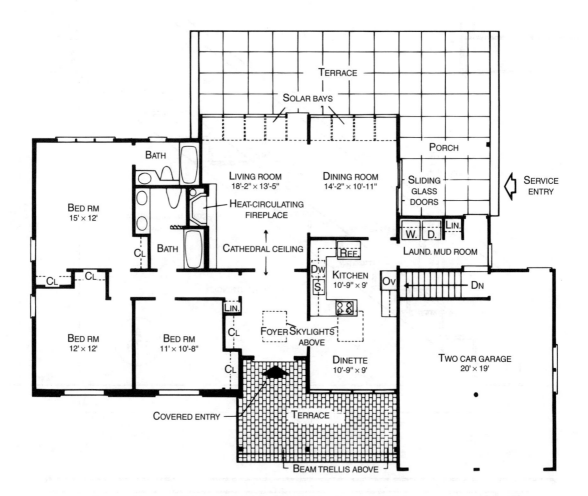

Hallway Modification

Name_____

Date _____

Examine this partial plan of a kitchen adjacent to a small hallway connecting the service entrance to a basement stairwell. Imagine the homeowners want to remove the kitchen door so they can exit the house through just one door. Recommend some options for achieving this goal as well as new treatments to the hallway that will visually blend the transformed area into the kitchen. (Note: The stairwell leads to an unfinished, unheated basement.) Write your recommendations on a separate sheet of paper and attach it to this page.

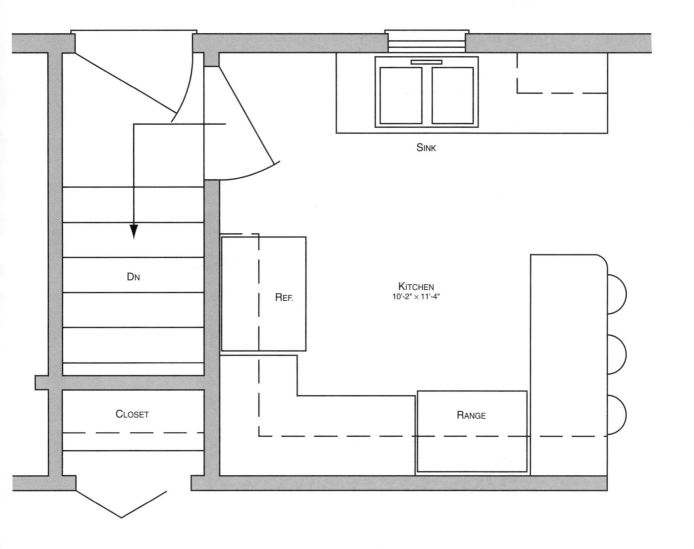

SINK

DN

REF.

KITCHEN
10'-2" × 11'-4"

CLOSET

RANGE

Stairs and Halls
Chapter 17
Mastery Test

Name _____

Date _____

Score _____

Multiple Choice: Select the best response and write the letter in the preceding blank.

_____ 1. The distance from the top surface of one tread to the top surface of the next is the _____.
A. run
B. span
C. rise
D. tread

_____ 2. The total horizontal length of a stairway is _____.
A. the total rise
B. equal to the stairwell opening
C. 10½ in.
D. the total run

_____ 3. Main stairways are generally made of _____.
A. prefabricated parts
B. typical construction materials
C. softwoods
D. None of the above.

_____ 4. The stairs that should be avoided whenever possible are _____ stairs.
A. circular
B. winder
C. spiral
D. double-L

_____ 5. The recommended angle of the ideal stairs is _____ degrees.
A. 20 to 25
B. 25 to 30
C. 30 to 35
D. 35 to 40

_____ 6. The decorative treatment of the stairway should generally be coordinated with the _____.
A. room at the lowest level
B. living room
C. room with the greatest view of the stairway
D. foyer

_____ 7. When covering stair treads, it is important to remember _____.
A. the covering should be skidproof
B. carpeting should have a short, tight pile
C. padding should not be too thick
D. All of the above.

Completion: Complete the following sentences by writing the missing words in the preceding blanks.

_____ 8. A housing unit with a first and second floor has a _____ stairway between those levels.

_____ 9. Structures with a basement have a _____ stairway from the first level to the basement.

_____ 10. The type of stairs that has two flights of steps parallel to each other with one landing between them is the _____ stairs.

_____ 11. Generally, a safe and comfortable stairway should have a riser height of about _____ in. and a run of _____ in.

(continued)

Name _____

_____ 12. At least one side of a stairway requires a _____.

_____ 13. A vertical distance of _____ is the accepted minimum headroom for a stairway.

_____ 14. Standard residential hallways range in width from _____ to _____ in.

_____ 15. The recommended slope for a ramp is _____.

Short Answer: Provide brief answers to the following questions or statements.

16. How is the headroom of a stairway defined? _____

_____

17. What are open stairs? _____

_____

18. List the seven basic design shapes used for stairways. _____

_____

_____

_____

_____

_____

_____

_____

19. What are some points that need to be considered concerning the width of a stairway? _____

_____

_____

_____

20. List four factors that affect stair safety. _____

_____

_____

_____

_____

21. When is stair headroom *not* a problem? _____

_____

22. When should the stairway become a focal point? _____

_____

_____

(continued)

Name _____

23. How do stairs designed for individuals with special physical needs differ from typical stairs?

_____

_____

_____

Chapter 18
Lighting

Objectives

After studying this chapter, students will be able to
- explain how natural light can be used to enhance the decor of a home.
- list the advantages and disadvantages of incandescent, halogen, and fluorescent lights.
- explain the difference between general, task, and accent lighting, and list types of fixtures that can be used to create each type of lighting.
- evaluate the appropriateness of lighting sources for the activities of a room.

Teaching Materials

Text, pages 325–340

Student Activity Guide

Check Your Understanding
18-1, *Light Sources*
18-2, *Types of Lighting*
18-3, *Footcandle Needs*
18-4, *Lighting Fixtures*
18-5, *Lighting Application*

Instructor's Resources

Lighting Efficacy, transparency master 18-A
Energy-Saving Lighting Examples, reproducible master 18-B
Types of Lighting Fixtures, transparency master 18-C
Lighting Guidelines for Saving Energy, reproducible master 18-D
Chapter 18 Mastery Test

Instructional Concepts and Student Activities

1. Have students read Chapter 18 in the text and complete the review questions.
2. Ask students to collect pictures, illustrations, and technical information about residential lighting. Have them add this material to their housing notebooks.

Natural Light

3. Lead a class discussion on natural light in terms of amount, effect, glare, room orientation, colors, and textures.
4. Demonstrate how some fabrics and objects change appearance when subjected to natural light.

Artificial Light

5. Discuss incandescent, halogen, and fluorescent light. Demonstrate how objects differ in appearance under the three lighting sources.
6. Show the *Interior Lighting: Bringing Rooms to Life* video from Learning Seed's catalog and have the class discuss it.
7. Discuss with the class the different applications of lighting: general, task, and accent lighting.
8. *Light Sources,* Activity 18-1, SAG. Students are to discuss the characteristics, advantages, and disadvantages of natural, incandescent, halogen, and fluorescent lighting.
9. *Lighting Efficacy*, transparency master 18-A, IR. Have the class discuss the definition of *lighting efficacy* and its application to incandescent and fluorescent lamps.
10. *Energy-Saving Lighting Examples*, reproducible master 18-B, IR. Use the handout to help students recognize the many benefits of replacing common incandescent bulbs with comparable fluorescent lamps.

Selection and Placement

11. *Types of Lighting Fixtures,* transparency master 18-C, IR. Use the transparency as a guide for describing to students the various structural and portable lighting fixtures, their proper placement, and use.
12. *Types of Lighting*, Activity 18-2, SAG. Students are to match the three basic types of lighting with descriptions of their applications.
13. *Footcandle Needs*, Activity 18-3, SAG. Students are to match descriptions of various activities with their recommended light levels.
14. *Lighting Fixtures*, Activity 18-4, SAG. Students are to identify illustrations of lighting fixtures.
15. Lead a class discussion on the different lighting needs that exist within each room of the house. Have students recommend ways to address each need.

16. *Lighting Application*, Activity 18-5, SAG. Students are to plan the lighting for a grand foyer with specific features and dimensions.
17. *Lighting Guidelines for Saving Energy*, reproducible master 18-D, IR. Use the handout to discuss ways to save energy with interior and exterior lighting.
18. Assign one or more tasks listed in the text's *Suggested Activities* section at the end of the chapter.

Suggested Evaluation Techniques

19. *Check Your Understanding*, SAG. Have students complete as many questions as possible without referring to the text. Then have them find answers to questions they do not know.
20. Administer the *Chapter 18 Mastery Test*.

Answer Key

Text

Review Questions, page 339

1. through the size, number, and arrangement of windows; the type of window treatments used; and window placement
2. Incandescent light is produced by heating a wire until it glows, while fluorescent light is produced by creating ultraviolet rays.
3. incandescent advantages: does not hum or flicker, does not interfere with electrical devices, is less expensive than fluorescent lights, and flatters skin tones
disadvantages: uses more electricity and produces more heat
fluorescent advantages: disperses light over a larger area, causes less glare, and requires less electricity
disadvantages: hums, flickers, interferes with electrical devices, is more expensive than incandescent lights, and produces light less flattering to skin tones
4. produces bright light comparable to daylight, makes colors look their best, and lasts three times longer than incandescent bulbs while using about 40 percent less energy
5. have a warm-white light and use less energy than the old bulbs known for their cold, bluish light
6. general, task, and accent
7. increased wattage, smooth surfaces, light colors, and the use of white versus color light

8. indirect: wall-focused recessed lights and track lighting, and ceiling-focused wall fixtures
direct: luminous ceilings, recessed lights focused downward, chandeliers, and standard wall and ceiling fixtures
9. track lighting, recessed lights, chandeliers, hanging lights, strip lighting, and minilights
10. a lampshade with the bottom edge at eye level to the seated person, an opaque shade with a white lining, and a stable base
11. Decide how the room will be used, define specific lighting needs for each area within the room, and choose the most functional lighting fixtures to meet the needs of each area.
12. A kitchen needs direct general lighting with good task lighting above each work area. A living room needs indirect general lighting, task lighting for reading or conversation, and accent lighting on focal points and prized possessions.
13. by emphasizing architectural features, highlighting landscape features, making social areas and walkways usable, and increasing safety

Student Activity Guide

Check Your Understanding, pages 159–162

1. natural
2. deciduous
3. incandescent
4. fluorescent
5. direct
6. indirect
7. footcandle
8. halogen
9. recessed
10. portable
11. 42
12. controls

13. D	21. C
14. A	22. A
15. C	23. D
16. B	24. C
17. B	25. B
18. B	26. D
19. C	27. A
20. A	28. C

29. General lighting provides an even amount of light throughout the room, task lighting provides light for a specific activity, and accent lighting uses a highly concentrated beam of light to highlight an object.

30. Direct lighting produces the strongest illumination from the light source to the object, while indirect lighting is directed toward an intermediate surface that reflects the light into the room.
31. Decide how the room will be used, define specific lighting needs for each area within the room, select the basic types of lighting required, and choose the most functional lighting fixtures to meet the needs of each area.
32. small yard lights spaced evenly along the sidewalk or a decorative lamp post near the sidewalk at the front of the property
33. produce bright light comparable to daylight, make colors look their best, and last three times longer than incandescent bulbs while using about 40 percent less energy
34. different uses of the same fixtures, decorative effects, conserved energy, and increased bulb life

Types of Lighting, Activity 18-2
1. C, E, I
2. A, D, F, H, K
3. B, G, J

Footcandle Needs, Activity 18-3
1. A
2. A
3. B
4. B
5. C
6. C
7. C
8. B
9. D
10. C
11. C
12. C
13. D

Lighting Fixtures, Activity 18-4
1. undercabinet lighting
2. task lighting
3. strip lighting
4. track lighting
5. recessed lighting
6. luminous ceiling

Instructor's Resources

Chapter 18 Mastery Test
1. C
2. C
3. B
4. A
5. C
6. A
7. A
8. C
9. B
10. C

11. shiny
12. artificial
13. incandescent
14. two
15. halogen
16. 12
17. general
18. footcandle
19. track
20. portable
21. to enable a person to perform tasks safely and efficiently without eyestrain and to enhance the mood and decorative scheme of a home
22. by using window treatments and exterior foliage to filter the sunlight
23. size, wattage, shape, and surface treatment of the bulb
24. in a glass tube by releasing electricity through a mercury vapor to make invisible ultraviolet rays
25. produce bright light comparable to daylight, make colors look their best, last three times longer and use about 40 percent less energy than incandescent bulbs
26. general, task, and accent lighting
27. for highlighting an area or object by focusing a highly concentrated beam of light or by using minilights
28. They make different uses and decorative effects possible from the same fixtures.
29. task lighting over the dinner table
30. diffused general lighting

Lighting Efficacy

Lighting efficacy = ratio of <u>light output</u> (lumens) to the <u>electricity used</u> (watts)

Incandescent lamps = 15 to 20 lumens per watt

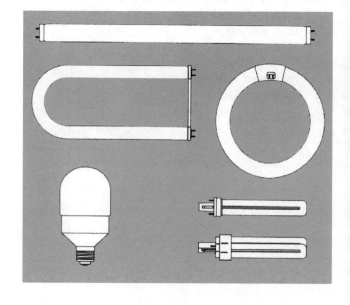

Fluorescent lamps = 60 to almost 100 lumens per watt

Source: American Lighting Association

Energy-Saving Lighting Examples

Incandescent Wattage	Fluorescent Replacement (Type)	(Rated Life)	Annual Dollar Savings
Two 60W	20-W straight tube	9,000	$21.17
100W	Two 20W straight tubes	9,000	11.96
Two 75W	40W straight tube	20,000	23.21
Two 60W	32W circle tube	12,000	18.57
Three 60W	32W and 40W circle tubes	12,000	22.08
Two 100W	Two 40W U-tubes	12,000	24.53
60W	13W compact twin	10,000	10.01
100W	Two 13W compact twins	10,000	15.34
75W	18W compact quad	10,000	12.09
60W	15W compact screw-in	9,000	9.53

Notes: W = wattage. Savings are based on 6 hours of daily use at the electricity rate of 10¢ per kilowatt-hour.

Source: American Lighting Association

Types of Lighting Fixtures

Structural Fixtures

Luminous ceilings

Recessed lights

Track lighting

Strip lighting

Portable Fixtures

Lamps

Wall fixtures

Ceiling fixtures

Undercabinet (and undershelf) fixtures

Lighting Guidelines for Saving Energy

Indoors

- Turn lights off when not in use. Consider installing timers, photocells, or occupancy sensors to reduce the length of time lights are on.
- Use task lighting to focus light where needed instead of brightly lighting an entire room.
- Consider three-way lamps because they help keep lighting levels low when brighter light is not needed.
- Replace the five incandescent bulbs you use most frequently with compact fluorescents (CFLs), which use much less energy. Plan to replace the remaining incandescents as they burn out.
- Consider carefully the size and fit of CFLs for table and floor lamps since certain fixtures may not accommodate some larger CFLs.
- For spot lighting, consider CFLs with reflectors since they provide a very directed light in a range of intensities.
- Replace incandescent nightlights with 4-watt minifluorescent or electro-luminescent lights.
- Use 4-foot fluorescent fixtures with reflective backing for the garage, laundry, and workroom areas. Select them with electronic ballasts since these do not flicker and hum as some magnetic ballasts do.
- Consider replacing halogen torchiere fixtures with compact fluorescent torchieres, which use 60 to 80 percent less energy and can produce more light.
- Allow daylight into the room by using light-colored, loose-weave curtains on windows while preserving privacy. Decorate the living space with lighter colors that reflect daylight.

Outdoors

- Use outdoor lights with a photocell unit or timer so they turn off during the day.
- Turn off decorative outdoor gas lamps. Eight gas lamps burning year-round use as much natural gas as it takes to heat an average-size home during an entire winter.
- CFLs are ideal for exterior lighting because of their long life. For cold climates, buy one with a cold-weather ballast.

Source: U.S. Office of Energy Efficiency and Renewable Energy

Lighting
Chapter 18
Mastery Test

Name _____

Date _____

Score _____

Multiple Choice: Select the best response and write the letter in the preceding blank.

_____ 1. When planning a residential lighting scheme, _____ should be considered.
  A. natural lighting
  B. artificial lighting
  C. Both of the above.
  D. None of the above.

_____ 2. For most households, the area of the house that benefits most from an eastern exposure is the _____.
  A. master bedroom
  B. living room
  C. breakfast area
  D. family room

_____ 3. When electricity passes through a fine tungsten filament in a vacuum bulb, _____ light is produced.
  A. fluorescent
  B. incandescent
  C. halogen
  D. mercury vapor

_____ 4. The type of incandescent bulb that does the best job of dispersing light evenly and decreasing glare is a _____ bulb.
  A. frosted
  B. pear-shaped, general service
  C. cone-shaped
  D. flame-shaped

_____ 5. Of the following, _____ is the false statement about incandescent bulbs.
  A. incandescent lights are less expensive to install and replace than fluorescent lights
  B. incandescent lights do not interfere with other electrical devices
  C. incandescent lights use less electricity than fluorescent lights
  D. incandescent lights produce more heat than fluorescent lights

_____ 6. Rooms with windows facing the _____ side of the house have the most-even natural lighting.
  A. north
  B. south
  C. east
  D. west

_____ 7. When a lighting source is directed toward an intermediate surface that reflects the light into the room, it is called _____.
  A. indirect lighting
  B. local lighting
  C. accent lighting
  D. downlighting

_____ 8. The light that shows colors at their truest values and produces the most illumination in a room is _____ light.
  A. blue
  B. yellow
  C. white
  D. pink

(continued)

Name _____

_____ 9. The type of lighting that uses transparent or translucent panels lit from behind is _____.
   A. strip lighting
   B. a luminous ceiling
   C. recessed downlights
   D. accent lighting

_____ 10. For reading, the bottom edge of a lampshade should be _____.
   A. above a seated person's head
   B. 48 in. above the floor
   C. at a seated person's eye level
   D. at a seated person's shoulder level

Completion: Complete the following sentences by writing the missing words in the preceding blanks.

_____ 11. Rooms that receive full sunlight for most of the day should not be decorated with many smooth or _____ surfaces.

_____ 12. _____ sources of light change the appearance of colors.

_____ 13. Globe, flame, teardrop, and pear shapes describe _____ bulbs.

_____ 14. Three-way incandescent bulbs contain _____ filaments to provide three different levels of lighting.

_____ 15. Of all the different types of lightbulbs available for use in the home, those that produce the brightest light are _____ bulbs.

_____ 16. Straight fluorescent tubes range in length from _____ to 48 in.

_____ 17. A basic type of lighting that produces a comfortable, even amount of brightness throughout a room is _____ lighting.

_____ 18. The amount of illumination produced by a standard plumber's candle at a distance of one foot is _____.

_____ 19. _____ lighting is mounted on a metal strip that allows fixtures to be placed anywhere along the strip.

_____ 20. _____ lighting fixtures are *not* part of a home's architectural structure.

Short Answer: Provide brief answers to the following questions or statements.

21. What is the purpose of proper home lighting? _____

_____

_____

22. How can glare from the sun be reduced in a room without changing the location or height of the windows? _____

_____

_____

23. What four factors affect the light intensity emitted from an incandescent lamp? _____

_____

_____

_____

_____

(continued)

Name_____

24. How is fluorescent light produced?_____

_____

_____

_____

25. What are some advantages of halogen bulbs? _____

_____

_____

_____

_____

26. List the three main applications of lighting. _____

_____

_____

_____

27. Describe how accent lighting is used. _____

_____

_____

_____

28. Identify the key benefits of lighting controls. _____

_____

_____

_____

_____

29. What is the main source of light in a typical dining room?_____

_____

30. What is the most suitable type of lighting for bedrooms?_____

_____

Chapter 19
Electrical and Plumbing Systems

Objectives

After studying this chapter, students will be able to

- list the three main components of the wiring system and explain how they operate.
- evaluate the adequacy of a wiring system in relation to a household's needs.
- trace the flow of the water-supply system into and out of the house, explaining the functions of its various components.
- evaluate a house's plumbing system according to basic guidelines for planning a system.

Teaching Materials

Text, pages 341–353

Student Activity Guide

Check Your Understanding
19-1, *Electrical Circuits*
19-2, *Receptacles and Switches*
19-3, *Electrical Plan*
19-4, *Plumbing System*

Instructor's Resources

Electrical Branch Circuits, transparency
    master 19-A
Garage Electrical Plan, reproducible master 19-B
Wastewater-Removal System, transparency
    master 19-C
Chapter 19 Mastery Test

Instructional Concepts and Student Activities

1. Have students read Chapter 19 in the text and complete the review questions.
2. Ask students to collect articles and manufacturers literature about residential electrical and plumbing systems, materials, appliances, and fixtures. Have students add these materials to their housing notebooks.

The Electrical System

3. Define and explain the components of a residential electrical system. Be sure to include the service-entrance panel, branch circuits, receptacles, and switches.
4. *Electrical Branch Circuits*, transparency master 19-A, IR. Examine the three types of electrical circuits found in a residence, discussing wire size, overcurrent protection, and voltage.
5. Show students how to calculate the amount of wattage a given circuit can provide. The formula is *amperes × volts = watts*.
6. Show the *Electrical (DIY-209)* video from Shopware Educational Systems and have the class discuss it.
7. *Electrical Circuits*, Activity 19-1, SAG. Students are to identify the components of a simple residential electrical system.
8. Discuss with students the planning of the electrical system in terms of circuitry requirements, receptacles, and switches. Let students examine a typical electrical plan.
9. *Receptacles and Switches*, Activity 19-2, SAG. Students are to identify specific types of receptacles and switches.
10. *Electrical Plan*, Activity 19-3, SAG. Students are to plan the outlets and switches for a given room and specify the circuit requirements.
11. Lead a class discussion on signal and communication systems.
12. *Garage Electrical Plan*, reproducible master 19-B, IR. Students are to color-code outlets and switches in a given room to demonstrate knowledge of electrical symbols.

The Plumbing System

13. Lead a class discussion on the water-supply system, wastewater-removal system, and plumbing fixtures.
14. Show the *Plumbing (DIY-204)* video from Shopware Educational Systems and have the class discuss it.
15. *Plumbing System*, Activity 19-4, SAG. Students are to identify the parts of the residential plumbing system using a schematic diagram.

16. Discuss with students the planning of the plumbing system. Let students examine a typical plumbing plan.

17. *Wastewater-Removal System*, transparency master 19-C, IR. Have students examine a partial plan view of a wastewater-removal system that links the home's laundry room, kitchen, and half bath. Ask students to name other key components of the system that lie beyond the view. (answer: traps below fixtures, soil stacks for other water closets, the house trap, and sewer line)

18. Assign one or more tasks listed in the text's *Suggested Activities* section at the end of the chapter.

Suggested Evaluation Techniques

19. *Check Your Understanding*, SAG. Have students complete as many questions as possible without referring to the text. Then have them find answers to questions they do not know.

20. Administer the *Chapter 19 Mastery Test*.

Answer Key

Text

Review Questions, page 352

1. the building's main electrical distribution box that receives electricity from the power company and sends it throughout the home through branch circuits

2. by stopping the current with circuit breakers or fuses when the circuit becomes overloaded

3. three individual-appliance circuits (one apiece for the range, refrigerator, and dish-washer), one or more small-appliance circuits for using small kitchen appliances, and one general-purpose circuit for kitchen lighting

4. adhering to the specifications of the National Electrical Code, providing enough electrical capacity for the household's short-term and long-term needs, placing additional recepta-cles and switches as needed, and installing them in accessible and convenient locations

5. water supply: has separate water mains for hot and cold water and is pressurized wastewater removal: has larger pipes, contains soil stacks, depends on gravity for removal of wastewater, and is not pressurized

6. clustering rooms that require plumbing, deciding how much hot water will be needed at one time, and providing enough water-service capacity for the household's short-term and long-term needs

7. 42 gallons

8. indicates that a visitor is present, allows family members to communicate within the home, and permits the homeowner to monitor the various systems on the property

Student Activity Guide

Check Your Understanding, pages 169-172

1. J
2. G
3. F
4. M
5. O
6. L
7. A
8. D
9. B
10. E
11. H
12. K
13. N
14. C
15. I

16. to receive electricity from the power company and distribute it throughout the house, and to monitor the home's electrical system and prevent electrical overload

17. Small-appliance circuits power small appliances, such as blenders and toasters, that require moderate amounts of current. Individual-appliance circuits power permanently installed appliances that require large amounts of electricity, such as water heaters, washers, and dryers.

18. Receptacles with grounding terminals accommodate three-prong plugs, while receptacles without grounding terminals accommodate two-prong plugs only.

19. a system of switches connected to relays that operate a line voltage switch controlling a fixture; because it uses smaller, less costly wire that allows all electrical appliances to be operated from a master panel or home computer

20. present and future electrical needs

21. The building main brings water from the city water main or private well to the house. It may then pass through a treatment system. A cold water branch line carries it to each cold water fixture.

22. The water-supply system uses pressure to move water through pipes that are horizontal; have a ½ to ¾ in. diameter; and are made of copper tubing, plastic pipe, or galvanized steel. The wastewater-removal system uses gravity to move wastewater through pipes that are sloped; have a 3 or 4 in. diameter; and are made of cast iron, copper and brass alloy, or plastic.

23. locating areas that require plumbing close together to avoid the higher costs of extra pipes and a larger water heater

24. 49 gallons

25. indicate that a visitor is present, allow people to communicate within the home, and permit the owner to monitor the various systems within the dwelling and property
26. breakers
27. 240
28. 120
29. two
30. individual
31. shock
32. three
33. flat
34. 500
35. light
36. 8
37. 12

Electrical Circuits, Activity 19-1

Solution on page 266

Receptacles and Switches, Activity 19-2

1. simplex receptacle
2. duplex receptacle
3. 240-volt receptacle
4. weatherproof receptacle
5. clock receptacle
6. GFCI receptacle
7. single-pole switch
8. three-way switch
9. dimmer switch
10. four-way switch
11. pull-chain switch

Electrical Plan, Activity 19-3

Solution on page 267

Plumbing System, Activity 19-4

Solution on page 268

Instructor's Resources

Garage Electrical Plan, Activity 19-B

Solution on page 269

Chapter 19 Mastery Test

1.	D	7.	C
2.	A	8.	A
3.	B	9.	C
4.	A	10.	B
5.	C	11.	C
6.	C	12.	C

13. service entrance
14. overcurrent
15. 120, 240
16. branch
17. 1,800
18. 1,440
19. three
20. dimmer
21. well
22. septic tank
23. gravity
24. ½
25. to be a safety device that opens an overloaded circuit by melting a fusible link
26. a circuit
27. service-entrance panel, branch circuits, receptacles, and switches
28. general-purpose circuits: to power structural lighting fixtures and receptacles used for devices that require little wattage
small-appliance circuits: to power appliances that require a moderate amount of current
individual-appliance circuits: to power permanently installed appliances that use a large amount of electricity
29. the duplex receptacle, also called simplex, triplex, and quad
30. ground fault circuit interrupter
31. 12 to 18 in., but 36 in. when it would be more convenient and provide easier access
32. water-supply system, wastewater-removal system, and plumbing fixtures
33. to work on one part of the plumbing system without shutting down the entire system
34. copper tubing, galvanized steel pipe, and plastic pipe (which is sometimes restricted)
35. to let water and waste drain down and gases vent up through the roof
36. by locating areas that require plumbing close together to avoid the higher costs of extra pipes and a larger water heater
37. indicate that a visitor is present, allow persons to communicate within the home, and permit the owner to monitor the various systems within the dwelling and property

Electrical Circuits
Activity 19-1

Solution

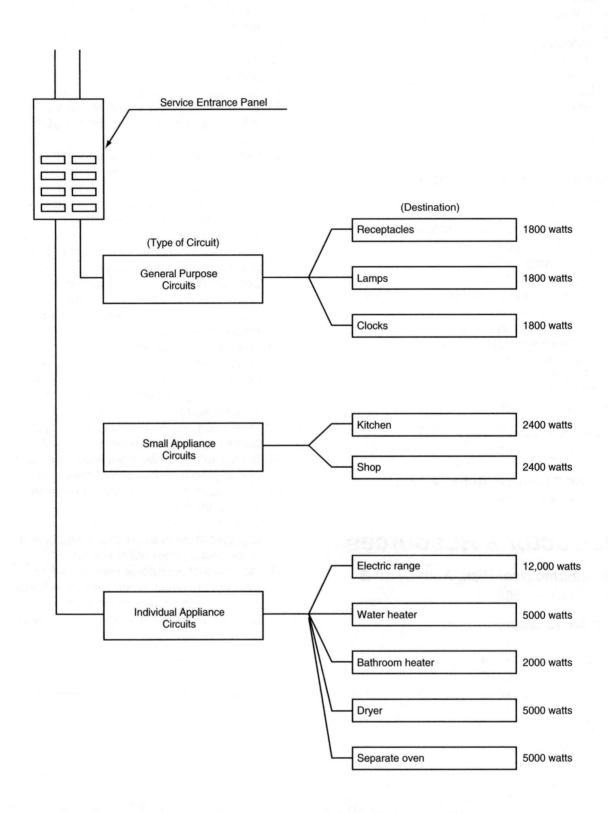

Electrical Plan
Activity 19-3

Solution

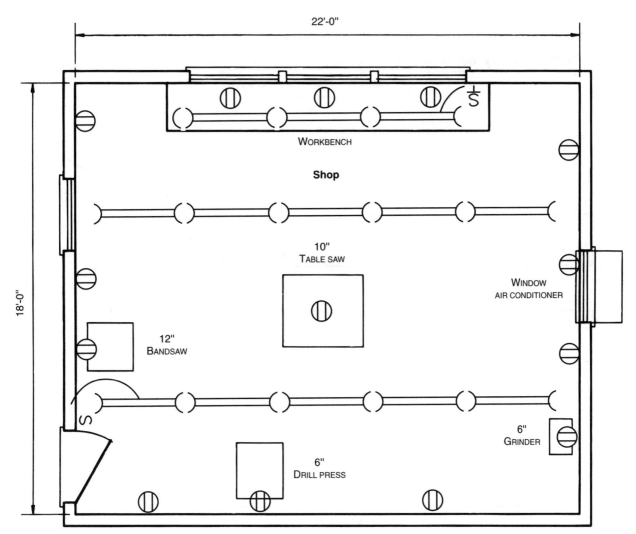

General purpose circuits:	Number: 1	Watts per circuit 1800
Small appliance circuits:	Number: 2	Watts per circuit 2400

Individual appliance circuits:

Window air conditioner	2400 watts
Table saw	2400 watts
Band saw	2400 watts
Drill press	2400 watts
Grinder	2400 watts

Plumbing System
Activity 19-4

Solution

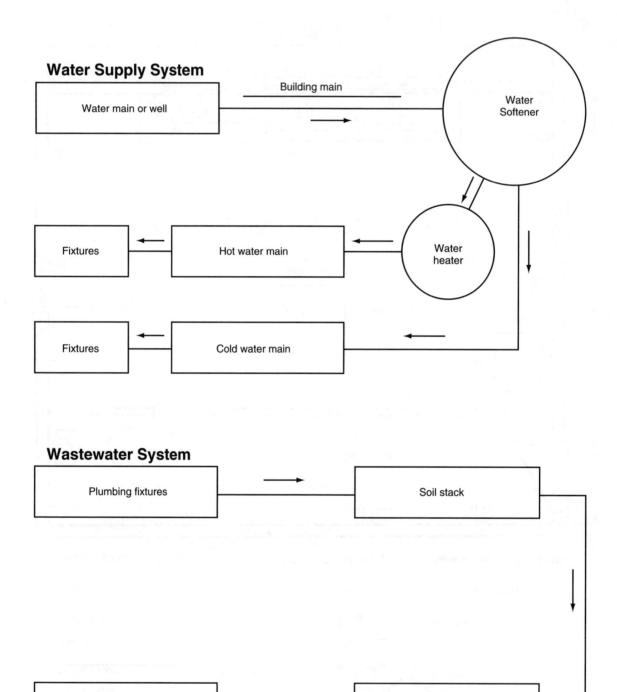

Water Supply System

| Water main or well |
Building main →

Water Softener

Water heater

Hot water main → Fixtures

Cold water main → Fixtures

Wastewater System

Plumbing fixtures →

Soil stack

House drain

House sewer ←

Garage Electrical Plan
Reproducible Master 19-B

Solution

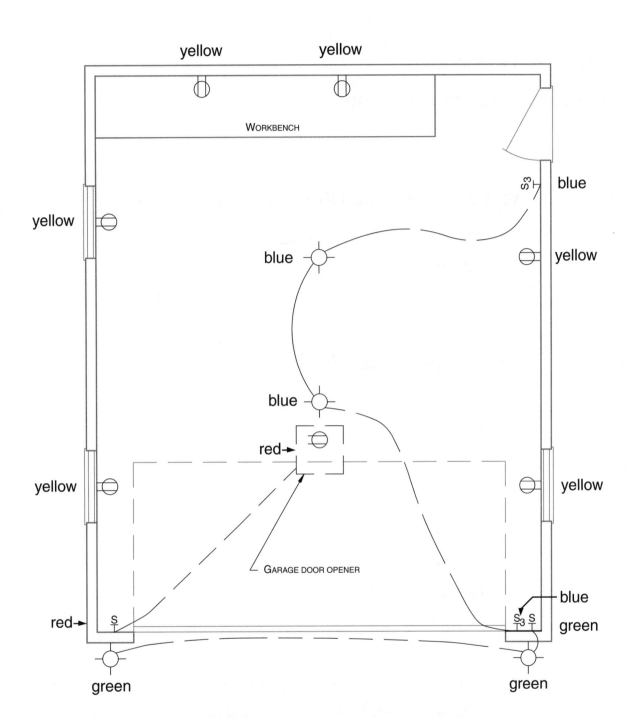

Electrical Branch Circuits

150 to 200 ampere

240-volt service to the house

General-Purpose Circuits (3 watts per sq. ft. minimum)

#12 wire, 20 amp breaker
120 volts

Small-Appliance Circuits

#12 wire, 20 amp breaker
120 volts

Individual-Appliance Circuits

120 or 240 volts depending on requirements
Typical: range, countertop oven, refrigerator,
    dishwasher,waste disposal, clothes washer, clothes
    dryer, water heater, furnace, air conditioner, heat
    pump, and attic fan
The electrical requirements must be determined for
    each individual appliance circuit since it is
    dedicated to a particular appliance.

Garage Electrical Plan

Name _____

Date _____

Identify the electrical symbols in the floor plan by referring to "A-4 Electrical Symbols" in the text's appendix. Color each symbol as indicated:

- Three-way switches that operate ceiling outlet fixtures (blue)

- A switch that operates outside lights by the garage door (green)

- Six duplex outlets on interior garage walls (yellow)

- An outlet and switch for a garage door opener (red)

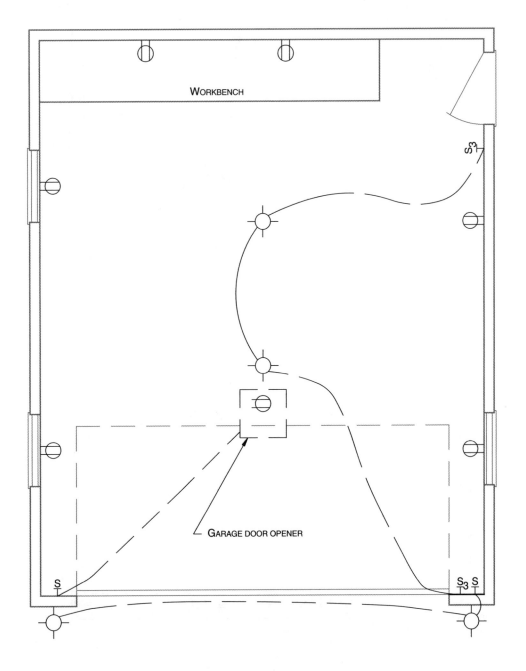

WORKBENCH

GARAGE DOOR OPENER

Wastewater-Removal System

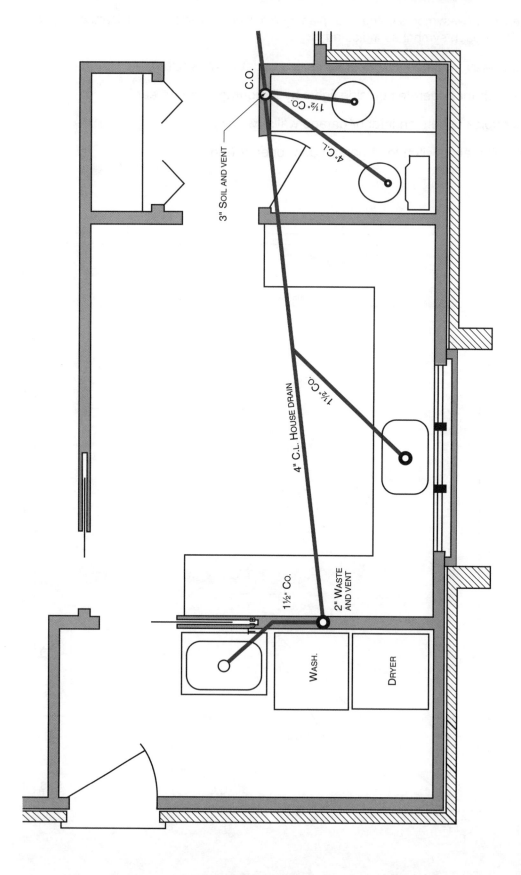

Electrical and Plumbing Systems

Name _____

Date _____

Score _____

Chapter 19 Mastery Test

Multiple Choice: Select the best response and write the letter in the preceding blank.

_____ 1. The unit of current used to measure the amount of electricity flowing through a wire during a specified amount of time is called _____.
A. voltage
B. watt
C. resistance
D. ampere

_____ 2. The measure of the pressure that forces current through a wire is _____.
A. voltage
B. watt
C. resistance
D. ampere

_____ 3. The single switch used to shut down the home's entire electrical system is the _____.
A. circuit breaker
B. main disconnect switch
C. panel monitor switch
D. service-entrance panel switch

_____ 4. Of the following groups of electrical devices, _____ would normally be connected to a general-purpose circuit.
A. a lamp, clock, and radio
B. a lamp, radio, and toaster
C. a clock, toaster, and electric fry pan
D. an electric fry pan, washer, and water pump

_____ 5. Circuits that provide electricity for electrical hand tools and portable kitchen appliances such as toasters and blenders are called _____ circuits.
A. light duty
B. appliance
C. small-appliance
D. individual-appliance

_____ 6. The home's _____ generally requires a 240-volt circuit.
A. gas clothes dryer
B. toaster
C. electric range
D. television set

_____ 7. The type of receptacle that is required in bathrooms and around pools is a _____ receptacle.
A. weatherproof
B. duplex
C. GFCI
D. triplex

_____ 8. The National Electrical Code requires a minimum lighting capacity for residential structures of _____.
A. 3 watts per sq. ft.
B. 4 watts per sq. ft.
C. 5 watts per sq. ft.
D. None of the above.

(continued)

Name _____

_____ 9.   The National Electrical Code does *not* require _____.
        A. receptacles to be placed along a wall so no point is more than 6 ft. from a receptacle
        B. each room to have at least three receptacles
        C. each room to limit the number of receptacles to 10
        D. receptacles to be planned for halls and closets

_____ 10. The hot water main begins at the _____.
        A. water storage tank
        B. water heater
        C. building main
        D. water softener

_____ 11. The types of materials commonly used for wastewater-removal pipes are _____.
        A. wood fiber, plastic, and lead
        B. plastic, lead, and copper
        C. copper, brass alloy, and plastic
        D. cast iron, copper, and wood fiber

_____ 12. A drain size of _____ in. is required for a water closet.
        A. 1 or 2
        B. 3
        C. 3 or 4
        D. 6

Completion: Complete the following sentences by writing the missing words in the preceding blanks.

_____ 13. The _____ _____ consists of the fittings and conductors that bring electricity into the building.

_____ 14. Fuses and breakers are types of _____ devices that prevent the overloading of a branch or circuit.

_____ 15. Both _____ -volt and _____ -volt service are available for residential use.

_____ 16. Once electricity passes the main disconnect switch, it is routed to several _____ circuits.

_____ 17. A 15-ampere circuit on a 120-volt line will provide _____ watts of power.

_____ 18. An individual-electrical circuit should be used with any permanent, motor-driven appliance that requires over _____ watts for operation.

_____ 19. A _____ -way switch controls one or more fixtures from two locations.

_____ 20. A _____ switch may be used with any incandescent lighting fixture to vary its intensity.

_____ 21. The residential water-supply system begins at a city water main or private _____.

_____ 22. Wastewater that is *not* carried to the sanitary sewer is carried to a private _____ _____.

_____ 23. The water-supply system is pressurized, but the wastewater system depends on _____ to carry the used water and waste to the sewer.

_____ 24. Water-supply lines to most fixtures have a _____ in. diameter.

(continued)

Name _____

Short Answer: Provide brief answers to the following questions or statements.

25. What is the purpose of a fuse? _____

_____

26. What is the path that electricity flows through from a source to one or more outlets and back?

_____

27. List the four main components of a residential electrical system. _____

_____

_____

_____

_____

28. What three general classes of branch circuits are commonly used in a residential structure? What is the function of each? _____

_____

_____

_____

_____

29. What is the most common type of electrical receptacle? What are its variations called?

_____

_____

30. What does GFCI mean? _____

_____

31. How far above the floor are receptacles usually placed? What is the exception and when is it made?

_____

_____

32. What are the three primary parts of a residential plumbing system? _____

_____

_____

_____

33. What is the purpose of a shutoff valve? _____

_____

_____

Name _____

34. What materials are commonly used for water-supply pipes? Which one is sometimes restricted by local code requirements? _____

_____

_____

35. What is the function of soil stacks in the wastewater-removal system?_____

_____

_____

_____

36. When planning a home plumbing system, how can its efficiency be increased and costs reduced?

_____

_____

37. What three functions does a home signal and communication system perform? _____

_____

_____

_____

_____

_____

Chapter 20
Climate Control, Fireplaces, and Stoves

Objectives

After studying this chapter, students will be able to

- evaluate the level of climate control in a house by determining the number and type of climate-control devices in the house.
- describe the operations of various heating and cooling systems.
- list the components and structural considerations involved in using solar heating systems.
- describe the construction of fireplaces and stoves and explain how they heat a room.

Teaching Materials

Text, pages 354–368

Student Activity Guide

Check Your Understanding
20-1, *Heating Systems*
20-2, *Masonry Fireplace*

Instructor's Resources

Residential Climate Control, transparency master 20-A

Forced Warm-Air System, transparency/ reproducible master 20-B

Climate-Control Plan, transparency/reproducible master 20-C

Active Solar Systems, transparency master 20-D

Warm-Air Solar System, reproducible master 20-E

Passive Solar Systems, transparency master 20-F

Types of Passive Solar Systems, transparency master 20-G

Chapter 20 Mastery Test

Instructional Concepts and Student Activities

1. Have students read Chapter 20 in the text and complete the review questions that follow.

2. Ask students to collect articles and manufacturers' literature about climate-control systems, fireplaces, and stoves. Have them add these materials to their housing notebooks.

Climate Control

3. *Residential Climate Control*, transparency master 20-A, IR. Use the transparency to lead a class discussion on the basic functions and components of a home's climate-control system.
4. Have students describe the most common heating systems: forced warm-air, hydronic, electric radiant, and central heat-pump systems.
5. *Heating Systems*, Activity 20-1, SAG. Students are to describe each of the common heating systems in terms of system components and method of heat delivery.
6. *Forced Warm-Air System*, transparency/ reproducible master 20-B, IR. Have students examine and discuss the ductwork components of a forced-air system. Ask students if they have seen this system in unfinished basements of homes.
7. *Climate-Control Plan*, transparency/reproducible master 20-C, IR. Have students examine and discuss the location of supply and cold-air return ducts and registers in a typical climate-control plan.
8. *Active Solar Systems*, transparency master 20-D, IR. Have students discuss the differences between the two basic types of active solar systems: warm-air versus warm-water.
9. *Warm-Air Solar System*, reproducible master 20-E, IR. Use the master as a handout for students to examine a basic depiction of the warm-air active solar system.
10. Ask students to write an essay describing the components of typical solar heating systems and explain the differences between passive and active systems.
11. *Passive Solar Systems*, transparency master 20-F, IR. Have students discuss the differences among three basic types of passive solar systems: direct-gain, indirect-gain, and isolated-gain systems.

12. *Types of Passive Solar Systems*, transparency master 20-G, IR. Have students discuss the basic differences among residential structures that rely on passive solar heating.
13. Lead a class discussion on residential cooling systems and the function of insulation in reducing cooling costs.
14. Demonstrate how to calculate the R-value of a wall. (Refer to Fig. 20-14 in the text.)

Fireplaces and Stoves

15. Lead a class discussion on the typical types of fireplaces found in homes: single-face, two-face opposite, two-face adjacent, and three-face.
16. *Masonry Fireplace*, Activity 20-2, SAG. Students are to identify the parts of a typical masonry fireplace.
17. Have students write a short essay describing how stoves transmit heat to the occupants of a room.
18. Describe the two basic types of stoves—radiant and circulating—and discuss with students the heating efficiency of various stoves.
19. Explain to students the safety precautions necessary when installing and operating wood or coal-burning stoves.
20. Assign one or more tasks listed in the text's *Suggested Activities* section at the end of the chapter.

Suggested Evaluation Techniques

21. *Check Your Understanding*, SAG. Have students complete as many questions as possible without referring to the text. Then have them find answers to questions they do not know.
22. Administer the *Chapter 20 Mastery Test*.

Answer Key

Text

Review Questions, page 367

1. (See Items 1-4 in Figure 20-1 in the text.)
2. Heat is absorbed from the sun by solar collectors on the roof, stored in an area filled with stones or water, and distributed through water pipes or a forced-air duct system.
3. a home with a southern exposure, no windows on the north side, and specially-built walls of concrete block with glass panels
4. Refrigerant passes through a compressor to become a pressurized hot gas, refrigerant is pumped to the condenser and cooled into a liquid state, liquid is pumped to the evaporator cooling coil to remove heat from the air, and ducts blow the cool air throughout the house.

5. systems that use the furnace blower to circulate cooled air versus systems that run independently of the furnace
6. the level of resistance to heat
7. Materials with higher R-values insulate better.
8. adds moisture to air, alone or as part of a heating unit
9. condenses the water droplets in humid air on cold coils for collection and removal
10. firebox: contains the fire and allows heat to enter the room
    damper: controls the burning rate and prevents downdrafts of cold air
    flue: facilitates a good draft to supply the fire with oxygen
11. A circulating stove is a radiant stove surrounded by a jacket with openings at the bottom and top to permit airflow, sometimes assisted by a small fan.
12. circulating stove

Student Activity Guide

Check Your Understanding, pages 177–179

1. One set carries heated air to the living space, while the other returns cold air from the living space to the furnace for heating.
2. because well water is warmer than outside air in cold weather and colder in warm weather
3. 96 cu. ft. of stone and 48 cu. ft. of water storage
4. hydronic heating system that uses copper tubing embedded in concrete floor or plastered ceiling, a central heat pump, and active solar heating
5. provides cool air; dehumidifies moist air in humid weather; and filters air contaminants including dirt, pollen, and dust
6. glass fiber, foamed glass, foamed plastics, and expanded minerals
7. throat and skin irritation and cracks in furniture
8. Sides and back consist of a double-wall passageway to heat cool air pulled from a room; air for combustion is piped into the sealed firebox from the outside; glass doors on the firebox prevent the loss of warm air up the chimney; and the tendency to pull cold air into a room through cracks around doors and windows is reduced.
9. circulating
10. by covering the opening with sheet metal to reflect the heat back into the room

11. C	16. D
12. D	17. A
13. D	18. D
14. C	19. C
15. C	

20. electricity
21. thermostat

22. radiators
23. absorber
24. three
25. heat
26. humidity
27. cleaning
28. draft
29. wood

Heating Systems, **Activity 20-1**

(Student response. See pages 354-360 in the text.)

Masonry Fireplace, **Activity 20-2**

1. smoke shelf
2. damper
3. cap
4. flashing
5. fire stop
6. flue lining
7. smoke chamber
8. mantle
9. angle steel lintel
10. firebrick
11. ash dump
12. outer hearth
13. concrete slab
14. clean-out door
15. basement floor
16. footing

Instructor's Resources

Chapter 20 Mastery Test

1.	B	6.	B
2.	C	7.	B
3.	D	8.	B
4.	C	9.	C
5.	D	10.	D

11. drops
12. hot water
13. resistance
14. refrigeration
15. south
16. copper
17. collect, store
18. insulation
19. higher
20. flue
21. temperature control, humidity control, air circulation, and air cleaning
22. furnace, blower, duct system, and thermostat
23. to eliminate cold floors and provide more-even heating
24. ceiling, floor, baseboard convectors
25. It uses an electric refrigeration unit to remove heat from outside air or well water, then pumps it into the house.
26. central air conditioner
27. A room air conditioner cools a room or local area. It consists of a compressor, condenser, cooling coil, and fan all in one unit.
28. by totaling the R-values of all the wall's components
29. Air becomes stale, but fans built into the central heating system or attic move the air and eliminate moisture, smoke, and fumes.
30. single-face fireplace because of good oxygen flow

Residential Climate Control

Temperature Control
Heating system

Cooling system

Ventilation

Solar orientation of the structure

Humidity Control
Humidifier

Dehumidifier

Air Circulation
Fans

Air Cleaning
Filters

Forced Warm-Air System

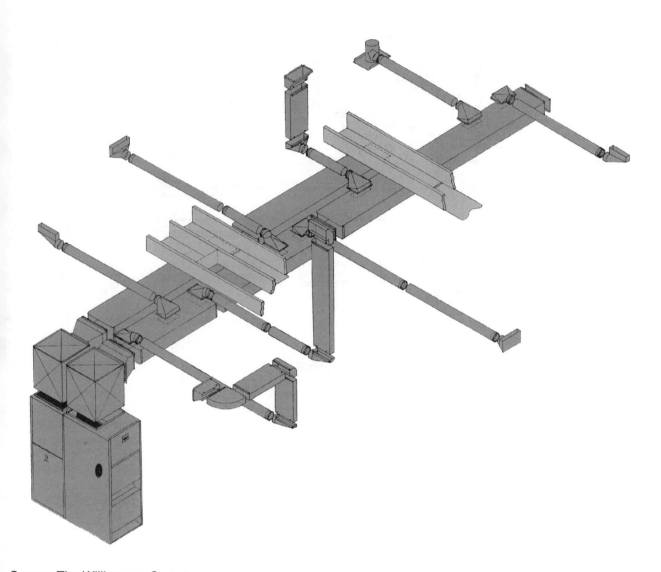

Source: The Williamson Company

Climate-Control Plan

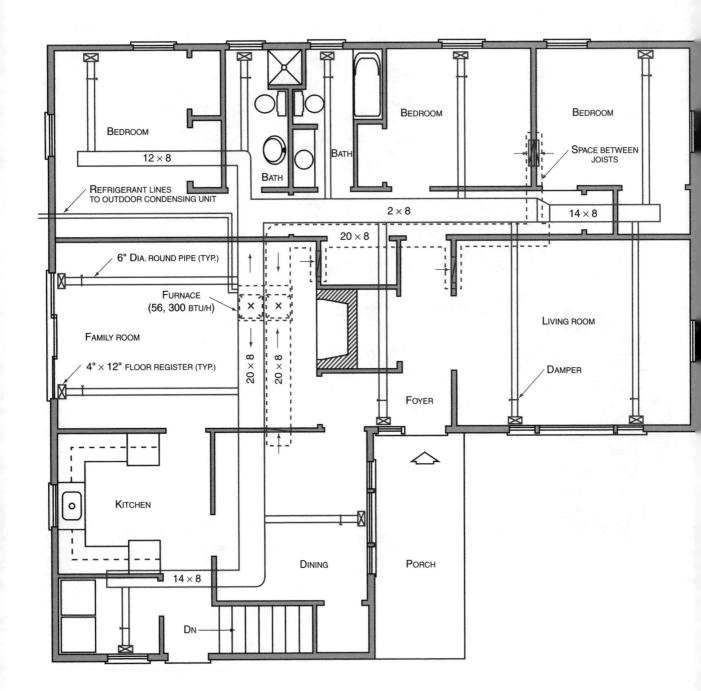

Active Solar Systems

General

- Contain an array of collectors (airtight boxes with absorbers).
- May use copper, the best absorber-plate material.
- Have an efficiency range of 15% to 65%.

Warm-Air System

- Uses a heat-storage box filled with stones or other thermal mass.
- Moves heated air through one or more blowers operated by controls.

Warm-Water System

- Uses a storage tank filled with water or other liquid.
- Moves heated water with a pump operated by controls.
- Is susceptible to problems with freezing.

Warm-Air Solar System

The design layout of this active solar system shows the following:

- 6 in. thick by 8 ft. long solar collector

- ducts with a 6 in. diameter

- 4 in. high by 8 ft. long thermal-storage area

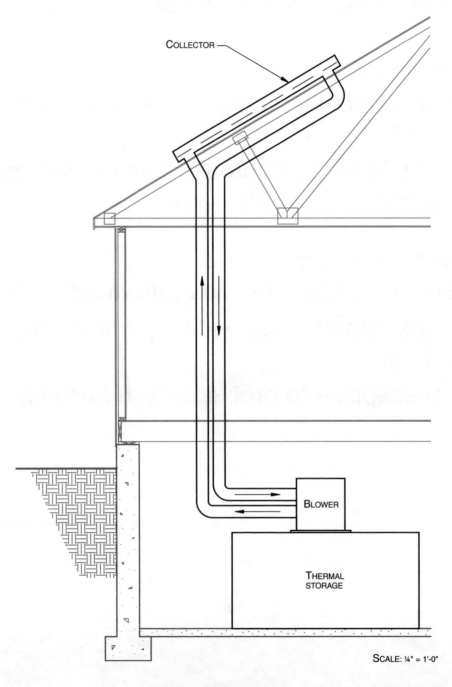

COLLECTOR

BLOWER

THERMAL STORAGE

SCALE: ¼" = 1'-0"

Passive Solar Systems

Direct-Gain System

- Is the most popular system.
- Uses a large south-facing glass area, allowing sunlight to directly penetrate living space.
- Needs a massive storage structure.
- Requires thick masonry walls and floors.

Indirect-Gain System

- Absorbs sunlight via a large thermal mass built between the sun and living space.
  - May be a trombe wall, which is a massive, dark colored, interior wall built next to a large window area.
  - Often is a wall of water-filled drums, but can contain other phase-change materials besides water.
- Relies on heat transfer from the thermal mass to the living space.

Isolated-Gain System

- Collects and stores energy outside the dwelling.
  - May become an attached sun space.
- Is more expensive to construct.
- Requires thick masonry walls and floors, but less interior space.
- May use solar collectors.
- More easily controls the heat collected.

Types of Passive Solar Systems

Direct Gain

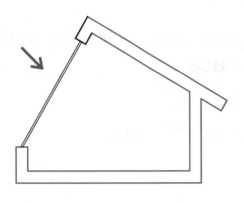

Sloped Wall

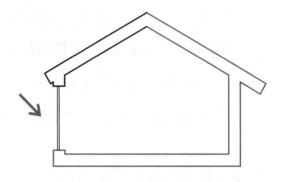

Vertical Wall

Indirect Gain

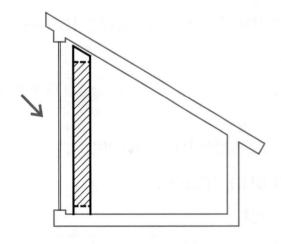

Trombe Wall

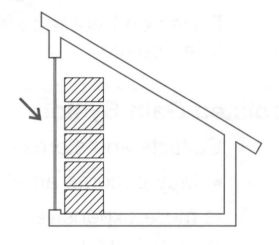

Drum Wall

Climate Control, Fireplaces, and Stoves
Chapter 20 Mastery Test

Name _____

Date _____

Score _____

Multiple Choice: Select the best response and write the letter in the preceding blank.

_____ 1. The structural element of a dwelling that helps temperature control systems work more efficiently is the _____.
  A. foundation
  B. insulation
  C. ceiling
  D. flooring

_____ 2. The common type of climate-control system that provides both heating and cooling in the same unit is the _____ system.
  A. forced warm-air
  B. hydronic
  C. central heat-pump
  D. active solar heating

_____ 3. Of the following components, a _____ is *not* a part of a typical hydronic heating system.
  A. boiler
  B. radiator
  C. pump
  D. blower

_____ 4. The two main types of solar heating systems are _____ systems.
  A. active and inactive
  B. passive and impassive
  C. active and passive
  D. active and impassive

_____ 5. Solar collectors range in efficiency from _____ percent.
  A. 70 to 80
  B. 50 to 65
  C. 20 to 90
  D. 15 to 65

_____ 6. The material that is frequently used to store the heat collected by warm-air solar collectors is _____.
  A. water
  B. stone
  C. rock salt
  D. earth

_____ 7. Of the following groups of materials, the best insulators are _____.
  A. glass fiber, foamed glass, and glass panels
  B. foamed plastics, expanded minerals, and glass fiber
  C. foamed glass, glass fiber, and concrete
  D. concrete, wood, and gypsum

_____ 8. Heating a home during the winter drops the indoor _____ to levels that can cause throat and skin irritation.
  A. airflow
  B. humidity
  C. air cleaning
  D. temperature

(continued)

Name _____

_____ 9. The three primary components of a traditional fireplace are _____.
A. inner hearth, outer hearth, and firebox
B. firebox, chimney, and ash dump
C. damper, flue, and firebox
D. outer hearth, flue, and damper

_____ 10. Of the following, the most efficient heating source is a _____.
A. traditional masonry fireplace
B. prefabricated heat circulating fireplace
C. Franklin stove
D. stove with baffles, a long smoke path, and a heat exchanger

Completion: Complete the following sentences by writing the missing words in the preceding blanks.

_____ 11. Efficiency of the central heat pump _____ considerably when temperatures fall below 30°F.

_____ 12. A hydronic heating system uses _____ _____ to heat the home.

_____ 13. Electric radiant heating systems use _____ wiring to produce heat.

_____ 14. The central heat-pump system uses an electric _____ unit to heat and cool a living space.

_____ 15. Solar collectors are generally installed on the roof facing _____ to receive maximum exposure to sunlight.

_____ 16. The most efficient and expensive material used for absorber plates is _____.

_____ 17. A passive solar heating system uses the structure of the house to both _____ and _____ heat.

_____ 18. A material that efficiently resists the flow of heat is called _____.

_____ 19. R-values are _____ for materials with greater insulative efficiency.

_____ 20. A _____ is needed to carry smoke to the outside of the house and facilitate a good draft for the fire.

Short Answer: Provide brief answers to the following questions or statements.

21. What are the components of a total climate-control system? _____

_____

_____

22. List the main components of a forced warm-air heating system. _____

_____

_____

23. Why are registers generally located close to the floor along the outside walls of a house?

_____

24. What are three common locations for heating wires for electric radiant systems? _____

_____

_____

_____

(continued)

Name _____

25. How does a central heat-pump system provide heat to a home in cold weather? _____

_____

_____

26. What is the most efficient type of residential cooling system?_____

_____

27. How does a room air conditioner differ from a central air conditioner? _____

_____

_____

_____

28. How is the R-value of a wall determined? _____

_____

_____

_____

29. What happens when the same air is continually used in a home without adding a fresh supply? How is this prevented? _____

_____

_____

_____

30. What is the most efficient type of masonry fireplace? Why? _____

_____

_____

_____

Chapter 21
Communication, Security, and Home Automation

Objectives

After studying this chapter, you will be able to

- determine the features related to information, communication, and security that should be considered when designing a new home or remodeling.
- define common terms associated with information, communication, security, and home automation.
- list the components of a security system designed to protect residential property.
- identify the components of a home-automation system.
- describe the elements of a low-voltage switching system.

Teaching Materials

Text, pages 369–381

Student Activity Guide

Check Your Understanding
21-1, *Types of System Functions*
21-2, *Security-System Components*
21-3, *Home Automation*

Instructor's Resources

Five System Functions, reproducible master 21-A
Protecting Occupants and Property, transparency master 21-B
Chapter 21 Mastery Test

Instructional Concepts and Student Activities

1. Have students read Chapter 21 in the text and complete the review questions.
2. Have students collect technical information about communication, security, and home automation systems and products. Have the students add this information to their housing notebooks.

Types of System Functions

3. Discuss modern technology features in terms of functions that might be considered when designing a new home.
4. *Five System Functions*, reproducible master 21-A, IR. Acquaint students with the basic types of system functions, their descriptions, and some examples. Ask students to identify more examples of each type of system function.

Information and Communication Systems

5. Lead a class discussion on residential telephone lines and typical communication systems and signaling circuits.
6. Show and/or demonstrate some typical information and communication systems used in homes.
7. *Types of System Functions*, Activity 21-1, SAG. Students match each situation with the type of system function it describes.

Structured Wiring

8. Discuss the advantages and capabilities of structured wiring.
9. Show examples of structured wiring components.

Security Systems

10. Lead a discussion about security systems in the home in terms of those that protect property versus those that protect occupants as well.
11. Show the students the components of a typical home security system and explain the function of each component.
12. *Protecting Occupants and Property*, transparency master 21-B, IR. Have students discuss the components of a complete at-home security system.
13. *Security-System Components*, Activity 21-2, SAG. Students are to match various security-system components with their descriptions.

Home Automation

14. Lead a class discussion on home automation in terms of early efforts to network appliances. Explore current types of home automation systems such as hard-wired systems, power line technology, structured wiring, and combination systems.
15. *Home Automation*, Activity 21-3, SAG. Have students locate each component for a home security and automation system on an approved floor plan.

Low-Voltage Switching

16. Discuss how low-voltage switching works.
17. Assign one or more tasks listed in the text's *Suggested Activities* section at the end of the chapter.

Suggested Evaluation Techniques

18. *Check Your Understanding*, SAG. Have students complete as many questions as possible without referring to the text. Then have them find answers to questions they do not know.
19. Administer the *Chapter 21 Mastery Test*.

Answer Key

Text

Review Questions, page 380

1. A. alarm function
   B. programming function
   C. switching function
   D. communication/recording function
   E. monitoring function
2. indicates that a visitor is present, allows family members to communicate within the home, permits the owner to monitor various systems within the dwelling and property
3. B
4. doors
5. to sense an entry made by breaking glass, which does not activate the magnetic switches on unopened doors and windows
6. a network
7. CEBus, SmartHouse®, Echelon®, and Integrated Networks
8. CEBus
9. hard-wired system, power line technology, structured wiring, and combination system
10. 24

Student Activity Guide

Check Your Understanding, pages 183–184

1. E
2. A
3. F
4. G
5. B
6. C
7. D
8. H
9. switching
10. two
11. fire
12. doors
13. perimeter
14. smoke
15. networking
16. X10
17. Category 5
18. PVC
19. remote control
20. B
21. D
22. A
23. C
24. B
25. C

Types of System Functions, 21-1

1. A	11. C
2. B	12. C
3. C	13. D
4. D	14. E
5. C	15. A
6. B	16. D
7. C	17. E
8. E	18. E
9. E	19. B
10. B	20. B

Security-System Components, Activity 21-2

1. touch pad
2. smoke detector
3. control panel
4. siren
5. motion detector
6. shock sensor
7. door sensor
8. panic button
9. glassbreak detector

Instructor's Resources

Chapter 21 Mastery Test

1. A
2. B
3. D
4. A
5. D
6. B
7. D
8. B
9. C
10. B
11. A
12. C

13. monitoring
14. programming
15. telephone
16. structured
17. perimeter
18. smoke inhalation
19. structured
20. bundled
21. when planning and designing a new home, because the cost is less and system integration is more efficient.
22. monitoring, switching (activating), programming, communication/recording, and alarm
23. provide a signal to an intruder alert, alert the homeowner to unsafe conditions from gas and smoke, and warn of a malfunctioning appliance
24. sensing visitors, allowing people to communicate within the home, and permitting the monitoring of systems in the dwelling and on the property
25. Category 5 cable
26. control panel, touch pad, siren, door sensors, motion sensor, and smoke detectors
27. through glassbreak and shock sensor detection
28. hard-wired systems, power line technology, structured wiring systems, and combination systems
29. hardware modules, computer interface, and a software program

Five System Functions

Function	Description	Examples
Monitoring	• Examine certain conditions. • Determine the status of each. • Report the status to the homeowner or another device.	• Measuring room temperature. • Detecting movement • Sensing carbon monoxide levels.
Switching	• Initiate an action based on data input.	• Turning the furnace on when the thermostat drops too low. • Shutting the clothes washer off when the last rinse cycle ends.
Programming	• Control a sequence of planned events.	• Turning lights off in 1 hr., and back on in 4 hr. • Lowering the house temperature at 10 p.m., and raising it at 8 a.m.
Communicating/ Recording	• Record, play back, and/or allow live voice, video, or data communication.	• Using an intercom. • Using a telephone. • Finding information on the Internet.
Alarm	• Send an alert based on information from a monitoring device.	• Sounding a siren when an intruder appears. • Flashing a warning when an appliance malfunctions.

Protecting Occupants and Property

A complete at-home security system has the following:

- **Exterior lights**—with sudden onset for intruders

- **Perimeter system**—that wires all doors and windows with magnetic switches and offers glassbreak protection

- **Indoor motion detectors**—to sense intruders who bypass the perimeter system

- **Emergency "alert"**—if fire or an intruder is detected

- **Panic button**—that activates a siren or sends an alarm to a monitoring station if the security system is somehow disarmed or disabled

- **Smoke detectors**—to provide fire protection

Communication, Security, and Home Automation
Chapter 21 Mastery Test

Name _____

Date _____

Score _____

Multiple Choice: Select the best response and write the letter in the preceding blank.

_____   1.   An example of an emerging technology is _____.
A.   security devices and cabling
B.   sound systems
C.   cable television
D.   telephone wiring

_____   2.   When the temperature in a house drops enough to switch the furnace on, this is an example of a _____ function.
A.   monitoring
B.   switching (activating)
C.   programming
D.   communication/recording

_____   3.   _____ are devices that perform communication/recording functions.
A.   Intercoms
B.   Voice or video phones
C.   Closed-circuit video cameras
D.   All of the above.

_____   4.   The telephone company's lines terminate at the _____.
A.   cable termination box outside the house
B.   buffalo box in the front yard
C.   wiring cabinet in the basement
D.   service-entrance panel

_____   5.   _____ are popular signal and communication system devices.
A.   Doorbells
B.   Buzzers
C.   Chimes
D.   All of the above.

_____   6.   The type of cable to use for digital satellite and digital cable is _____.
A.   Category 5 cable
B.   Radio grade 6 cable
C.   standard telephone cable
D.   speaker wire

_____   7.   The panic button in a security system may be used _____.
A.   after the intruder is inside the house
B.   when a perimeter switch fails
C.   when the system has been disarmed
D.   All of the above.

_____   8.   Hard-wired systems are used in security and surveillance applications because they _____.
A.   are cheap and dependable
B.   have a high level of reliability
C.   can easily be modified
D.   represent low-level technology

_____   9.   The type of home automation system popular in the home remodeling market is _____.
A.   the hard-wired system
B.   structured wiring
C.   power line technology
D.   combination systems

(continued)

Name _____

_____ 10. The preferred home automation system for new home construction seems to be _____.
  A. combination systems
  B. structured wiring
  C. power line technology
  D. hard-wired systems

_____ 11. The type of home automation system usually chosen for a totally customized installation is _____.
  A. a combination system
  B. structured wiring
  C. power line technology
  D. a hard-wired system

_____ 12. An advantage of low-voltage switching is _____.
  A. Category 5 cable is used
  B. electrical shock is eliminated
  C. fixtures located at various points in the house may be controlled from a single location
  D. the system is inexpensive to install

Completion: Complete the following sentences by writing the missing words in the preceding bank.

_____ 13. Devices that perform _____ functions examine certain aspects of the house to determine the status of each.

_____ 14. Devices that perform _____ functions can control a sequence of events.

_____ 15. A new home should have a minimum of two standard _____ lines.

_____ 16. An organized arrangement of high-quality cables and connections that distribute services throughout the home is an example of _____ wiring.

_____ 17. In a _____ security system, all doors and windows are wired with magnetic switches inside the frame.

_____ 18. Most deaths from nighttime fires are the result of _____ _____ because a victim does not wake up.

_____ 19. In a _____ wiring system, home security and home automation systems are joined in one network connection center.

_____ 20. When several conductors (wires) are placed inside one PVC jacket, this is an example of _____ cable.

Short Answer: Provide brief answers to the following questions or statements.

21. When is the best time to consider new technologies and why?_____

_____

_____

22. What are the five basic functions of modern technology systems? _____

_____

_____

_____

(continued)

298 Reproducible Test Master

Name _____

23. List three actions that an alarm device might perform. _____

_____

_____

24. What services are provided by signal and communication systems? _____

_____

_____

25. What type of cable is necessary for high-speed Internet access? _____

_____

26. What six components are generally recommended for a security system designed to protect property? _____

_____

_____

_____

_____

27. How is an intruder detected if entry is through a broken window? _____

_____

_____

28. What are the four types of home automation systems? _____

_____

_____

29. What are the three basic components generally included in a power line technology system?

_____

_____

Chapter 22
Energy and Water Conservation

Objectives

After studying this chapter, students will be able to

- evaluate the energy efficiency of a home according to its orientation, insulation, construction, and site.
- identify the efficiency of an appliance by using EnergyGuide and Energy Star labels and by checking for energy-saving features.
- list the advantages and disadvantages of using solar or wind energy for a home energy supply.
- list ways to use computers to decrease home energy consumption.
- list the residential water-saving measures required by law.
- explain how green building promotes conservation.

Teaching Materials

Text, pages 382–397

Student Activity Guide

Check Your Understanding
22-1, *Orientation*
22-2, *Insulation*
22-3, *Increasing Efficiency*

Instructor's Resources

Projected Residential Energy Use, reproducible master 22-A

Average Residential Energy Bill, transparency master 22-B

Air-Conditioning Suitability Checkpoints, transparency master 22-C

Nationwide View of Air-Conditioning Use, reproducible master 22-D

Energy-Saving Approaches, transparency master 22-E

Impact of Energy Alternatives, transparency master 22-F

Biomass Energy Sources, transparency master 22-G

Trends in U.S. Water Use, transparency master 22-H
Chapter 22 Mastery Test

Instructional Concepts and Student Activities

1. Have students read Chapter 22 in the text and complete the review questions.
2. Ask students to collect technical literature on insulation products (including information on efficiency and application) as well as energy-saving heating and cooling equipment and residential appliances. Have them add these materials to their housing notebooks.

Architectural and Site Considerations

3. Lead a class discussion on the effects of solar orientation, insulation, windows, doors, construction, heating and plumbing systems, and site considerations on energy conservation.
4. *Orientation*, Activity 22-1, SAG. Students are to specify the preferred orientation of various rooms of a house for both cold and warm climates.
5. Show the *Home Designs*, the *New Homes*, or *Older Homes* video from Utah State University. Have the class discuss it.
6. *Insulation*, Activity 22-2, SAG. Students are to match insulation terms with their descriptions.
7. *Projected Residential Energy Use*, reproducible master 22-A, IR. Have students discuss the estimates of total energy use by households in the near future, especially regarding space and water heating.

Energy-Saving Appliances

8. *Average Residential Energy Bill*, transparency master 22-B, IR. Have students discuss the appliances and activities responsible for various portions of the average household's energy bill.
9. *Air-Conditioning Suitability Checkpoints*, transparency master 22-C, IR. Have students discuss the house features that help retain the cooled air a central air conditioner generates.
10. Discuss EnergyGuide labels and how to save energy with refrigerators, freezers, dishwashers, clothes washers, and water heaters.

11. Have students discuss the reason for not labeling the energy use of ranges, ovens, clothes dryers, humidifiers, dehumidifiers, and space heaters. (The reason is: energy use varies little according to the model, but greatly according to user frequency.)

12. Show the *Cooktops and Cookware* or *Kitchen Appliances* video from Utah State University. Have the class discuss the video and opportunities for saving energy.

13. *Increasing Efficiency*, Activity 22-3, SAG. Students are to write an essay about how to increase the heating and cooling efficiency of a dwelling.

14. *Nationwide View of Air-Conditioning Use*, reproducible master 22-D, IR. Have students examine how long various parts of the country run their air conditioners. (Note: This map reflects the air-conditioning needs of average households, as satisfied by both central and room air conditioners.)

15. *Energy-Saving Approaches*, transparency master 22-E, IR. Have students review the list of ways to save energy. Based on information covered in this portion of the text, what additional recommendations would they add to the list?

Energy Alternatives

16. Have students form small groups to discuss alternative energy sources such as solar, wind, and geothermal energy. Have each group share its findings with the class.

17. *Impact of Energy Alternatives*, transparency master 22-F, IR. Have students discuss the contribution of alternate energy sources to the nation's total energy use. (Note: The next item features a transparency that explains *biomass*.)

18. *Biomass Energy Sources*, transparency master 22-G, IR. Acquaint students with biomass, which currently is the greatest source of renewable energy. (Note: Woodfuel, as in logs for fireplaces, is the only biomass used for energy in the residential sector.)

Water Conservation

19. *Trends in U.S. Water Use*, transparency master 22-H, IR. Have students examine how much U.S. water demands have increased over a recent 40-year period.

20. Have the class develop a list of ways that teenagers can help reduce water use at home and school. Write examples from the students on the board.

Green Building

21. Ask students to examine local newspapers to find examples of green building taking place in the local area, region, or state. Have students discuss their findings.

22. Assign one or more tasks listed in the text's *Suggested Activities* section at the end of the chapter.

Suggested Evaluation Techniques

23. *Check Your Understanding*, SAG. Have students complete as many questions as possible without referring to the text. Then have them find answers to questions they do not know.

24. Administer the *Chapter 22 Mastery Test*.

Answer Key

Text

Review Questions, page 396

1. with living areas on the south side and the garage and utility rooms on the north side
2. insulating boards
3. to let in sunlight and warmth
4. constructing a roof overhang of the proper length, using an appropriate roof color, double-framing the walls, and filling gaps in construction materials
5. by insulating air ducts in unheated spaces, locating ducts around the perimeter of the home, placing warm air registers near large glass areas, placing ductwork directly under floor panels, and installing dampers in ducts
6. by centrally locating plumbing mains, insulating very long pipes, insulating pipes or water heaters in unheated areas, and installing flow restrictors in faucets and showerheads
7. by forming a windbreak along the north side of a house with evergreens, by blocking the summer sun on the south side of a house with deciduous trees, and by using earth berms to block wind
8. by comparing the estimated energy use and operating cost of an appliance to that of all similar models
9. advantages: conserves nonrenewable fuels, uses an inexhaustible and freely available fuel source, and produces no waste products disadvantages: very expensive to install, requires an auxiliary heating system for cloudy days, and requires considerable space for heat-storage facilities

10. advantages: conserves nonrenewable fuels, uses an inexhaustible fuel source, and generates a power source that can be sold to power companies
    disadvantages: requires a very large windmill and is expensive to install
11. by determining optimum site orientation, window placement, and other factors in designing a home for maximum energy efficiency; by shutting appliances off when not in use; and by adjusting the home's lights, air and water temperatures, and exterior shades as needed
12. 1.6 gallons per flush
13. 2.5 gallons per minute at a line pressure of 80 lb. per sq. in.
14. reduce energy and water use, use clean energy, provide a healthy indoor environment, and use environmentally friendly materials

Student Activity Guide

Check Your Understanding, pages 189–191

1. to have the living space surrounded with a thermal blanket that keeps the home warm in cold weather and cool in warm weather
2. loose fill
3. It prevents moisture condensation in winter and reduces heat buildup in summer.
4. electronic igniters on gas-fired furnaces and automatic flue dampers
5. (Student response. See pages 390-392 in the text.)
6. provides heat only in moderately cold weather, needs a conventional heating system for backup during very cold weather, is not functional in areas with little sunshine, is very expensive to install, and requires considerable space for heat storage facilities
7. They can be used to design energy-efficient homes. In the home, they can turn off appliances not in use, raise and lower thermostat temperatures as needed, turn on water heaters as needed, raise and lower shades to permit sunlight or block cold air, automatically turn lights on or off as people enter or leave rooms, and adjust heating and cooling systems to outdoor temperatures for more efficient energy use.
8. B
9. D
10. C
11. C
12. B
13. A
14. C
15. B
16. A

17. 13
18. higher
19. double
20. 30
21. 1.6
22. green

Orientation, Activity 22-1

1. south, north
2. southeast, north
3. east, east
4. west, west
5. southwest, northeast
6. south, north
7. north, southwest
8. north, south
9. In cool climates, the living areas of the home are placed on the south side to take advantage of warm sunlight, while the garage and utility room are placed on the north side to buffer the cold. In warm climates, the living areas are placed on the north side to take advantage of less sunlight and heat, while the garage and utility room are often placed on the south side.

Insulation, Activity 22-2

1. B
2. A
3. J
4. F
5. E
6. G
7. C
8. I
9. H
10. D

Instructor's Resources

Chapter 22 Mastery Test

1. C
2. C
3. A
4. D
5. D
6. D
7. B
8. B
9. C
10. A
11. C
12. orientation
13. south
14. north
15. wind
16. insulation
17. R-value
18. polyurethane
19. moisture
20. 10, 15
21. berm

22. 2.5
23. (List four:) orientation of a home, type and amount of insulation, placement and construction of windows and doors, construction of roof and walls, placement of heating and plumbing systems
24. because the east side receives full sunlight in the morning, which brightens rooms and helps to warm them after a cool evening
25. by having a vestibule at the main entrance to prevent outdoor air from entering the living areas and/or by locating a garage, utility room, or porch with a wind screen on the windy side of the house to serve as a buffer
26. (Student response. See pages 383-385 in the text.)
27. loose fill
28. It should fit snugly in ceilings, floors, and walls and should not block air circulation vents in eaves.
29. Place most windows on the south side of the home, have few or no windows on the north side, avoid large window areas on the windy side, and use insulating windows.
30. A proper overhang shades south windows from the high summer sun, but allows the low winter sun to enter.
31. (Student response. See pages 382-384 in the text.)
32. to compare the efficiency and energy use of an appliance to all similar models
33. that the appliance or product is at least 10 percent more energy efficient than competing products
34. that no more than 1.6 gallons of water per flush could be used in all new toilets in residential construction
35. a way for builders to minimize the environmental impact of their construction projects

Projected Residential Energy Use (Quadrillion Btu per Year)

Use	2005	2010	2015	2020
Space heating	6.73	6.99	7.10	7.27
Water heating	2.55	2.58	2.54	2.52
Lighting	2.54	2.73	2.84	2.95
Space cooling	2.13	2.19	2.23	2.32
Refrigeration	1.27	1.16	1.10	1.09
Clothes dryer	0.86	0.89	0.89	0.91
Cooking	0.58	0.61	0.63	0.66
Color television	0.47	0.58	0.68	0.78
Freezer	0.39	0.37	0.36	0.36
Furnace fan	0.26	0.28	0.30	0.32
Personal computer	0.20	0.25	0.30	0.35
Clothes washer	0.10	0.12	0.15	0.18
Dishwasher	0.08	0.08	0.09	0.09
Other uses	3.60	4.22	4.76	5.29
Total	21.75	23.06	23.98	25.10

Source: U.S. Energy Information Administration

Average Residential Energy Bill

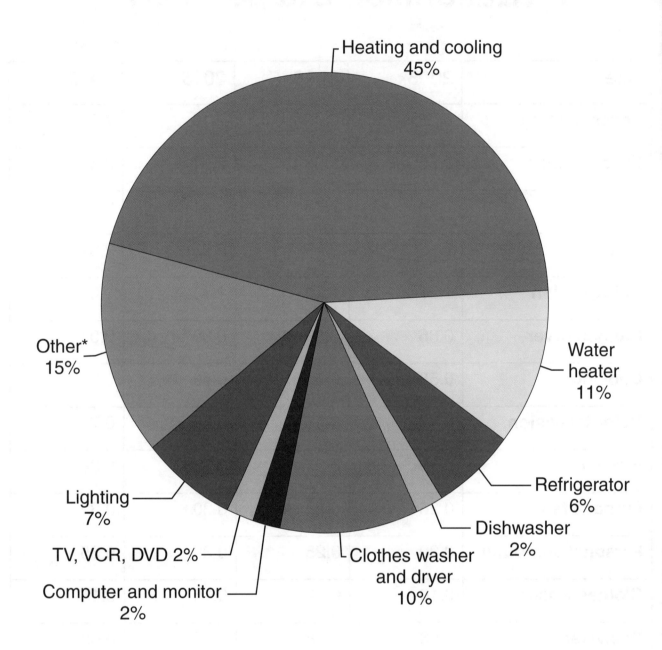

* = Includes ranges, ovens, microwave ovens, and small appliances.

Source: U.S. Department of Energy

Air-Conditioning Suitability Checkpoints

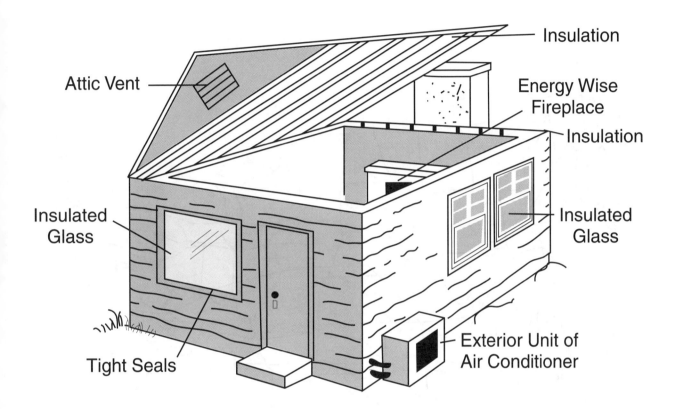

Source: Air Conditioning and Refrigeration Institute

Nationwide View of Air-Conditioning Use
(Cooling Hours per Year)

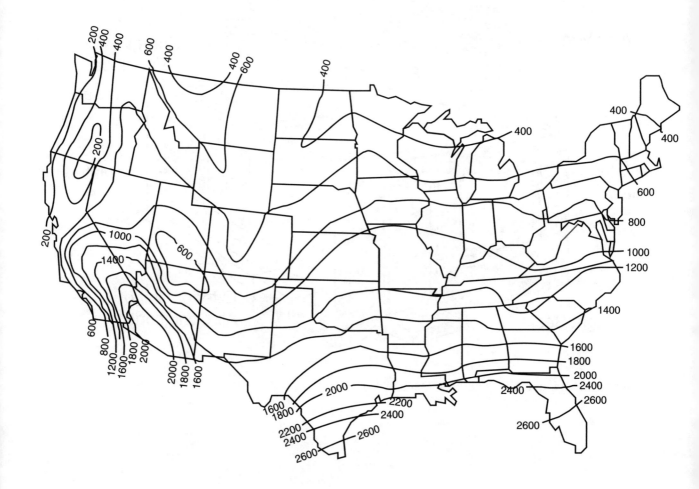

Source: Air Conditioning and Refrigeration Institute

Energy-Saving Approaches

- Purchase appliances with high energy ratings.

- Add insulation to a water heater to increase its energy efficiency.

- Use on-demand water heaters whenever possible.

- Cook with convection and microwave ovens since they need less energy than conventional cooking appliances.

- Consider heat pumps for increased efficiency.

- Automatic flue dampers reduce heat loss.

- Run appliances during off-peak hours when utilities often charge lower electric rates.

Impact of Energy Alternatives

Total = 97.551 Quadrillion Btu   Total = 5.881 Quadrillion Btu

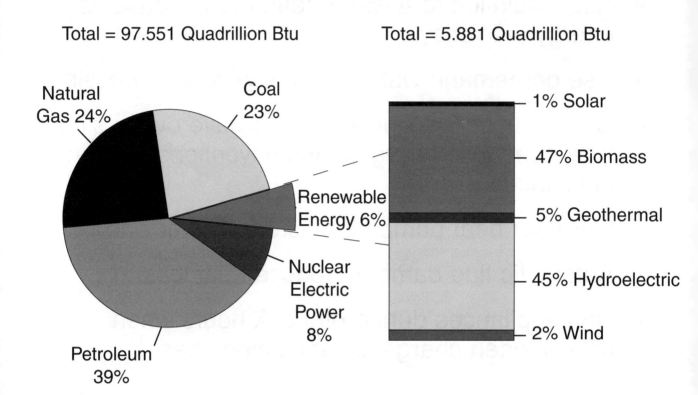

Natural Gas 24%

Coal 23%

Renewable Energy 6%

Nuclear Electric Power 8%

Petroleum 39%

1% Solar

47% Biomass

5% Geothermal

45% Hydroelectric

2% Wind

Based on 2002 U.S. energy consumption
Source: U.S. Energy Information Administration

Biomass Energy Sources

Biomass = the use of plants, plant waste, and animal waste for fuel.

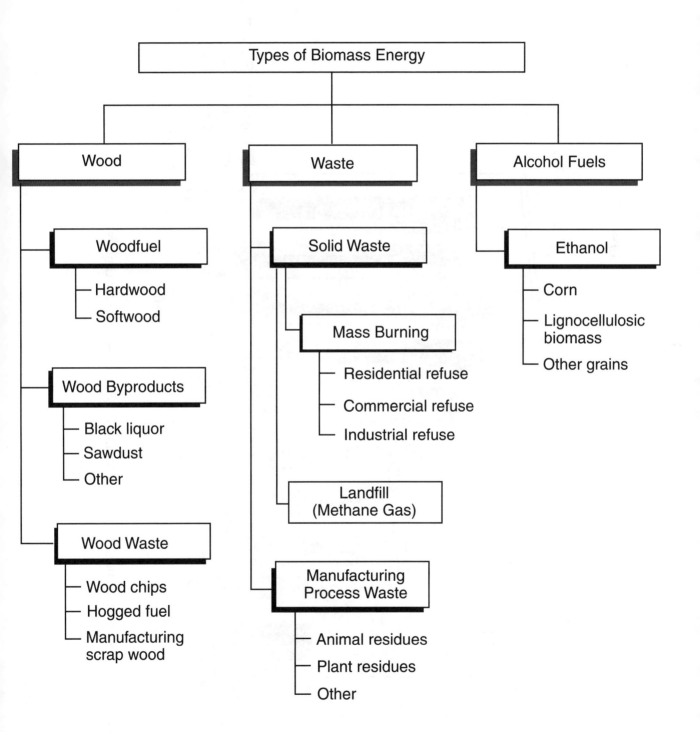

Trends in U.S. Water Use
(Billion Gallons per Day)

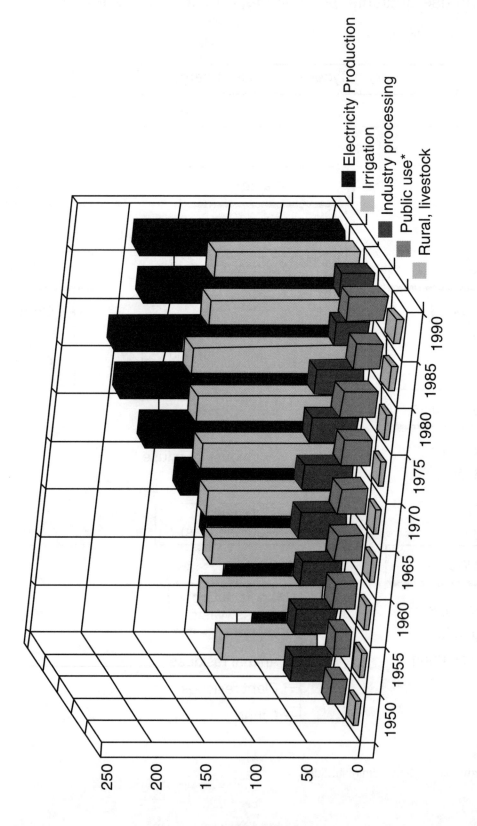

Source: U.S. Geological Survey

* = Water supplied in homes, restaurants, and businesses for everyday use

Energy and Water Conservation
Chapter 22 Mastery Test

Name _____

Date _____

Score _____

Multiple Choice: Select the best response and write the letter in the preceding blank.

_____ 1. Of all the energy used in this country, the portion used by homes is approximately _____ percent.
    A. 33
    B. 25
    C. 20
    D. 12

_____ 2. The two sides of a home that are generally the warmest are the _____ sides.
    A. north and east
    B. south and east
    C. south and west
    D. north and west

_____ 3. In cool climates, the garage and utility room should be placed on the _____ side of the house.
    A. north
    B. east
    C. south
    D. west

_____ 4. The rooms that are generally placed on the east side of the house are the _____.
    A. bedrooms
    B. bathrooms
    C. living room and family room
    D. dining room and kitchen

_____ 5. Blanket insulation is produced in _____.
    A. boards and loose fill
    B. rolls and boards
    C. batts and loose fill
    D. rolls and batts

_____ 6. In a residential structure, board insulation is generally used _____.
    A. around foundations
    B. between studs in side walls
    C. between studs and siding
    D. All of the above.

_____ 7. The vapor barrier should be placed _____.
    A. next to the insulation, facing away from the interior
    B. between the interior and the insulation
    C. between two layers of insulation
    D. All of the above.

_____ 8. Exterior doors that make the best insulators are _____.
    A. solid wood doors
    B. steel doors with a plastic foam core
    C. hollow-core doors with storm doors
    D. solid vinyl doors

_____ 9. The largest energy user in the home is the _____.
    A. range and oven
    B. hot water heater
    C. heating/cooling system
    D. clothes dryer

(continued)

Name _____

_____ 10. The label that appears on most major appliances to help compare the energy efficiency of
different models is the _____ label.
A. EnergyGuide
B. efficiency rating
C. operating costs
D. cost comparison

_____ 11. The average cost of a windmill per kilowatt of capacity is _____.
A. $200
B. $1,000
C. $2,000
D. $3,000

Completion: Complete the following sentences by writing the missing words in the preceding blanks.

_____ 12. The placement or alignment of rooms within the structure as well as the
placement of the structure on a site is called _____.

_____ 13. In cool climates, the living areas of the house should be placed on the
_____ side.

_____ 14. In warm climates, the living areas of the house should be placed on the
_____ side.

_____ 15. In addition to the sun, the _____ affects the amount of energy required to
heat or cool a home.

_____ 16. Surrounding the living space as a thermal blanket to keep the home
warm in cold weather and cool in warm weather is the reason for _____.

_____ 17. The term used to identify the amount of insulation needed is _____.

_____ 18. Rigid, foamed plastics are usually made from _____ or polystyrene.

_____ 19. Air movement in the attic prevents _____ buildup in cold weather.

_____ 20. The cost of heating water accounts for _____ to _____ percent of the
average household energy bill.

_____ 21. An earth _____ can be used to protect the north side of a home from
winter winds.

_____ 22. The flow rate of showerheads and faucets used in homes is limited to
_____ gallons per minute at a line pressure of 80 lb. per sq. in.

Short Answer: Provide brief answers to the following questions or statements.

23. List four architectural considerations that can decrease a home's energy use._____

_____

_____

_____

_____

24. Why are kitchens and dining rooms often placed on the east side of the house?_____

_____

_____

(continued)

Name _____

25. In a home, how can cold winds be blocked to reduce heat loss? _____

_____

_____

26. How do the three types of insulation differ? _____

_____

_____

_____

_____

_____

27. What type of insulation is used in inaccessible spaces, such as attic floors or cores of concrete
blocks? _____

_____

28. How should insulation be used to reduce heating or cooling losses? _____

_____

_____

_____

_____

29. How should windows be used to help reduce heat loss in northern climates? _____

_____

_____

_____

_____

30. How can the length of a roof overhang control the amount of heat gain in a home? _____

_____

_____

_____

31. How can site considerations be used to decrease a home's energy use? _____

_____

_____

_____

_____

_____

(continued)

Name _____

32. How can consumers use EnergyGuide labels? _____

_____

_____

_____

33. What does an Energy Star label indicate? _____

_____

_____

_____

34. What did the National Energy Policy Act of 1994 specify with regard to water closets? _____

_____

_____

_____

35. What is green building? _____

_____

_____

_____

Chapter 23
Designing for Health and Safety

Objectives

After studying this chapter you will be able to

- identify fire hazards around the home and explain preventive measures.
- explain the hazards associated with carbon monoxide and ways to prevent them.
- explain the hazards associated with radon in residential housing and identify preventive measures.
- point out problems in residential structures associated with excess moisture.
- describe the dangers associated with weather- and nature-related events such as earthquakes, floods, tornadoes, and hurricanes.
- list steps that can be taken to lessen the damage and destruction of weather- and nature-related events.

Teaching Materials

Text, pages 398–419

Student Activity Guide

Check Your Understanding
23-1, *Fire, Gas, and Mold*
23-2, *Preventing Property Damage and Injury*

Instructor's Resources

Using a Fire Extinguisher, reproducible master 23-A

Sources of Water Vapor in the Home, transparency master 23-B

Top Ten U.S. Natural Disasters, reproducible master 23-C

U.S. Tornado Activity, transparency master 23-D

Chapter 23 Mastery Test

Instructional Concepts and Student Activities

1. Have the students read Chapter 23 in the text and complete the review questions.

2. Ask students to collect technical information about health and safety. Have them add this information to their housing notebooks.

Smoke and Fire Detection

3. Lead a class discussion on smoke and fire detection including fire prevention, smoke detectors, fire safety code requirements, and fire extinguishers.
4. Provide smoke detectors and fire extinguishers for student examination.
5. Invite the local fire chief to discuss fire prevention and fire safety code requirements.
6. Prepare a bulletin display that shows the key elements of a home fire-prevention program.
7. *Using a Fire Extinguisher,* reproducible master 23-A, IR. Use the handout for a class discussion on the proper use of fire extinguishers.

Carbon Monoxide Detection

8. Lead a class discussion on carbon monoxide detection including carbon monoxide poisoning and CO detectors.
9. Provide an opportunity for students to become familiar with typical CO detectors.

Radon Detection

10. Lead a class discussion on radon detection including radon in the home, radon testing, and radon mitigation.
11. Have the students explain how an active, fan-driven, vent-pipe system removes radon.

Moisture and Mold Problems

12. *Sources of Water Vapor in the Home,* transparency master 23-B, IR. Have the class review and discuss the major sources of water vapor in the home.
13. Lead a class discussion on moisture and mold problems including migration of water vapor, preventative measures, ventilation, health hazards associated with mold, and mold prevention and removal.
14. Ask the students to bring in samples or take photos of molds found around their residences for class discussion and identification.

15. *Fire, Gas, and Mold*, Activity 23-1, SAG. Students are to demonstrate their understanding of fire, carbon monoxide, radon, and mold by matching descriptions to the correct hazards.

Weather- and Nature-Related Safety

16. Lead a class discussion on weather- and nature-related safety including earthquakes, floods, tornadoes, and hurricanes.
17. *Top Ten U.S. Natural Disasters*, reproducible master 23-C, IR. Use the handout to review U.S. natural disasters that required the greatest amount of relief from the U.S. Federal Emergency Management Agency. Ask students if anyone personally experienced a similar type of natural disaster.
18. Ask students to identify methods of reducing damage inside the home from earthquakes.
19. Have students research additional ways to reduce earthquake damage to dwellings. (An excellent reference is *Earthquake Safe: A Hazard Reduction Manual for Homes* published by David Helfant, available at www.buildersbooksite.com.)
20. *U.S. Tornado Activity,* transparency master 23-D, IR. Have students study the map to determine how their community ranks in terms of tornado activity. (Note: White areas of the map may occasionally have a tornado, but too infrequently to average one per 1,000 sq. mi.)
21. Prepare a large U.S. map that shows the areas most prone to damage from flooding, hurricanes, and earthquakes.
22. Ask students to list techniques that may be used to reduce damage to dwellings from severe weather and the forces of nature.

General Home Safety

23. Discuss general home safety. What are some common ways in which people are injured around the home?
24. *Preventing Property Damage and Injury*, Activity 23-2, SAG. Students match nature-related and general household hazards to the relevant safety practices.
25. Assign one or more tasks listed in the text's *Suggested Activities* section at the end of the chapter.

Suggested Evaluation Techniques

26. Check your Understanding, SAG. Have students complete as many questions as possible without referring to the text. Then have them find answers to questions they do not know.

27. Administer the Chapter 23 Mastery Test.

Answer Key

Text

Review Questions, page 418

1. D
2. in the living or family room, at the top of the stairwell between the first and second floors, and outside each bedroom
3. two
4. Class B
5. carbon monoxide (CO)
6. lung cancer
7. by sealing joints, cracks, and other openings; installing an active, fan-driven radon-removal vent-pipe system; and reducing the "stack" or "chimney" effect in basements
8. (List four:) damp spots on ceilings and the room side of exterior walls; water and frost on the inside surfaces of windows; moisture on basement sidewalls and floors; water-filled blisters on outside paint surfaces; marbles of ice on attic floors resulting from condensation of water on points of nails through roof sheathing.
9. D
10. by controlling the moisture (or water vapor) that encourages its growth
11. allergy-type symptoms
12. *Stachybotrys atra*
13. flooding
14. New Madrid
15. April, May, and June
16. 74 mph
17. August and September
18. B

Student Activity Guide

Check Your Understanding, pages 195–198

1. D
2. D
3. C
4. B
5. C
6. D
7. B
8. D
9. C
10. C
11. grease
12. oxygen
13. uranium
14. mitigation
15. mold

16. falls
17. digestion
18. (List two:) falling asleep while smoking; improperly using flammable materials to start a fire; operating unsafe electrical or heating equipment; placing materials that burn too close to a potential source of ignition
19. an expired battery, which signals a warning that battery replacement is needed
20. at least 3 ft.
21. paper, wood, fabric, and other ordinary combustible materials
22. an odorless gas that is potentially deadly
23. headaches, drowsiness, fatigue, nausea, and vomiting
24. through cracks in solid floors, construction joints, cracks in walls, gaps in suspended floors, gaps around service pipes, cavities inside walls, and the water supply
25. when it is occupied for the duration of the test
26. formation of water or frost on the glass in a window during cold weather
27. people, bathing facilities, cooking processes, laundry, and open gas flames
28. to allow escape of moisture from the crawlspace
29. through the production of spores
30. upper respiratory infections, breathing difficulties, coughing, sore throat, nasal and sinus congestion, skin and eye irritation
31. install flexible connections and/or breakaway gas shutoff devices
32. a high volume of fast-moving water
33. the area is likely to flood at least once every 100 years
34. between noon and midnight
35. June 1st through November 30th
36. to reduce damage to property during hurricanes
37. falls, burns, electrical shock, and poisoning

Fire, Gas, and Mold Hazards, Activity 23-1

1.	A	9.	D
2.	B	10.	C
3.	C	11.	D
4.	B	12.	C
5.	A	13.	D
6.	C	14.	B
7.	D	15.	A
8.	A	16.	A

Preventing Property Damage and Injury, Activity 23-2

1. F, J
2. A, C, E, H
3. A, D, E, H
4. B, G, I

Instructor's Resources

Chapter 23 Mastery Test

1.	C	7.	A
2.	C	8.	D
3.	D	9.	C
4.	C	10.	B
5.	D	11.	B
6.	D	12.	A

13. home
14. fire
15. creosote
16. photoelectric
17. combustion (or burning)
18. oxygen
19. Radon
20. Flash
21. safe
22. surge
23. November
24. Falls
25. (List two:) falling asleep while smoking, improperly using flammable materials to start a fire, operating unsafe electrical or heating equipment, placing materials that will burn too close to a potential source of ignition
26. (List three:) on each floor of the house including the basement and finished attic; in the living room or family room; at the top of the stairwell between the first and second floors; outside each bedroom when far apart
27. (List four:) headaches, drowsiness, fatigue, nausea, vomiting.
28. because water vapor is not visible or easily detected until it condenses
29. (List four:) upper respiratory infections, breathing difficulties, coughing, sore throat, nasal and sinus congestion, skin and eye irritation
30. foundation; horizontal members such as floors; columns, posts, and other vertical members that transfer the weight of the structure to the foundation; and all points of connection
31. two
32. the misuse of household appliances

Using a Fire Extinguisher

A portable fire extinguisher can put out a small fire or contain it until the fire department arrives. However, the number one priority is making sure everyone safely escapes.

Before a Fire

- Buy a multipurpose extinguisher (Class ABC) big enough to put out a small fire, but not so heavy as to be hard to handle.

- Choose a model that carries the label of an independent testing laboratory.

- Always read the instructions for the extinguisher beforehand and become familiar with its parts.

- Get hands-on training before operating a fire extinguisher, if possible. Most local fire departments offer this service.

- Install fire extinguishers close to exits.

During a Fire

- Keep your back to a clear exit when using the extinguisher so escape is possible if a fire cannot be controlled.

- Stand at a safe operating distance, usually several feet away.

- Hold the extinguisher with the nozzle pointed away from you and pull the pin on top to release the locking mechanism.

- Aim at the base of the fire, not the flames.

- Squeeze the lever slowly to release the extinguishing agent. (A typical fire extinguisher contains 10 seconds of extinguishing power, possibly less if already partially discharged.)

- Sweep from side to side until the fire is completely out.

- Move toward the fire as it starts to diminish, but do not walk away. Watch the area for a few minutes in case it re-ignites.

- If the room fills with smoke, leave immediately.

After the Fire

- Recharge the extinguisher immediately after use.

- Return the extinguisher to its proper location.

Source: National Fire Protection Association

Sources of Water Vapor in the Home

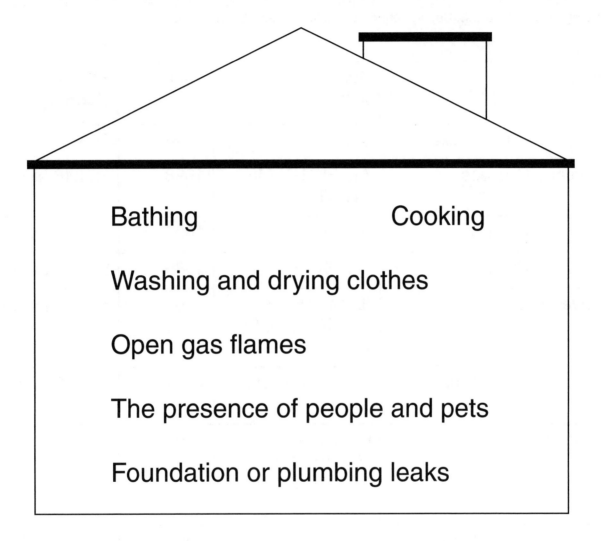

Bathing   Cooking

Washing and drying clothes

Open gas flames

The presence of people and pets

Foundation or plumbing leaks

Top Ten U.S. Natural Disasters

The following 10 disasters are ranked according to the relief costs provided by the Federal Emergency Management Agency (FEMA) as of July 31, 2003. Figures do not include funding provided by private insurance or by other participating federal agencies such as the Small Business Administration's disaster loan programs and the U.S. Department of Agriculture's Farm Service Agency.

Event	States Affected	Year	FEMA Funding
Northridge Earthquake	CA	1994	$6.981 billion
Hurricane Georges	AL, FL, LA, MS, PR, VI	1998	$2.246 billion
Hurricane Andrew	FL, LA	1992	$1.813 billion
Hurricane Hugo	NC, SC, PR, VI	1989	$1.308 billion
Midwest Floods	IL, IA, KS, MN, MO, NE, ND, SD, WI	1993	$1.141 billion
Tropical Storm Allison	FL, LA, MS, PA, TX	2001	$1.180 billion
Hurricane Floyd	CT, DE, FL, ME, MD, NH, NJ, NY, NC, PA, SC, VT, VA	1999	$1.066 billion
Loma Prieta Earthquake	CA	1989	$865.9 million
Red River Valley Floods	MN, ND, SD	1997	$740.1 million
Hurricane Fran	MD, NC, PA, VA, WV	1996	$621.8 million

Source: Federal Emergency Management Agency

U.S. Tornado Activity

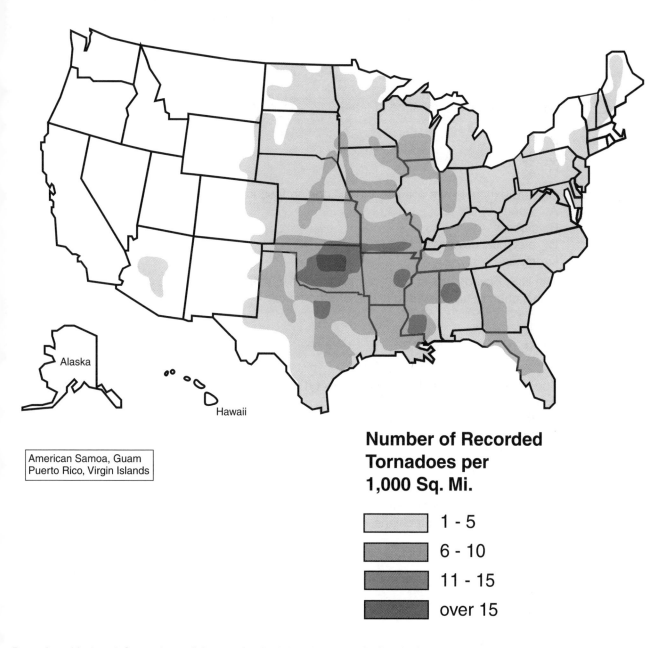

American Samoa, Guam
Puerto Rico, Virgin Islands

**Number of Recorded
Tornadoes per
1,000 Sq. Mi.**

1 - 5

6 - 10

11 - 15

over 15

Based on National Oceanic and Atmospheric Administration (NOAA), Storm Prediction Center Statistics

Source: U.S. Federal Emergency Management Agency

Designing for Health and Safety
Chapter 23 Mastery Test

Name _____

Date _____

Score _____

Multiple Choice: Select the best response and write the letter in the preceding blank.

_____ 1. The percentage of fire deaths that occur in the U.S. home is _____ percent.
   A. 50
   B. 70
   C. 80
   D. 90

_____ 2. All residential stairs must be at least _____ in. wide.
   A. 24
   B. 30
   C. 36
   D. 42

_____ 3. Class B extinguishers are used to extinguish fires involving _____.
   A. wood
   B. paper
   C. electrical devices
   D. grease

_____ 4. The U.S. Environmental Protection Agency has estimated that one of every _____ homes in this country has elevated levels of radon gas.
   A. 5
   B. 10
   C. 15
   D. 20

_____ 5. The greenish-black mold that can grow on material with a high-cellulose and low-nitrogen content is _____.
   A. the *Cladosporium* species
   B. the *Pencillum* species
   C. *Alternaria alternata*
   D. *Stachybotrys atra*

_____ 6. Of the following, the area *not* located in an earthquake zone is _____.
   A. along the Mississippi River
   B. the southern Appalachians
   C. New England
   D. the southern half of Texas

_____ 7. Of the following, _____ has caused a greater loss of life and property than all other natural hazards.
   A. floods
   B. tornadoes
   C. hurricanes
   D. earthquakes

_____ 8. The area of the country that runs north from Texas through eastern Nebraska and northeast to Indiana is called _____.
   A. a natural flood plain
   B. the New Madrid earthquake zone
   C. hurricane row
   D. tornado alley

(continued)

Name _____

_____ 9. Records show that about _____ percent of all reported tornadoes have wind speeds of
112 mph or less.
A. 65
B. 75
C. 85
D. 95

_____ 10. The three months of the U.S. tornado season are _____.
A. January, February, and March
B. April, May, and June
C. July, August, and September
D. October, November, and December

_____ 11. New garage doors built and installed to resist hurricane forces should be certified to
withstand _____ mph winds.
A. 100
B. 110
C. 120
D. 130

_____ 12. A tropical storm is considered a hurricane when winds have reached a constant _____
mph speed.
A. 74
B. 84
C. 94
D. 104

Completion: Complete the following sentences by writing the missing words in the preceding blanks.

_____ 13. More injuries occur in the _____ than anywhere else.

_____ 14. U.S. statistics show that someone is killed by _____ every two hours.

_____ 15. Burning unseasoned wood in a fireplace or wood-burning stove will
create a _____ buildup and lead to a chimney fire.

_____ 16. There are two basic types of smoke detectors: ionization and _____.

_____ 17. Carbon monoxide is produced from incomplete _____.

_____ 18. Carbon monoxide poisoning reduces the blood's ability to transport
_____.

_____ 19. The natural decay of uranium found in soil, rocks, and water
causes _____.

_____ 20. A high volume of fast-moving water that appears suddenly is a _____
flood.

_____ 21. Some newer homes have a _____ room constructed within the structure
to withstand tornado-force winds.

_____ 22. Nine of 10 hurricane fatalities can be attributed to a dome of ocean water
called a storm _____.

_____ 23. The hurricane season lasts from June through _____.

_____ 24. About one-third of all accidental deaths occurring annually in the home
are due to _____.

(continued)

Name _____

Short Answer: Provide brief answers to the following questions or statements.

25. Name two of the leading causes of residential fires. _____

_____

_____

_____

26. Name three recommended locations for placement of smoke detectors in the home. _____

_____

_____

_____

_____

27. Identify four symptoms of carbon monoxide poisoning. _____

_____

_____

28. Why are occupants generally *not* aware of a water vapor problem in their house? _____

_____

_____

_____

_____

29. Identify four health problems caused by indoor molds. _____

_____

_____

30. What four structural elements of a house need to be strengthened to reduce damage from an earthquake? _____

_____

_____

_____

_____

31. What is the minimum number of exits required for each occupied room in a residence? _____

_____

_____

32. What is the source of most electrical shocks in the home? _____

_____

Chapter 24
Exterior Design

Objectives

After studying this chapter, students will be able to
- identify distinguishing features of traditional styles of homes.
- describe the designs of ranch and split-level homes, and list their advantages and disadvantages.
- determine the main purpose of a contemporary design, and list its design features, advantages, and disadvantages.

Teaching Materials

Text, pages 421–437

Student Activity Guide

Check Your Understanding
24-1, *Architectural Style Identification*
24-2, *House Styles*
24-3, *Contemporary Homes*

Instructor's Resources

Traditional Housing Styles, reproducible master 24-A

Modern Home Designs, transparency master 24-B

Chapter 24 Mastery Test

Instructional Concepts and Student Activities

1. Have students read Chapter 24 in the text and complete the review questions.
2. Ask students to collect pictures of basic residential styles or designs and identify each one. Then have them include these materials in their housing notebooks.

Traditional Styles

3. *Traditional Housing Styles*, reproducible master 24-A, IR. Use the handout to acquaint students with the distinguishing feature(s) of each traditional style of housing exteriors. Have students refer to the handout as they progress through the chapter.
4. Show slides of each traditional exterior house style to serve as the basis for a class discussion. During this discussion, help students form a mental picture of each style and list several features of each style.
5. Invite a local architect to speak to the class and show examples of traditional exterior home styles.
6. Plan a field trip to see examples of traditional exterior home styles in your community.
7. *Architectural Style Identification*, Activity 24-1, SAG. Students are to take a photograph, select a picture, or sketch an example of a residence that clearly illustrates a basic architectural style. They are to identify the style and list the key characteristics.
8. *House Styles*, Activity 24-2, SAG. Students are to identify sketches of several basic architectural styles.

Modern Designs

9. *Modern Home Designs*, transparency master 24-B, IR. Have students compare and discuss the fundamental designs on which many modern homes are based.
10. Lead a class discussion on basic home designs by showing illustrations of the ranch house and the split-level house.
11. Have students share, identify, and discuss pictures from their housing notebooks with the class.

Contemporary Designs

12. Show illustrations of contemporary designs, such as geodesic domes, foam domes, solar homes, and underground structures, to serve as the basis for a class discussion.

13. *Contemporary Homes*, Activity 24-3, SAG. Students are to select one of the contemporary designs discussed in the text and write an essay describing why they would like to live in it.
14. Assign one or more tasks listed in the text's *Suggested Activities* section at the end of the chapter.

Suggested Evaluation Techniques

15. *Check Your Understanding*, SAG. Have students complete as many questions as possible without referring to the text. Then have them find answers to questions they do not know.
16. Administer the *Chapter 24 Mastery Test*.

Answer Key

Text

Review Questions, page 436

1. white or tinted stucco walls; low-pitched tile roofs; broad roof overhangs; colorful tile on floors and around windows; arched windows, doors, and colonnades; wrought iron railings and grilles; exposed roof beams; balconies; wide porches; and inner patio or courtyard
2. A Dutch house has a gambrel roof with Dutch kick and open porch, while the Pennsylvania Dutch house has a pent roof and unsupported hood over front door.
3. French plantation house
4. A half-house has one main room, a double house has a second room added on, and the saltbox has a lean-to structure added to half-house or double house.
5. overhanging second story
6. steep gable roof with little overhang, 1 or 1½ stories high, central chimney, narrow wood siding or split shingles, central doorway, and small-paned windows
7. A Cape Ann home has a larger central chimney and a gambrel roof.
8. symmetry, simple exterior lines, 2½ or 3 stories high with a band of stone between stories, high hip or gable roof (may have balustrade), central main door with pilasters on both sides, a pediment above the door, and large chimneys at each end of the roof
9. The Federal style adds Greek and Roman features to the Georgian house. Greek Revival homes have the symmetry of Georgian homes, but Greek proportions and decorations, a white exterior, and a two-story portico. Southern Colonial homes are similar to Greek Revival homes, but the portico is extended and often has upper and lower balconies.

10. square tower on the roof
11. advantages: has no stairs, is easily expanded, takes many shapes, and is convenient for indoor/outdoor living
disadvantages: is more expensive per sq. ft. than two-story homes
12. advantages: a perfect solution for a hilly site, provides separation of family functions, and requires little hall space
disadvantages: more expensive to build than ranch or two-story homes and often requires zoned heating
13. Triangular frames are bolted together to form a self-reinforcing sphere.
14. fewer building materials needed per sq. ft., reduced heat loss, and great flexibility in floor plan design
15. A giant inflated balloon is sprayed with polyurethane foam and dried.
16. large areas of glass on the south side of the house, masonry floors and/or walls, minimum air infiltration, double-wall construction, and individual heating zones
17. reduced heating and cooling costs, site remains more natural, requires little exterior maintenance, is safer then traditional homes, and is quiet and private

Student Activity Guide

Check Your Understanding, pages 201–203

1. J
2. C
3. H
4. E
5. G
6. D
7. F
8. B
9. I
10. A
11. A
12. B
13. C
14. D
15. C
16. B
17. A
18. B

19. (List three:) white or tinted stucco walls; low pitched tile roofs; broad roof overhangs; Mexican barrel tile or mission tile on roof; colorful tile on floors and around windows; arched windows, doors, and colonnades; wrought iron railings and grilles; exposed roof beams; balconies and wide porches; inner patios or courts
20. a gambrel roof that flares out at the bottom and extends to cover an open porch
21. Half-timber walls have large, rough, wood support beams with plaster or masonry filled in-between.
22. raised brick or stone basement to protect house from floods, balconies with lacy ironwork railings, white stucco walls, and hip roofs with two chimneys
23. half-timber construction and two or three stories

24. (List two:) designed for a sloping or hilly site; sleeping, living, and recreation areas placed on different levels; little hall space required
25. to have it blend well with the natural surroundings
26. masonry floors, masonry walls, barrels of water
27. south side
28. the southern side of a hill

House Styles, Activity 24-2

1. Cape Ann
2. Dutch Colonial
3. Spanish
4. Tudor
5. Federal
6. Pennsylvania Dutch
7. Southern Colonial
8. Saltbox

Instructor's Resources

Chapter 24 Mastery Test

1.	B	6.	D
2.	C	7.	B
3.	A	8.	C
4.	D	9.	B
5.	C	10.	D

11. French
12. garrison
13. Georgian
14. Federal
15. Southern Colonial
16. intermediate
17. contemporary
18. solar
19. simple in design and fairly small, one main floor with a tiny entrance and a steep stairway to the attic, fireplace and chimney on a side wall, a steep shingled roof, and brick or stone walls
20. The Cape Ann, a variation of the Cape Cod, has a larger central chimney and a gambrel roof.
21. Italianate
22. Victorian
23. overabundance of decorative trim, high porches, steep gabled roofs, tall windows, towers, and gingerbread trim surrounding exterior elements
24. A hillside ranch is built on a hill so part of the basement is exposed and can be used for a garage or a living area with a panoramic view. A raised ranch has part of the basement above ground, which allows windows in the basement walls.
25. An engineered system of triangular frames create self-reinforcing roof and wall units based on mathematically precise divisions of a sphere.
26. greatly reduced heating and cooling costs; more room for landscaping, gardening, and activities in the yard; little exterior maintenance needed; safer than traditional homes from fire, tornadoes, and burglars; and a quiet, private interior

Traditional Housing Styles

- **Native American**—adobe

- **Spanish**—stucco walls, tile roofs, and courtyards

- **Swedish**—log cabin

- **Dutch**—gambrel roof and dormers

- **German**—pent roof

- **French**—half-timber home, the French manor, and the Mansard roof

- **English**—Tudor and Elizabethan homes, and the Cotswold cottage

- **Colonial**—English half-house

- **Saltbox**—lean-to

- **Garrison**—overhanging second story

- **Cape Cod**—small cottage with steep gable roof

- **Georgian**—large and symmetrical with simple lines

- **Federal**—Greek and Roman features

- **Greek Revival**—two-story portico with Greek columns

- **Southern Colonial**—front colonnade with two-story portico

- **Italianate**—square tower on roof

- **Victorian**—abundant decorative trim

Modern Home Designs

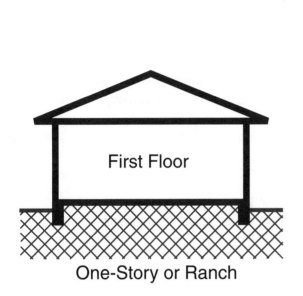

One-Story or Ranch

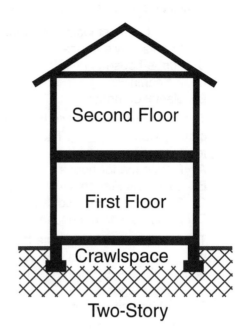

Two-Story

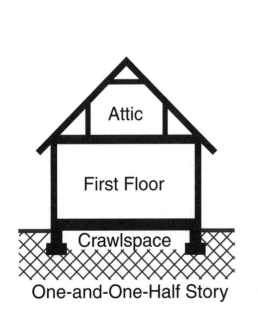

One-and-One-Half Story

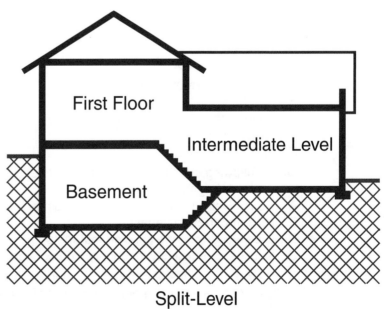

Split-Level

Exterior
Design
Chapter 24 Mastery Test

Name _____

Date _____

Score _____

Multiple Choice: Select the best response and write the letter in the preceding blank.

_____ 1. Probably the most lasting adaptation of a Native American style home is the _____.
   A. Spanish style house
   B. adobe house
   C. log cabin
   D. plantation house

_____ 2. The traditional home style brought to America by the Huguenots in the seventeenth century was the _____. The turret is the standard feature and walls are often half-timber for decoration.
   A. French manor house
   B. Louisiana French style house
   C. French Normandy cottage
   D. French plantation house

_____ 3. The traditional style of home that predominated in England in the late 1500s was the _____. It was usually two or three stories tall with an overhanging second story, gables, chimneys, columns, and decorative masonry.
   A. Tudor manor
   B. Elizabethan manor
   C. Cotswold cottage
   D. garrison house

_____ 4. Of the following, _____ does *not* describe a Cape Cod home style.
   A. small cottage having a steep gable roof with little overhang
   B. 1 or 1½ stories with a central chimney
   C. walls with narrow wood siding or split shingles
   D. an overhanging second story

_____ 5. The basic one-story home design that was inspired by ranchers' homes in the southwest is the _____.
   A. Spanish colonial
   B. split-level house
   C. ranch house
   D. Arizona bungalow

_____ 6. A variation of split-level design is the _____ house style.
   A. side-to-side
   B. front-to-back
   C. back-to-front
   D. All of the above.

_____ 7. Of the following qualities, _____ does *not* describe a home designed by Frank Lloyd Wright.
   A. blends well with the natural surroundings
   B. uses imported materials
   C. uses wood or stone building materials
   D. focuses on efficiency, economy, and comfort

_____ 8. Compared to designs of conventional homes, dome designs reduce the quantity of building materials needed per square foot of usable area by _____ percent.
   A. 10
   B. 20
   C. 30
   D. 40

(continued)

Name _____

_____ 9. The geodesic dome was developed by _____.
  A. Frank Lloyd Wright
  B. R. Buckminster Fuller
  C. Thomas Jefferson
  D. ranchers in the southwest

_____ 10. Examining the topography of the land's surface involves studying _____ on the site.
  A. trees
  B. streams and rocks
  C. other manufactured structures
  D. All of the above.

Completion: Complete the following sentences by writing the missing words in the preceding blanks.

_____ 11. With its distinguishing Mansard roof, the _____ manor is a stately home more common in the northern part of the country.

_____ 12. The _____ style house is noted for an overhanging second story borrowed from medieval English architecture.

_____ 13. A large, formal-looking house that is symmetrical with simple exterior lines is the _____ style house.

_____ 14. The _____ style home was designed by Thomas Jefferson and represented an official architectural style for the newly formed country.

_____ 15. The _____ _____ style is an outgrowth of the Greek revival style and features a front colonnade with a giant two-story portico.

_____ 16. The second level of a split-level design is called the _____ level and usually incorporates the garage, recreation room, and foyer.

_____ 17. Homes of _____ designs are built with the effect of environmental conditions in mind.

_____ 18. A true _____ home has special design features that use sunlight for maximum energy efficiency.

Short Answer: Provide brief answers to the following questions or statements.

19. List the characteristics of a half-house. _____

_____

_____

_____

20. What is the difference between Cape Cod and Cape Ann houses? _____

_____

_____

21. From what housing style was the city brownstone adapted? _____

_____

(continued)

Name _____

22. Which traditional house style became popular after the Civil War and was strongly influenced by the English? _____

_____

23. What are the characteristics of a Victorian house? _____

_____

_____

_____

24. How do the two variations of the ranch house differ? _____

_____

_____

_____

_____

_____

_____

25. How is the geodesic dome designed? _____

_____

_____

_____

_____

_____

26. What are the advantages of an earth-sheltered home? _____

_____

_____

_____

_____

Chapter 25
Landscaping

Objectives

After studying this chapter, students will be able to

- describe physical factors outside the house that affect housing choices.
- list the main characteristics and functions of grass, ground covers, trees, shrubs, and vines.
- name and describe manufactured elements in a landscape and explain why they might be used.
- list the activities required to plan a landscape.
- evaluate the quality of a landscape according to the elements and principles of design.

Teaching Materials

Text, pages 438–460

Student Activity Guide

Check Your Understanding
25-1, *Ornamental Plants*
25-2, *Landscape Plan*
25-3, *Planning a Landscape*

Instructor's Resources

Landscape Plants, transparency master 25-A
Basic Tree Shapes, transparency master 25-B
Elements and Principles of Design, transparency master 25-C
Chapter 25 Mastery Test

Instructional Concepts and Student Activities

1. Have students read Chapter 25 in the text and complete the review questions.
2. Ask students to collect information about landscape plants that thrive in the area. They should include ideal types of plants and interesting planting arrangements, architectural elements in the landscape, and landscaping techniques. Have them add these materials to their housing notebooks.

Landscape Plants

3. *Landscape Plants*, transparency master 25-A, IR. Acquaint students with the basic categories of landscape plants covered in the text.
4. Show pictures of landscaping plants common to the area, including grasses, ground covers, trees, shrubs, and vines. Have the pictures serve as the basis for class discussion.
5. *Basic Tree Shapes*, transparency master 25-B, IR. Have students review the basic contours associated with different species of trees. Ask students which shapes they see in the community.
6. Invite an owner of a local plant nursery or garden-supply center to speak to the class on various plants available in the area.
7. Plan a field trip to a local plant nursery to let students see plants that are suited to the area's climate.
8. Plan a field trip to a local botanical garden, state park, or historic site that has identified plants used in landscaping.
9. Show the *Basic Landscaping* video from Hobar Publications and have the class discuss it.
10. *Ornamental Plants*, Activity 25-1, SAG. Students are to prepare a chart of landscape plants that are appropriate for their area of the country.

Other Landscape Elements

11. Discuss items other than plants, such as paths, steps, walls, patios, game areas, and pools, that can be used to make the landscape more unified and functional.
12. Ask students to select a picture of one or more landscape elements that interests them. Have students share their selections with the class and explain the function each performs.

Planning the Landscape

13. *Elements and Principles of Design*, transparency master 25-C, IR. Have students review the design elements and principles they learned in Chapter 6 and discuss their application to landscape plans.

14. Lead a class discussion on what needs to be considered when planning a landscape. Review how the elements and principles of design may be used in landscaping.
15. *Landscape Plan*, Activity 25-2, SAG. Students are to create a landscape plan, using plants that thrive in the area.
16. *Planning a Landscape*, Activity 25-3, SAG. Students are to plan a landscape of their own design, following the suggestions presented in the text. They are to use the chart developed in Item 8 to help choose appropriate plants.
17. Assign one or more tasks listed in the text's *Suggested Activities* section at the end of the chapter.

Suggested Evaluation Techniques

18. *Check Your Understanding*, SAG. Have students complete as many questions as possible without referring to the text. Then have them find answers to questions they do not know.
19. Administer the *Chapter 25 Mastery Test*.

Answer Key

Text

Review Questions, page 459

1. provide wind protection, reduce glare from sun, shield street noise, provide privacy, absorb pollutants, provide oxygen, and provide habitats for birds and animals
2. grasses: grow from the bottom up, are finely textured, and facilitate walking and recreation areas
   ground covers: have thicker foliage, vary in texture, often grow where grasses do not grow well, and are not good for areas where walking and recreation take place
3. Native deciduous trees grow naturally in a given area and have spectacular foliage in the fall. Ornamental trees have an outstanding shape, leaf color, blossom, or other qualities that makes them focal points. Narrow-leaved evergreens have thin green needles, which remain all year. Broad-leaved evergreens do not lose leaves, grow in many shapes, and may have blossoms or fruit. Palms have single or clumped trunks with leaves varying in shape from broad fans to featherlike fronds.
4. as hedges, singular focal points, group plantings, or background plants
5. Paths are less formal, less permanent, and narrower than walks.

6. paths: loose stone, wood chips, and laid flagstones separated by grass
   walks: concrete, asphalt, masonry paving, and planks
7. to define boundaries, provide protection and privacy, and block sun and wind
8. Those used for safety or privacy should be constructed of very durable materials.
9. weak and strong features, impact of the elements, location of the three zones, and city zoning restrictions
10. by using a variety of deciduous and evergreen plants with some manufactured elements
11. (Student response. See pages 454-458.)
12. 5:3
13. There is no point of emphasis, no color or texture variety, and little variation in height.

Student Activity Guide

Check Your Understanding, pages 207–210

1. C
2. B
3. A
4. D
5. B
6. C
7. A
8. A
9. B
10. C
11. D

12. (List five:) provide wind protection, reduce glare from sun, shield street noise, provide privacy, absorb pollutants, provide oxygen, provide habitats for birds and animals
13. in shady areas or where mowing would be difficult
14. Narrow-leaved evergreen trees have needles, color, and mass all year; have three basic shapes (broad conical, narrow conical, and columnar); and are generally native to northern states. Broad-leaved evergreen trees have leaves and a variety of shapes, may have fragrant blossoms or colorful berries, and are generally native to southern states.
15. broad conical
16. as hedges, singular focal points, group plantings, or background plants
17. Narrow-leaved evergreen shrubs are used as foundation plants around structures, as taller ground covers, and as low bushes lining paths. Broad-leaved evergreen shrubs are used individually or in groups with ample spacing for visual impact.
18. loose stone, wood chips, and laid flagstones separated by grass
19. appearance, durability, and cost
20. Decks are built above ground, often of pressure treated wood, while patios are built at ground level, usually of concrete or masonry.

21. Consider strong and weak points of the site; determine impact of the elements; note city zoning restrictions; consider the location of the three main zones; determine placement of landscape elements; and choose and place the specific landscape elements.
22. public, private, and service
23. to create patterns and to direct the viewer's attention to a focal point
24. by using a variety of shades and hues of green and by using colors from flowering plants as accents
25. full-grown plant sizes
26. informal

Instructor's Resources

Chapter 25 Mastery Test

1. C
2. A
3. D
4. B
5. A
6. B
7. C
8. A
9. D
10. grasses
11. ground cover
12. native deciduous
13. focal point
14. narrow
15. broad
16. 3
17. private
18. emphasis
19. to create a personal, pleasant, and functional environment
20. suitable height and spreading ability, proper lighting conditions, and soil moisture and richness
21. to contrast a large, open area; to form a background for a house; or to serve as focal points
22. Hawaii, most of California, parts of the Southwest, and the Gulf Coast states including Florida
23. to form the intermediate plantings between trees and grasses or ground covers
24. deciduous, narrow-leaved evergreen, and broad-leaved evergreen
25. (List six): garden paths, walks, steps, banks, walls, fences, patios, decks, paved game areas, decorative pools, and fountains
26. (List three): cost, durability, maintenance, texture, appearance
27. before the house is sited

Landscape Plants

Grasses

Ground Covers

Trees
Native deciduous

Ornamental

Narrow-leaved evergreen

Broad-leaved evergreen

Palm

Shrubs
Deciduous

Narrow-leaved evergreen

Broad-leaved evergreen

Vines

Basic Tree Shapes

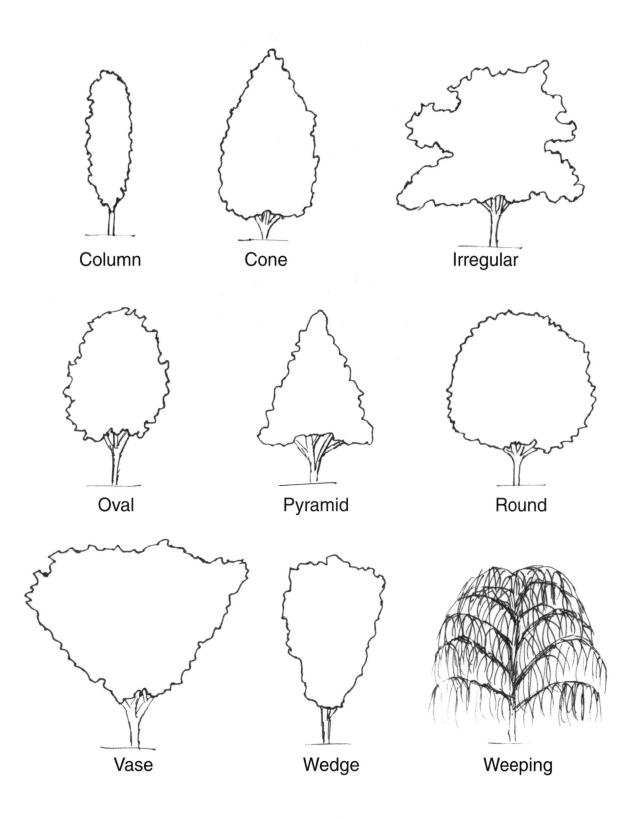

Column

Cone

Irregular

Oval

Pyramid

Round

Vase

Wedge

Weeping

Elements and Principles of Design

Elements of Design
Space

Line

Shape and Form

Texture

Color

Principles of Design
Proportion and Scale

Balance

Emphasis

Rhythm

Landscaping
Chapter 25
Mastery Test

Name _____

Date _____

Score _____

Multiple Choice: Select the best response and write the letter in the preceding blank.

_____ 1. When choosing lawn grass, the most important factor to consider is _____.
A. resistance to insects
B. depth of rooting
C. tolerance for a given climate
D. density of the turf

_____ 2. Of the following, _____ is *not* one of the three main categories of grasses used in North America.
A. wetland grasses
B. warm climate grasses
C. cool climate grasses
D. dry land grasses

_____ 3. A grass that thrives in both full sun and dense shade is _____.
A. Bermuda grass
B. carpet grass
C. Kentucky blue grass
D. zoysia grass

_____ 4. Of the following plants, the true ground cover is _____.
A. St. Augustine carpet grass
B. English ivy
C. incense cedar
D. privet

_____ 5. Of the following, _____ is *not* a common quality of broad-leaved evergreen trees.
A. hardiness in colder climates
B. a variety of shapes and heights
C. fragrant blossoms or colorful berries
D. an ability to serve various purposes in the landscape

_____ 6. Shrubs that have spectacular spring and summer blossoms are _____.
A. ornamental
B. deciduous
C. narrow-leaved evergreens
D. broad-leaved evergreens

_____ 7. The function of banks, walls, and fences in the landscape is to _____.
A. provide a focal point
B. connect two or more areas
C. separate distinct areas
D. provide unity to the landscape plan

_____ 8. The first step in planning a good landscape is to _____.
A. evaluate the site
B. check to see what plants are available
C. determine the location of the home
D. survey the neighborhood for ideas

_____ 9. The element or principle of design that reduces confusion within a landscape by providing a feeling of order is _____.
A. color
B. proportion
C. line
D. rhythm

(continued)

Name _____

Completion: Complete the following sentences by writing the missing words in the preceding blanks.

_____ 10. Both the leaves and stems of _____ grow from the bottom up, which allows frequent cutting without damaging the plant.

_____ 11. The purpose of a _____ _____ is to prevent erosion, control weeds, and reduce soil temperatures and loss of ground moisture.

_____ 12. The five main categories of trees include: narrow-leaved evergreens, broad-leaved evergreens, _____ _____ trees, flowering or ornamental trees, and palms.

_____ 13. Ornamental trees have outstanding qualities that makes them a _____ _____ in a landscape.

_____ 14. Firs, hemlocks, spruces, cedars, and pines have needles rather than leaves and are categorized as _____-leaved evergreen trees.

_____ 15. Because _____-leaved evergreen shrubs have showy flowers or berries, they are usually planted individually or with ample spacing for visual impact.

_____ 16. A garden path should be at least _____ ft. wide to allow room for work tools.

_____ 17. The _____ zone of a landscape includes a garden or pool, a patio or entertaining area, or a game area.

_____ 18. A unique plant or structural feature can serve as the object of _____ in a good landscape plan.

Short Answer: Provide brief answers to the following questions or statements.

19. What is the purpose of landscaping? _____

_____

_____

20. Besides their suitability to the climate, what points should be considered when choosing ground covers for a landscape? _____

_____

_____

_____

21. List three ways that trees may be used in the landscape. _____

_____

_____

_____

_____

_____

(continued)

Name _____

22. In what geographic area of the United States can palm trees generally be found? _____

_____

_____

23. What is the purpose of shrubs? _____

_____

_____

24. What are the three broad categories of shrubs? _____

_____

_____

_____

25. List six landscape elements other than plants that can be used to make a landscape more unified
and functional. _____

_____

_____

_____

_____

_____

26. List three factors to consider when choosing materials for paths, walks, or steps. _____

_____

_____

_____

27. When planning to build a new home, what is the best time to consider a lot's landscape
possibilities? _____

_____

Chapter 26
Remodeling, Renovation, and Preservation

Objectives

After studying this chapter, students will be able to

- list the reasons that people remodel and the factors they should consider before beginning a remodeling project.
- compare the five main types of remodeling according to cost, complexity, and time required.
- evaluate the remodeling needs of a family and select an appropriate type of remodeling.
- explain renovation.
- identify three types of historical preservation.
- explain the role of the family, interior designer, architect, and contractor in remodeling, renovation, or preservation projects.

Teaching Materials

Text, pages 461–477

Student Activity Guide

Check Your Understanding
26-1, *Remodeling an Attic*
26-2, *Planning an Addition*

Instructor's Resources

Types of Remodeling, transparency master 26-A
Remodeling Costs Versus Value, reproducible master 26-B
Top Signs of an Untrustworthy Contractor, reproducible master 26-C
Chapter 26 Mastery Test

Instructional Concepts and Student Activities

1. Have students read Chapter 26 in the text and complete the review questions.
2. Ask students to collect articles related to remodeling, renovation, and preservation costs; materials; and design ideas. Have them add these materials to their housing notebooks.

Choosing to Remodel

3. Lead a class discussion on the reasons for remodeling. List the reasons on the board during the discussion.

Types of Remodeling

4. *Types of Remodeling*, transparency master 26-A, IR. Acquaint students with the basic categories of remodeling projects covered in the text.
5. Lead a class discussion on the basic types of remodeling. Be sure to include changing lived-in areas, such as kitchens, bathrooms, or other rooms; making unused space livable, such as garages, porches, basements, and attics; adding on ground-level and second-story additions; and buying to remodel.
6. Invite a local building contractor to speak to the class about factors to consider in the remodeling process.
7. Show the *Attic Conversions* or *Kitchens* video from Shopware Educational Systems and have the class discuss it.
8. *Remodeling an Attic*, Activity 26-1, SAG. Students are to write a short essay discussing what needs to be considered when planning to remodel an attic into a studio work space.
9. Show the *Finishing a Basement* video from Hobar Publications and have the class discuss it.
10. *Remodeling Costs Versus Value*, reproducible master 26-B, IR. Use the handout to have students discuss common remodeling projects that increase a home's sales value. The chart shows the average percent of remodeling costs recovered at the time of sale due to the property's increased value from each improvement. (To find more information about this annual listing from *Remodeling* Magazine, search its Web site: remodeling.hw.net.)

Renovation

11. Lead a class discussion on renovation.

Historic Preservation

12. Lead a class discussion on historical preservation including restoration, preservation through remodeling, and adaptive reuse.

Preparing Remodeling, Renovation, and Preservation Plans

13. Discuss the steps in planning and the roles of the interior designer, architect, and contractor in preparing remodeling plans.
14. *Planning an Addition*, Activity 26-2, SAG. Students are to plan a family room addition for a specific house and sketch their plans in the space provided.
15. *Top Signs of an Untrustworthy Contractor*, reproducible master 26-C, IR. Use the handout to review characteristics of contractors who should not be chosen to do any type of remodeling work. Have students discuss the importance of a competent, trustworthy contractor to a consumer's ultimate satisfaction with the remodeling work.
16. Assign one or more tasks listed in the text's *Suggested Activities* section at the end of the chapter.

Suggested Evaluation Techniques

17. *Check Your Understanding*, SAG. Have students complete as many questions as possible without referring to the text. Then have them find answers to questions they do not know.
18. Administer the *Chapter 26 Mastery Test*.

Answer Key

Text

Review Questions, page 476

1. new family members need their own rooms, more entertaining, increased income to update styles, a more efficient house is needed, or more energy-efficient equipment is needed
2. close ties with schools and community, sentimental attachment to the house, much time and money invested in landscaping, or the high cost of buying a new house
3. length of time the family will continue to live in the house, local building ordinances, property taxes, estimated costs, and the time and effort required to remodel
4. changing lived-in areas, making unused space livable, adding on, buying to remodel, and preserving a historic home
5. simplest: changing lived-in areas; most complex: preserving a historic home

6. making unused space livable by remodeling the attic since construction of an exterior entrance would be needed to put a bedroom in the basement.
7. providing shoring while the wall is removed, and watching for and rerouting plumbing and wiring lines
8. The less expensive house may have very costly problems to correct, such as an unsound foundation, weak floor substructure, rotted support beams, faulty wiring, unsound roofing, weak walls, or inadequate insulation.
9. Adaptive reuse significantly changes a structure for an entirely different use, while remodeling modifies a structure to enhance its current use.
10. Determine weak and strong points of the present home; evaluate heating, wiring, plumbing, and insulation; draw a sketch of the original space that shows all architectural details; add and evaluate desired changes; and draw a finished plan.
11. (Student response. See pages 474-475.)

Student Activity Guide

Check Your Understanding, pages 215–219

1. A
2. C
3. B
4. A
5. C
6. B
7. A
8. B
9. A
10. A
11. C

12. (List three:) close ties with neighbors, schools, and community organizations; sentimental attachment to home; investment of time and money on landscaping; high cost of building or buying another home; amount of time involved in obtaining another home
13. yes because the family would benefit from the change and would probably realize a higher price when the house is sold
14. (List two:) local building ordinances, higher property taxes, insufficient space to build, overall cost, costly building permits
15. all the costs involved with remodeling, including building materials, utility additions, and labor
16. advantages: saves money in labor costs and yields more personalized results
disadvantages: requires more time than a professional would take and may result in serious errors
17. (List two:) kitchen, bathroom, bedroom
18. updated or added appliances, improved traffic patterns and work triangles, added counter and cabinet space, new wiring or circuits, changed plumbing, new ventilation, and new windows

19. (List three:) garage, porch, basement, attic
20. possibly a deeper foundation to meet local building codes, a moisture barrier between the foundation and flooring materials, insulation that meets the R-value recommended for living spaces, and wiring for lighting and outlets
21. a 7 ft. height from floor to finished ceiling that may slope to 5 ft.
22. adequate insulation and proper ventilation
23. Rainy or very hot or cold weather should be avoided since remodeling will require an opening in the house's exterior.
24. If it is a bearing wall, temporary supports should be used when the wall is removed, and some type of permanent support should be in place before the remodeling is finished.
25. Remove and replace the roof, make the foundation and first-floor walls strong enough to support the weight of a second story, and build a stairway connecting the two floors.
26. foundation and floor substructure for soundness, wood for insects and dry rot, wiring, heating, roofing, walls, and insulation
27. Determine weak and strong points of the present home; evaluate heating, wiring, plumbing, and insulation; draw a rough sketch of the original space; draw desired changes; and draw a finished plan.
28. A
29. B
30. C
31. D
32. A

Instructor's Resources

Chapter 26 Mastery Test

1.	D	4.	A
2.	D	5.	B
3.	D	6.	A

7. kitchen
8. rewiring
9. architect
10. outside entrance
11. remodeling
12. contractor
13. sound
14. finished plan
15. if planning to move within a year or two, or if trying to anticipate the desires of future homeowners who may prefer making different changes
16. to assure safe construction, yield the best results for the cost, accomplish the job relatively quickly, and eliminate frustration with jobs too difficult for the amateur
17. (List three:) garages, porches, attics, basements
18. by adding skylights, windows, or dormers
19. not enough yard space available for a ground-level addition
20. Determine the weak and strong points of the present home. If certain changes or repairs are being considered for attention at a later date, they may be inexpensively and conveniently incorporated into the remodeling project.
21. Renovation is returning an old home to its previous, but not necessarily original condition, while historic preservation is returning a structure to its original condition and maintaining traditional styles, materials, and in some cases, furnishings.
22. to change the function of a building, such as converting an old factory to a housing complex

Types of Remodeling

Changing Lived-In Areas

Kitchens (usually involves appliances and possibly lighting and plumbing fixtures)

Bathrooms (usually involves plumbing fixtures)

All other rooms

Making Unused Space Livable

Garages

Porches

Unfinished basements

Attics

Adding On

Ground-level additions

Second-story additions

Buying to Remodel

Remodeling Costs Versus Value

The following percentages indicate how common remodeling investments add to the value of a home. The percentages result from comparing average construction costs to the added resale value of homes due to specific remodeling projects. For example, adding a new deck addition increases the resale value of a home enough to recover all (actually, 104.2 %) of the costs involved.

For the projects listed here, the message is clear. A homeowner can remodel a home for greater comfort and convenience now, and recoup most of the associated costs when the house is sold.

Percent of Cost Recovered	
Deck addition	104.2%
Siding replacement	98.1
Bathroom addition, midrange	95.0
Attic bedroom	92.8
Bathroom remodel, upscale	92.6
Bathroom remodel, midrange	89.3
Window replacement, upscale	87.0
Window replacement, midrange	84.8
Bathroom addition, upscale	84.3
Family room addition	80.6
Major kitchen remodel, upscale	79.6
Basement remodel	79.3
Master suite, upscale	76.9
Master suite, midrange	76.4
Major kitchen remodel, midrange	74.9

Based on 2003 figures

Source: *Remodeling* Magazine

Top Signs of an Untrustworthy Contractor

- You can't verify the name, address, telephone number, or credentials of the remodeler.

- A salesperson tries to pressure you into signing a contract.

- A salesperson tells you a special price is available only if you sign the contract *today*.

- No references are furnished, and no examples of previous projects are available.

- Information you receive from the contractor is out-of-date or no longer valid.

- You are unable to verify the license or insurance information.

- You are asked to pay for the entire job in advance, or to pay in cash to a salesperson instead of by check or money order to the company itself.

- The company cannot be found in the telephone book, or is not listed with the local Better Business Bureau or with a local trade association such as NARI.

- The contractor does not offer, inform, or extend notice of your right to cancel the contract within three days. (Law requires notification in writing of your "Right of Recision." This grace period allows you to change your mind and declare the contract null and void without penalty.)

- You are given vague or reluctant answers, or your questions are not answered to your satisfaction.

- The contractor exhibits poor communication skills, is impatient and does not listen to you, or is inaccessible.

If licensing is required in your state, ask the contractor if he or she is licensed and call to verify compliance with the law. Also ask the contractor if he or she or any employees are certified in remodeling or have any special training or education, such as earning one or more of the following designations:

- Certified Remodeler (CR)

- Certified Kitchen and Bath Remodeler (CKBR)

- Certified Remodeler Specialist (CRS)

- Certified Lead Carpenter (CLC)

Source: National Association of the Remodeling Industry (NARI)

Remodeling, Renovation, and Preservation

Chapter 26 Mastery Test

Name _____

Date _____

Score _____

Multiple Choice: Select the best response and write the letter in the preceding blank.

_____ 1. The least complex type of remodeling generally involves _____.
   A. restoration
   B. adding on
   C. adaptive reuse
   D. changing lived-in areas

_____ 2. When considering remodeling to add space and deciding where to add it, _____ should be considered.
   A. the type of space needed
   B. the current location of rooms
   C. the availability of space in the existing house
   D. All of the above.

_____ 3. To convert garages and porches into living space, professional help is generally needed for _____.
   A. checking foundations for compliance with local building codes
   B. placing a moisture barrier between the foundation and flooring material
   C. adding wiring for lighting and outlets
   D. All of the above.

_____ 4. When converting an attic into a bedroom, a(n) _____ is also required.
   A. bathroom
   B. fire escape
   C. outside entrance
   D. dormer

_____ 5. If a structure is returned to its original condition, it is _____.
   A. adapted for reuse
   B. restored
   C. rebuilt
   D. remodeled

_____ 6. The professional who provides advice on appropriate floor and wall treatments, furnishings, and accessories within a given budget is a(n) _____.
   A. interior designer
   B. architect
   C. building contractor
   D. carpenter

Completion: Complete the following sentences by writing the missing words in the preceding blanks.

_____ 7. The _____ is the most remodeled room in the house and usually the most expensive to remodel.

_____ 8. When remodeling a kitchen, _____ is necessary if several new appliances are added or major appliances are moved.

_____ 9. The professional who makes final drawings of a proposed remodeling plan and writes specifications for the materials needed is the _____.

_____ 10. When a bedroom is located in the basement, sufficient lighting and a(n) _____ _____ should be provided to meet local fire protection laws.

_____ 11. Adding livable space to an existing house is more complex and expensive than other types of _____ projects.

(continued)

Name _____

_____ 12. The professional who obtains necessary building permits and schedules the work of subcontractors needed for a project is the _____.

_____ 13. Before buying an old home to remodel, very careful inspection is necessary to make sure the structure is _____ and worth remodeling.

_____ 14. When planning to remodel, showing all aspects of the project in a _____ _____ is needed for consulting contractors, ordering materials, and applying for building permits.

Short Answer: Provide brief answers to the following questions or statements.

15. When should a family *not* remodel their home? _____

_____

_____

_____

16. Why should professionals be hired to do the most difficult remodeling jobs? _____

_____

_____

_____

17. Name three areas of the home that are *not* used as living spaces but may be remodeled for that purpose. _____

_____

_____

_____

18. How can natural lighting be added to an attic space? _____

_____

_____

19. Why might a family choose to add a second story to the home? _____

_____

_____

20. What is the first step in planning a remodeling job? Why is this step necessary? _____

_____

_____

_____

_____

_____

(continued)

Name _____

21. How does renovation differ from historic preservation? _____

_____

_____

_____

_____

_____

22. What is the purpose of adaptive reuse? _____

_____

_____

_____

Chapter 27
Presenting Housing Ideas

Objectives

After studying this chapter, students will be able to

- explain how presentation methods can help the design professional communicate ideas.
- list the seven types of drawings used to present design ideas and describe how each is used in clarifying a design.
- identify the materials and methods used to make a rendering.
- determine how presentation boards, models, slides, and PowerPoint® presentations can help a client visualize a finished project.

Teaching Materials

Text, pages 479-493

Student Activity Guide

Check Your Understanding
27-1, *Presentation Drawings*
27-2, *Rendering*
27-3, *Presentation Board*
27-4, *Architectural Model*

Instructor's Resources

Two-Point Exterior Perspective, transparency master 27-A
Presentation Floor Plan, transparency master 27-B
Pencil Rendering, transparency master 27-C
Ink Rendering, transparency master 27-D
Airbrush Rendering, transparency master 27-E
Chapter 27 Mastery Test

Instructional Concepts and Student Activities

1. Have students read Chapter 27 in the text and complete the review questions.
2. Using magazines, ask students to clip illustrations that represent effective forms of communicating housing ideas. Have them add these to their housing notebooks.

Presentation Drawings

3. Lead a class discussion on the various types of presentation drawings. Be sure to include exterior perspectives, interior perspectives, presentation floor plans, presentation elevations, presentation plot plans, presentation landscape plans, and presentation sections.
4. *Two-Point Exterior Perspective*, transparency master 27-A, IR. Have students examine the drawing of a home used in a real estate ad, while they review the common characteristics of two-point exterior perspectives.
5. *Presentation Floor Plan*, transparency master 27-B, IR. Have students examine the black/white copy of a color drawing that shows the room layout of a home. Ask students to identify other features that a presentation floor plan may show.
6. Provide examples of typical interior perspectives, presentation elevations, presentation plot plans, presentation landscape plans, and presentation sections for students to examine.
7. Invite an architect or interior designer to show examples of his or her work to students. Allow time for questions and answers.
8. *Presentation Drawings*, Activity 27-1, SAG. Students are to match the types of presentation drawings with their descriptions.

Rendering

9. Discuss and demonstrate the standard rendering techniques using the following: pencil, ink, watercolor, colored pencil, felt-tip marker, appliqué, and airbrush. An art teacher or architectural drafting instructor may be a valuable resource for this content area.
10. *Pencil Rendering*, transparency master 27-C, IR. Have students notice the masterful use of light and shadow in these student drawings using ordinary pencils with soft lead. A home and common building materials are shown.
11. *Ink Rendering*, transparency master 27-D, IR. Have students examine the crisp lines typical of an ink drawing. This one shows an earth-sheltered home.
12. *Airbrush Rendering*, transparency master 27-E, IR. Have students examine the photolike quality of an airbrush rendering.

13. *Rendering*, Activity 27-2, SAG. Students are to apply rendering techniques on given architectural features using pencil, ink, and colored pencil.

Other Presentation Methods

14. Lead a class discussion on how communication devices, such as presentation boards, models, and slides, help clients. Provide examples for students to examine.
15. *Presentation Board*, Activity 27-3, SAG. Students are to prepare a presentation board for a room of their design and explain the key points of their presentation.
16. *Architectural Model*, Activity 27-4, SAG. Students are to build a model of a cabinet, table, chair, or appliance and sketch their plan in the space provided.
17. Assign one or more tasks listed in the text's *Suggested Activities* section at the end of the chapter.

Suggested Evaluation Techniques

18. *Check Your Understanding*, SAG. Have students complete as many questions as possible without referring to the text. Then have them find answers to questions they do not know.
19. Administer the *Chapter 27 Mastery Test.*

Answer Key

Text

Review Questions, page 492

1. exterior perspectives, interior perspectives, presentation floor plans, presentation elevations, presentation plot plans, presentation landscape plans, and presentation sections
2. exteriors: exterior perspectives, presentation elevations, presentation plot plans, presentation landscape plans, and presentation sections
   interiors: interior perspectives, presentation floor plans, presentation elevations, and presentation sections
3. Elevations show one side of an object with no depth, while perspective drawings show more than one side of the object for a realistic appearance.
4. A two-point perspective shows two sides of a building with the corner appearing closest, while a one-point perspective shows three walls, the ceiling, and the floor of a room with the back wall appearing the farthest away.

5. Interior perspectives use a one-point perspective, while exterior perspectives use a two-point perspective.
6. pencil, ink, colored pencil, felt-tip marker, watercolor, appliqué, and airbrush
7. simplest: pencil; most complex: airbrush
8. because it produces a sharper line and finer detail
9. colored pencil, because shading techniques can be mastered more easily with it than other methods
10. airbrush
11. presentation boards, models, slides, and PowerPoint® presentation graphics software
12. as a developmental tool for designers to explore ideas, and as a finished model for clients to see the precise detailing and proper scaling of the final structure

Student Activity Guide

Check Your Understanding, pages 223–225

1. presentation
2. exterior
3. vanishing
4. two-point
5. one-point
6. elevation
7. section
8. rendering
9. airbrush
10. to communicate ideas to prospective clients and investors, for advertising purposes
11. to emphasize certain areas of the structure, such as the design of the sides or the roof of a house
12. interior perspective
13. presentation floor plan
14. (List two): may be cut to the size needed and transferred to a rendering; assures bold, uniform colors and patterns; reproduces well; available in many common rendering symbols, such as trees, people, furniture, building materials, and doors
15. It helps clients better understand how the finished area will appear and how the various colors, textures, and designs will relate.
16. It lets the designer see the plan from all sides, which helps to perfect the design, remedy potential design problems, and show proposed projects to clients.
17. They help effectively communicate design ideas to the client, show examples of the designer's previous work, recommend successful ideas used in similar situations, and compactly store a record of the designer's work.

18. D
19. B
20. C
21. A
22. D
23. C
24. B

Presentation Drawings, Activity 27-1

1.	I	6.	C
2.	B	7.	D
3.	H	8.	F
4.	E	9.	G
5.	A		

Instructor's Resources

Chapter 27 Mastery Test

1.	B	6.	B
2.	C	7.	C
3.	C	8.	C
4.	B	9.	D
5.	D		

10. two
11. symbols
12. one
13. plot
14. section
15. shading, texturing
16. water
17. appliqué

18. airbrush
19. to present ideas to clients and investors in nontechnical language and to use for advertising
20. Parts of the drawing meant to appear closest to the viewer are drawn in the largest scale, while adjacent parts farther away are drawn gradually smaller. Lines extended from the closest parts of the drawing past the farthest parts eventually meet at a vanishing point.
21. presentation floor plan; by showing placement of walls and doors and the arrangement of furniture and appliances
22. kitchens, bathrooms, and walls with built-in cabinets
23. the entire landscape plan, which includes the placement of trees, shrubs, flowers, pools, walks, fences, drives, the house, and all other important features
24. to offer flexibility in communicating with clients
25. because ink produces a sharper line and finer detail
26. because of the smooth gradation of tones and realistic appearance
27. floor plans, elevations, and other drawings and information to help the client visualize the finished product as well as manufacturers' samples of carpeting, draperies, upholstery, paint, and other prominent surface treatments

Two-Point Exterior Perspective

Source: Terre Haute Parade of Homes

Presentation Floor Plan

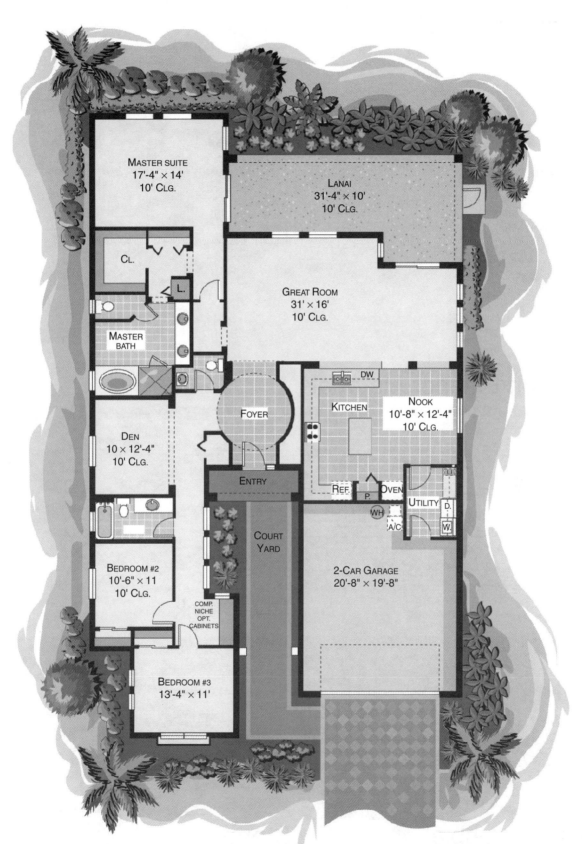

MASTER SUITE
17'-4" × 14'
10' CLG.

LANAI
31'-4" × 10'
10' CLG.

CL.

L.

GREAT ROOM
31' × 16'
10' CLG.

MASTER
BATH

DW

KITCHEN

NOOK
10'-8" × 12'-4"
10' CLG.

FOYER

DEN
10 × 12'-4"
10' CLG.

ENTRY

REF.   OVEN
P.

UTILITY

D.

WH
W.

A/C

COURT
YARD

BEDROOM #2
10'-6" × 11
10' CLG.

2-CAR GARAGE
20'-8" × 19'-8"

COMP.
NICHE
OPT.
CABINETS

BEDROOM #3
13'-4" × 11'

Source: WCI Communities, Inc.

Pencil Rendering

Exterior Perspective

Common Exterior Materials

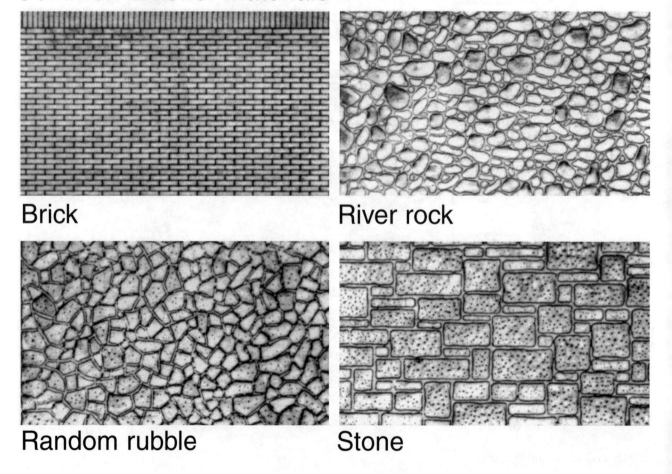

Brick

River rock

Random rubble

Stone

Ink Rendering

Source: The Garlinghouse Company

Airbrush Rendering

Source: Progress Lighting

Presenting Housing Ideas
Chapter 27 Mastery Test

Name _____

Date _____

Score _____

Multiple Choice: Select the best response and write the letter in the preceding blank.

_____   1.   The main purpose of presentation drawings is to show _____.
   A.   what materials will be used in the dwelling
   B.   how the finished project will appear
   C.   the builder how to build the house
   D.   how much the project will cost

_____   2.   The device that makes drawing one-point perspectives easier is a _____.
   A.   curved blade T-square
   B.   protractor
   C.   grid
   D.   pen

_____   3.   Related areas, similar functions, or convenience features are best communicated on a presentation floor plan through the use of _____.
   A.   notes
   B.   an appendix
   C.   color
   D.   key symbols

_____   4.   The normal scale of residential floor plans is _____.
   A.   ¼ in. = 1 in.
   B.   ¼ in. = 1 ft.
   C.   ½ in. = 1 ft.
   D.   1 in. = 1 ft.

_____   5.   The scale of a presentation plot plan often uses an inch to equal _____.
   A.   10 ft.
   B.   20 ft.
   C.   30 ft.
   D.   Any of the above.

_____   6.   The specific tool used to produce pencil renderings is a _____.
   A.   very hard lead pencil
   B.   soft lead pencil
   C.   special rendering pencil
   D.   number 4 pencil

_____   7.   The rendering technique that gives a realistic appearance to a presentation is _____ rendering.
   A.   appliqué
   B.   pencil
   C.   watercolor
   D.   ink

_____   8.   The primary disadvantage of felt-tip marker rendering is that the _____.
   A.   renderings fade quickly
   B.   technique is very difficult to master
   C.   errors are very difficult to correct
   D.   range of colors is limited

_____   9.   Of the following statements about architectural models, _____ is *not* correct.
   A.   they allow the client to view all sides of a proposed project
   B.   they may be used by the designer to perfect the design
   C.   they may be built to any scale
   D.   they are never useful for finding defects in a plan

(continued)

Name _____

Completion: Complete the following sentences by writing the missing words in the preceding blanks.

_____ 10. Most exterior perspectives of residential structures are drawn in _____-point perspective.

_____ 11. Windows, doors, types of floor coverings, and shelves may be indicated in _____ on presentation floor plans.

_____ 12. A presentation elevation shows _____ side(s) of the object but no depth.

_____ 13. A presentation _____ plan is used to show the relationship between the site and the structure.

_____ 14. A presentation _____ drawing shows a cutaway view of a house or a series of rooms in a house in order to show the internal layout of the structure.

_____ 15. A series of dots, parallel lines, or other types of markings are used to produce _____ and _____ in ink renderings.

_____ 16. A watercolor pencil rendering may be given the appearance of a watercolor rendering by adding _____ with a brush.

_____ 17. A(n) _____ is a pressure-sensitive transfer material with a printed pattern or color on one side.

_____ 18. Professional illustrators generally prefer _____ rendering over other rendering methods.

Short Answer: Provide brief answers to the following questions or statements.

19. Why are presentation drawings, boards, and models of housing ideas developed? _____

_____

_____

20. How do vanishing points give drawings perspective? _____

_____

_____

_____

_____

_____

21. What type of presentation drawing would most likely be used to show a traffic-flow analysis in the house? How? _____

_____

_____

_____

(continued)

Name _____

22. Identify three areas inside the house that are frequently shown by using presentation elevations.

_____

_____

_____

23. What is shown on a presentation landscape plan? _____

_____

_____

_____

_____

24. Why should a design professional master several rendering techniques? _____

_____

_____

25. Why are ink renderings generally more suitable for reproduction than pencil renderings?

_____

_____

26. Why may professional illustrators generally prefer airbrush rendering over other methods?

_____

_____

27. What is contained on a typical presentation board? _____

_____

_____

_____

_____

_____

_____

Chapter 28
Computer Applications

Objectives

After studying this chapter, students will be able to

- identify the four basic categories of computer applications in housing.
- list several benefits of computer applications in housing design and analysis.
- determine several applications of the computer in the selection of construction elements and processes.
- describe how the computer is used to serve clients and customers.
- explain how the computer is useful in project management.

Teaching Materials

Text, pages 494–512

Student Activity Guide

Check Your Understanding
28-1, *Computer Programs*
28-2, *Application-Specific Software*

Instructor's Resources

Benefits of CADD, transparency master 28-A
Kitchen Design Software, transparency master 28-B
Interior Design Software, transparency master 28-C
Chapter 28 Mastery Test

Instructional Concepts and Student Activities

1. Have students read Chapter 28 in the text and complete the review questions.
2. Ask students to collect advertisements, reviews, and technical information about computer applications in the housing and interior design fields. Have them add this material to their housing notebooks.

Design and Analysis

3. Lead a class discussion on design and analysis including computer-assisted drafting and design (CADD); plot, site, and landscape planning; kitchen and bath design; and energy analysis.
4. *Benefits of CADD*, transparency master 28-A, IR. Acquaint students with the benefits of CADD in the architecture and construction industries.
5. Demonstrate a CADD program so the class can see how drawings are made using the computer.

Selection of Construction Elements and Processes

6. Lead a class discussion on the types and uses of software programs for selecting the proper construction element or process. Be sure to cover structural analysis, which includes structural component selection, computer simulation, and window selection, as well as preferred construction and installation techniques.
7. *Kitchen Design Software*, transparency master 28-B, IR. Show students a black/white computer simulation displaying a kitchen layout designed around selected kitchen cabinets. Have students discuss the advantages of seeing detailed design results before materials are purchased and installed.
8. Demonstrate a software program designed to aid the designer in selecting appropriate construction elements.

Service to Clients and Customers

9. Lead a class discussion on how the computer can be used to better serve clients with designing, constructing, and decorating homes. Be sure to include home planning aids, interior design programs, CD-ROM marketing tools, Internet sources, and virtual reality models.

10. Demonstrate the use of a software program that is designed to aid in serving clients.
11. *Interior Design Software*, transparency master 28-C, IR. Show students the results of a black/white interior design program from a furniture company that allows customers to create room layouts with selected furnishings. Have students discuss the advantages of seeing detailed design results before furnishings are purchased or construction begins.
12. Have students explore the Internet for sources of information on housing and interior design. Compile a class list of reliable references.

Project Management

13. Lead a class discussion on the subject of project management. Concentrate on organization for retrieval and use as a database. Also include PERT and Gantt charts for scheduling, cost estimates, financial models; project data management; and computer usage by housing professionals.
14. *Computer Program*, Activity 28-1, SAG. Students are to match various tasks in the housing industry with the basic types of computer software programs that address them.
15. *Application-Specific Software*, Activity 28-2, SAG. Students are to imagine a change they would like to make to their respective homes and write an essay about the computer software programs to use for the project.
16. Assign one or more tasks listed in the text's *Suggested Activities* section at the end of the chapter.

Suggested Evaluation Techniques

17. *Check Your Understanding*, SAG. Have students complete as many questions as possible without referring to the text. Then have them find answers to questions they do not know.
18. Administer the *Chapter 28 Mastery Test*.

Answer Key

Text

Review Questions, page 511

1. for creating new drawings quickly, modifying existing symbols easily, reusing symbols as often as needed, and automatically adjusting scale
2. It enables designers to view results before structures or systems are built.

3. for providing accurate information about size and construction details, and for reducing mistakes in developing orders and specifications
4. more restrictive building codes and unfamiliar products and materials
5. It stores large amounts of information in very little space.
6. showing different plants with different symbols, placing plants in the landscape, showing plants as they mature, and creating a list of landscape elements
7. It allows the user to easily skip to information pertinent to his or her situation.
8. in revising drawings
9. to analyze all aspects of energy use and plan energy-efficient structures
10. a lifelike representation of the finished structure
11. a thorough understanding of the construction process, the construction drawings, and specifications
12. better organization of project plans and details, more accurate pricing, better cost control, increased productivity, faster response time, and improved customer service

Student Activity Guide

Check Your Understanding, pages 231–234

1. drafting, designing, rendering plans, adding color and shading to layouts, displaying plans in three dimensions, touring building interiors from a walk-through perspective, analyzing a housing structure's energy use, and generating all necessary reports
2. saves time and improves accuracy
3. (List three:) trees, furniture, doors, windows, common appliances
4. description of the shape, size, and important features on the site
5. kitchen and bathroom
6. kitchen cabinet manufacturers
7. It enables designers to view results before structures or systems are built.
8. for providing accurate information about size and construction details, and for reducing mistakes in developing orders and specifications
9. more restrictive building codes and unfamiliar products and materials
10. when there is a large amount of information to review before making an informed choice and when a multitude of choices are available
11. plot
12. topographical
13. landscape
14. simulation
15. interactive

16. PERT
17. Gantt
18. B
19. D
20. C
21. A
22. B
23. D
24. C
25. C

Computer Programs, Activity 28-1

1. B	9. A
2. A	10. C
3. C	11. D
4. E	12. D
5. B	13. A
6. D	14. B
7. C	15. D
8. E	16. E

Instructor's Resources

Chapter 28 Mastery Test

1. A	5. B
2. C	6. D
3. D	7. D
4. B	8. C

9. (List five:) drafting, designing, rendering plans, adding color and shading to layouts, displaying plans in three dimensions, touring building interiors from a walk-through perspective, analyzing a housing structure's energy use, generating all necessary reports
10. revising drawings
11. landscape plan
12. saves time and improves accuracy
13. to analyze all aspects of energy efficiency and plan energy-efficient structures
14. more restrictive building codes and unfamiliar products and materials
15. Most computer users possess the technology, and it stores large amounts of information in little space.
16. It enables designers to view results before structures or systems are built.
17. library
18. scaled
19. virtual reality
20. energy
21. structural
22. kitchen, bathroom
23. interactive
24. PERT
25. Gantt

Benefits of CADD

- Enables the drafter to develop and communicate ideas in precise and attractive graphics.

- Increases productivity and produces higher-quality work.

- Saves considerable time in making drawings with many repetitive features.

- Creates all types of construction drawings.

- Revises drawings quickly and easily.

- Generates schedules from drawings.

- Makes plots at any scale from a drawing or any part of it.

- Has become standard in architecture and construction industries.

Kitchen Design Software

Source: 20-20 Kitchen Design Software

Interior Design Software

Source: 20-20 Home Office Furniture Design Software

Computer Applications
Chapter 28 Mastery Test

Name _____

Date _____

Score _____

Multiple Choice: Select the best response and write the letter in the preceding blank.

_____ 1.   The greatest application of computers in the broad field of residential housing is _____.
   A.   design and analysis of plans
   B.   selection of construction elements and processes
   C.   management of project data
   D.   service to clients

_____ 2.   The plan view drawing that shows the site and location of the buildings on the property is the _____.
   A.   site plan
   B.   landscape plan
   C.   plot plan
   D.   All of the above.

_____ 3.   The advantage of project data management is _____.
   A.   quicker response time
   B.   more accurate pricing
   C.   improved customer service
   D.   All of the above.

_____ 4.   Of the following, the item that generally is *not* shown on a landscape plan is _____.
   A.   plants on the site
   B.   a typical floor plan
   C.   paved areas
   D.   fences

_____ 5.   The computer does a better job of communicating a plan to a client than hand-drawn methods do because _____.
   A.   most people now think in computer terms
   B.   the results appear more realistic
   C.   computer software offers better plans
   D.   it uses more symbols

_____ 6.   Of the following, the techniques used to improve the scheduling of a construction project are _____ charts.
   A.   ASID and PERT
   B.   AIA and Gantt
   C.   PERT and CADD
   D.   PERT and Gantt

_____ 7.   Software programs developed by manufacturers of windows, cabinets, furniture, and other housing materials allow computer users to _____.
   A.   see how their products can fit into various floor plans
   B.   create an order form for the items needed
   C.   calculate the total cost of ordered items
   D.   All of the above.

_____ 8.   A project-management computer program for the housing industry will *not* _____.
   A.   improve customer service
   B.   control costs better
   C.   create more accurate CADD drawings
   D.   reduce response time

(continued)

Name _____

Short Answer: Provide brief answers to the following questions or statements.

9. Identify five ways that computers are used in housing design and construction. _____

_____

_____

_____

_____

_____

10. When using CADD programs, what type of application results in the greatest time savings?

_____

_____

11. What plan view drawing shows all the plants on the site as well as paved areas, fences, and other landscape elements? _____

12. Name the two greatest advantages of computer-assisted drafting and design (CADD) over traditional manual drafting. _____

_____

_____

13. What is the purpose of an energy analysis? _____

_____

_____

_____

14. What two forces are causing design professionals and do-it-yourselfers to depend on application-specific software for selection of standard components? _____

_____

_____

15. Why is CD-ROM a useful medium for information storage? _____

_____

_____

16. Why is computer simulation important to housing designers? _____

_____

_____

_____

(continued)

Name _____

Completion: Complete the following sentences by writing the missing words in the preceding blanks.

_____ 17. Frequently used symbols are stored in the symbols _____ of most CADD software programs.

_____ 18. If symbols were originally drawn in a plan that has ¼ in. equaling 1 ft., they would need to be _____ for a plan with ¼ in. equaling a different dimension.

_____ 19. A _____ model is a computer-generated plan that appears lifelike.

_____ 20. Evaluating the thermal aspects of solar energy systems is one task performed by a program that provides a(n) _____ analysis.

_____ 21. Checking the strength of cables, beams, and columns is one of the tasks of a program that provides a(n) _____ analysis.

_____ 22. The two most expensive areas of the home to build are the _____ and

_____.

_____ 23. CD-ROMs can be _____, which means they can provide information specific to a user's response to questions or options.

_____ 24. A _____ chart provides step-by-step guidance in a project's construction.

_____ 25. A _____ chart is a graphic representation that illustrates comparisons of estimated schedules versus actual progress for each job associated with a given project.

Chapter 29
Careers in Housing

Objectives

After studying this chapter, students will be able to
- list various career options within the housing field.
- compare the duties and educational requirements of various occupations related to housing.
- determine typical career paths for entry-level, midlevel, and professional level positions.

Teaching Materials

Text, pages 514–525

Student Activity Guide

Check Your Understanding
29-1, *Local Housing Careers*
29-2, *Exploring Careers*

Instructor's Resources

Construction Trades and Related Workers, reproducible master 29-A

Career Levels, transparency master 29-B

Deciding a Career Direction, reproducible master 29-C

Chapter 29 Mastery Test

Instructional Concepts and Student Activities

1. Have students read Chapter 29 in the text and complete the review questions.
2. Ask students to collect brochures and articles about various careers in the housing field. Have them note the type of work performed by each professional and the required preparation. Then have them add this material to their housing notebooks.

Planners and Designers

3. Lead a class discussion on planners and designers in the housing field that includes the architect, architectural drafter, architectural illustrator, interior designer, model maker, and the landscape designer.

4. Show the *Careers in Interior Design* video from Learning Seed's catalog and have the class discuss it.

Building Tradespeople

5. Lead a class discussion about building tradespeople that includes the building contractor, construction technologist, skilled tradesperson, construction machinery operator, and land surveyor.
6. *Construction Trades and Related Workers*, reproducible master 29-A, IR. Introduce students to the many types of building trades working in the housing industry. With which categories of tradespeople are they unfamiliar?
7. Show the *Construction* video from the American Association for Vocational Instructional Materials and have the class discuss it.

Allied Careers

8. Discuss allied careers related to housing with the class. Include government positions and real estate positions.
9. Assign each student a career identified in the text or one in a field that interests him or her. Then have students research their careers and make brief presentations to the class. (Students may use visuals and/or handouts to enhance their presentations.)
10. Invite several housing professionals to speak to the class about their positions. (This could be organized as a panel discussion.) Help students prepare appropriate questions to ask the speakers.
11. *Local Housing Careers*, Activity 29-1, SAG. Students are to conduct an interview to examine local opportunities for a selected occupation in the housing field and write a summary of the findings.

Preparing for a Career Path in Housing

12. Discuss preparing for a career path in housing, being sure to include the definition of a career path, how to determine suitable jobs, and how a student can get the job he or she wants.

13. *Career Levels*, transparency master 29-B, IR. Have students discuss the characteristics of the three basic career levels. Ask students to describe, in general terms, how these levels relate to salary, education, and past experience.
14. *Exploring Careers*, Activity 29-2, SAG. Students are to select a housing career described in the text that appeals to them, research it, and record their findings. Have students focus their research on U.S. Department of Labor resources.
15. *Deciding a Career Direction*, reproducible master 29-C, IR. Use the handout to encourage students to examine qualities about themselves that can help them identify suitable careers. (Note: Have students keep their answers private, but encourage anyone having difficulty making a self-assessment to talk with the vocational counselor.)
16. Assign one or more tasks listed in the text's *Suggested Activities* section at the end of the chapter.

Suggested Evaluation Techniques

17. *Check Your Understanding*, SAG. Have students complete as many questions as possible without referring to the text. Then have them find answers to questions they do not know.
18. Administer the *Chapter 29 Mastery Test*.

Answer Key

Text

Review Questions, page 524

1. to work with clients, make preliminary sketches, suggest building materials, help clients choose satisfactory final designs, prepare working drawings, help clients select their building contractor, and possibly supervise contracted work
2. must fulfill the state's educational requirements, usually a bachelor's degree from an accredited college, and pass an examination to receive a license
3. architectural drafter and architectural illustrator
4. creativity; knowledge of design principles, construction, materials, textiles, furnishings, art, antiques, and other accessories; ability to work from blueprints to prepare presentation plans, presentation boards, and models; and the ability to work with people

5. must pass an examination to receive a license and have two years of postsecondary education in design, two years of practical work experience, and additional related education or experience to total six years of combined education and experience in design
6. building contractor, construction technologist, skilled tradesperson, and construction machinery operator
7. (Student response. See pages 517-520.)
8. building inspector, researcher, field representative, and community planner
9. real estate broker and real estate manager
10. to advance in the field

Student Activity Guide

Check Your Understanding, pages 237–239

1. J
2. A
3. M
4. D
5. L
6. B
7. K
8. C
9. G
10. F
11. I
12. H
13. E
14. N

15. An architect must fulfill the educational training requirements for the state in which he or she will work and pass an examination to obtain a license. Most states require at least a bachelor's degree from a college with an accredited architecture program. An architectural drafter needs a high school diploma with courses in architectural drawing and CADD and, for greater job opportunity, additional education at a community college, technical school, or university.
16. high degree of artistic skill, natural talent for freehand drawing, and a background in architectural drawing or commercial art
17. (List three:) works from blueprints to prepare presentation plans, presentation boards, and models; works with clients to choose furnishings and materials that meets their needs and tastes; selects and estimates costs of furniture, floor and wall coverings; arranges purchases; hires and supervises related workers
18. thorough knowledge of soil, plants, design, and construction
19. schedules work, obtains materials and equipment, checks that materials and construction comply with building codes, and makes sure the architect's and owner's specifications are met
20. apprentice, journeyman, and master

21. receive formal training, a bachelor's degree in some states, and training in other positions on the surveying team
22. broker: must pass a test to obtain brokerage license and may have a college degree; manager: requires no specified training
23. *Occupational Outlook Handbook, Guide for Occupational Exploration*, O*NET
24. (List five. See 29-16 in the text.)

Instructor's Resources

Chapter 29 Mastery Test

1. D
2. B
3. C
4. D
5. C
6. C
7. bachelor's
8. drafters
9. landscape designer
10. construction technologist
11. eyesight
12. land surveyor
13. creative ability, problem-solving skills, and knowledge and training in housing design
14. begins as a junior drafter; with more experience becomes an architectural drafter; and retains that position or, with more experience, becomes a registered architect
15. furniture, construction, textiles, design, art, antiques, cost estimating, and computer design applications
16. management, accounting, economics, construction law, and labor relations; because most building contractors are self-employed
17. carpenters, masons, electricians, plumbers, painters, and paperhangers
18. inspect construction for compliance to codes; inspect soil, water, and sewer components of sites; inspect materials, equipment, and workmanship on construction sites; monitor housing trends; provide loans; underwrite financing for low-cost housing; and sponsor research to improve housing
19. *Occupational Outlook Handbook*

Construction Trades and Related Workers

- Boilermakers

- Brickmasons and stonemasons

- Carpenters

- Carpet, floor, and tile installers and finishers

- Cement masons, concrete finishers, segmental pavers, and terrazzo workers

- Construction and building inspectors

- Construction equipment operators

- Construction laborers

- Drywall installers, ceiling tile installers, and tapers

- Electricians

- Glaziers

- Hazardous materials removal workers

- Insulation workers

- Painters and paperhangers

- Pipelayers, plumbers, pipefitters, and steamfitters

- Plasterers and stucco masons

- Roofers

- Sheet metal workers

- Structural and reinforcing iron and metal workers

Source: U.S. Department of Labor

Career Levels

Professional Positions
- key decision-makers
- key coordinators
- extensive independence

Midlevel Positions
- some independence
- many support tasks
- some supervisory tasks

Entry-Level Positions
- little independence
- many repetitive tasks

Deciding a Career Direction

Considerations	Your Response
Basic interests Do you prefer working with just people, data, or tools? a combination of two of these? all three?	
Aptitudes and abilities What can you do well compared to the efforts of others?	
Personality How do the people who best know you describe your personality?	
Personal priorities What is your idea of the perfect work setting?	
Career preferences What career interests you most, and what types of tasks do you want to perform?	

Careers in Housing

Chapter 29 Mastery Test

Name _____

Date _____

Score _____

Multiple Choice: Select the best response and write the letter in the preceding blank.

_____ 1. Of the following skills and abilities, _____ is *not* required to become an architect.
A. thorough understanding of construction technology
B. knowledge of building codes
C. knowledge of laws pertaining to construction
D. skill in designing and decorating interiors

_____ 2. The design and decoration of building interiors is planned and supervised by _____.
A. architects
B. interior designers
C. architectural illustrators
D. construction technologists

_____ 3. Of the following, _____ is *not* required to become a successful model maker.
A. manual dexterity
B. proficiency in reading drawings
C. a degree in architecture
D. a thorough knowledge of building materials

_____ 4. The _____ is a professional who coordinates the construction of buildings.
A. architect
B. interior designer
C. construction technologist
D. building contractor

_____ 5. The highest level of education typically achieved by a construction technologist results in a(n) _____.
A. high school diploma
B. associate's degree
C. bachelor's degree
D. master's degree

_____ 6. A building inspector's duty is to _____.
A. check water on the site
B. check sewer lines on the site
C. verify that local codes are followed
D. monitor housing trends

Completion: Complete the following sentences by writing the missing words in the preceding blanks.

_____ 7. Most states require at least a _____ degree to become licensed as an architect.

_____ 8. Architectural _____ draw the details of working drawings and make tracings from original drawings prepared by an architect or designer.

_____ 9. A _____ _____ plans the arrangement and composition of landscape elements on a site.

_____ 10. A _____ _____ specializes in estimating and bidding, quality control, site supervision, specifications writing, expediting, purchasing, and managing construction.

_____ 11. Construction machinery operators must have good _____ and physical coordination.

(continued)

Name _____

_____ 12. A _____ _____ locates property boundaries, measures distances, establishes contours, and makes drawings of the site.

Short Answer: Provide brief answers to the following questions or statements.

13. What kind of knowledge, skills, and training do occupations involved with the planning and design of buildings require? _____

_____

_____

_____

14. What is the career path of an architectural drafter? _____

_____

_____

_____

_____

15. A four-year degree in interior design is recommended for professional designers. Knowledge in what areas is needed? _____

_____

_____

16. What type of course work is needed to become a building contractor? Why are these courses necessary? _____

_____

_____

_____

17. Identify several types of skilled tradespeople associated with the building industry. _____

_____

_____

18. What roles do government agencies play in the housing industry?_____

_____

_____

_____

_____

19. What U.S. Department of Labor resource describes what workers do on a job, its working conditions, the training and education required, and average earnings?_____

_____

Chapter 30
Keeping a Job and Advancing a Career

Objectives

After studying this chapter, you will be able to

- identify factors that affect job performance.
- list the steps in meeting a client's needs through a functional plan.
- determine why ethics is an important consideration to the workplace.
- list common characteristics of a good leader.
- describe the typical process of conflict resolution.
- explain the concept of entrepreneurship.
- explain the need to manage home and work responsibilities.

Teaching Materials

Text, pages 526–540

Student Activity Guide

Check Your Understanding
30-1, *Working with Clients*
30-2, *Model Ethics Code*

Instructor's Resources

Reasons for Poor Listening Skills, transparency master 30-A

Meeting Client Needs, transparency master 30-B

Qualities of an Entrepreneur, transparency master 30-C

Chapter 30 Mastery Test

Instructional Concepts and Student Activities

1. Have students read Chapter 30 in the text and complete the review questions.
2. Ask students to collect information about jobs and careers and add this material to their housing notebooks.

Job Performance

3. Lead a class discussion on job performance and be sure to include the importance of employees developing good work habits, practicing safety on the job, and using good communication techniques.
4. *Reasons for Poor Listening Skills,* transparency master 30-A, IR. Acquaint students with common reasons for not listening effectively. Have them recommend ways for improving their communication skills by listening better.
5. Invite a local human resources expert to speak to the class about job performance issues.
6. Lead a class discussion on the importance of meeting client needs and the relationship of this task to good job performance.
7. *Meeting Client Needs,* transparency master 30-B, IR. Have students discuss the steps that housing professionals must take to meet client needs.
8. *Working with Clients*, Activity 30-1, SAG. Students are to imagine working for a design firm and interviewing a new client. They are to write a description of actions they would take and comments they would make during various points in the conversation.
9. Lead a class discussion on the relationship between better job performance through continuing education.

Ethics

10. Lead a class discussion on ethics, including work ethic.
11. *Model Ethics Code*, Activity 30-2, SAG. Each student is to identify 10 items to include in a model ethics code for a housing career of his or her choice.

Teamwork and Leadership

12. Discuss teamwork and leadership with the class in terms of attributes and expectations.

13. Have students discuss their most memorable experiences, both positive and negative, in working as part of a team. What could have been done to prevent the negative experiences?

Conflict Resolution

14. Lead a class discussion about conflict resolution with emphasis on suggestions for resolving conflicts.
15. Have students discuss the roles they believe individual employees should take when they observe conflict developing around them.

Entrepreneurship

16. *Qualities of an Entrepreneur,* transparency master 30-C, IR. Lead a class discussion on entrepreneurship that includes the characteristics of entrepreneurs and self-employed individuals.
17. Have students discuss examples of entrepreneurship in the community.

Managing Home and Work Responsibilities

18. Lead a class discussion on managing home and work responsibilities.
19. Assign one or more tasks listed in the text's *Suggested Activities* section at the end of the chapter.

Suggested Evaluation Techniques

20. *Check your Understanding,* SAG. Have students complete as many questions as possible without referring to the text. Then have them find answers to questions they do not know.
21. Administer the *Chapter 30 Mastery Test.*

Answer Key

Text

Review Questions, page 539

1. could result in greater appreciation of the individual's work, increased pay, and a promotion
2. construction
3. barely listening, pretending to listen, selective listening, and attentive listening
4. determining the needs of the client and the ultimate purpose or goal of the design plan
5. *Ethics* pertains to the conduct of the members of a profession, while *work ethic* pertains to an individual.

6. (Identify five. See 30-11.)
7. mediation
8. risk of failure
9. (Name five:) goal oriented, good health, knowledgeable, good planner, willing to take calculated risks, innovative, responsible
10. (Name two:) hiring outside help, adjusting work responsibilities, working from home, starting a home-based business, working part-time

Student Activity Guide

Check Your Understanding, pages 243–244

1. D
2. A
3. A
4. B
5. C
6. D
7. B
8. actions
9. structural
10. ethics
11. work
12. vision
13. delegate
14. conflict
15. entrepreneur
16. determining the needs of the client
17. reading, writing, speaking, and listening
18. (List five:) having vision, communicating well, staying persistent, having good organizational ability, showing responsibility, delegating authority
19. (List five:) goal oriented, good health, knowledgeable, good planner, willing to take calculated risks, innovative, responsible
20. (List two:) keeping an organized home, having family members help with the care of the home, hiring outside help, having friends and extended family provide extra support, adjusting work responsibilities, working part-time, working from home, starting a business from home

Instructor's Resources

Chapter 30 Mastery Test

1. D
2. B
3. A
4. C
5. B
6. C
7. A
8. emphatic
9. prototype

10. ethics
11. manager
12. poor communication
13. mediator
14. risks
15. (List four:) knowing the employer's policies and observing them, giving their best efforts to each job, planning and executing work efficiently, keeping the work area clean and organized, observing safety rules

16. reading, writing, speaking, and listening
17. determining the needs of the client
18. to show the construction of a product
19. (List four:) has vision, speaks clearly and directly, is persistent, has organizational ability, accepts responsibility, delegates authority
20. lack of adequate financing, poor management, and lack of the knowledge required

Reasons for Poor Listening Skills

- Interruptions

- Distraction caused by a speaker's manner or appearance

- Not understanding the words

- "Tuning out" because of disagreement with what is said, or thinking one already knows what will be said

- Daydreaming

- A hearing difficulty

Meeting Client Needs

1. Determine the client's needs.

2. Research potential design elements.

3. Formulate a preliminary plan.

4. Present the preliminary plan.

5. Seek client input.

6. Modify the plan to incorporate client input.

7. Present the final plan.

8. Seek client approval.

Qualities of an Entrepreneur

- Is goal oriented
- Maintains good health
- Stays knowledgeable
- Is a good planner
- Willingly takes calculated risks
- Is innovative
- Acts responsibly

Keeping a Job and Advancing a Career
Chapter 30 Mastery Test

Name _____

Date _____

Score _____

Multiple Choice: Select the best response and write the letter in the preceding blank.

_____ 1. Of the following, _____ is *not* a measure of job performance.
   A. developing general work habits
   B. practicing safety on the job
   C. using good communication techniques
   D. playing golf with the supervisor

_____ 2. Keeping the work area clean and organized is a desirable work habit because _____.
   A. it impresses the boss
   B. a cluttered workplace encourages accidents and slows work
   C. it looks better when people visit
   D. None of the above.

_____ 3. Statistics show that _____ percent of all accidents are caused by unsafe actions.
   A. 95
   B. 85
   C. 75
   D. 65

_____ 4. The most dangerous occupational area in the United States, as determined by OSHA, is _____.
   A. manufacturing
   B. transportation
   C. construction
   D. engineering

_____ 5. An example of a poor work ethic is _____.
   A. treating others with respect
   B. complaining to the boss
   C. admitting mistakes and learning from them
   D. avoiding gossip and criticism of others

_____ 6. Negotiation of a dispute with the impartial assistance of someone unaffected by the outcome is _____.
   A. arbitration
   B. going to court
   C. mediation
   D. resolution

_____ 7. The greatest risk associated with ownership of a business is _____.
   A. the risk of failure
   B. a stress-related heart attack
   C. ruining one's marriage
   D. losing the investment

Completion: Complete the following sentences by writing the missing word(s) in the preceding blank.

_____   8. Listening with the intent to understand is _____ listening.

_____   9. A model that is suitable for complete evaluation of a housing plan's form, design, and performance is a _____.

_____   10. The term that means "the rules or standards governing the conduct of the members of a profession" is _____.

(continued)

Name _____

_____ 11. A _____ is one who makes and implements decisions and who accomplishes desired results through others.

_____ 12. Many conflicts are the result of _____ _____.

_____ 13. In negotiated conflicts, the _____ looks for a compromise position that considers both parties' limits and needs.

_____ 14. An entrepreneur is someone who starts, manages, and assumes the _____ of a new business.

Short Answer: Provide brief answers to the following questions or statements.

15. List four general work habits that help workers make good progress on the job. _____

_____

_____

_____

16. List the four basic types of communication. _____

_____

_____

_____

17. What is the first step in meeting a client's needs? _____

_____

18. What is the purpose of a structural model? _____

_____

_____

19. Name four primary qualities that a good leader usually possesses. _____

_____

_____

_____

20. List the three primary reasons why new businesses fail. _____

_____

_____

_____